Tax and Transfer Tensions

Tax and Transfer Tensions

Designing Direct Tax Structures

John Creedy

Victoria University of Wellington and
New Zealand Treasury

Edward Elgar

Cheltenham, UK • Northampton, MA, USA

Published by
Edward Elgar Publishing Limited
The Lypiatts
15 Lansdown Road
Cheltenham
Glos GL50 2JA
UK

Edward Elgar Publishing, Inc.
William Pratt House
9 Dewey Court
Northampton
Massachusetts 01060
USA

A catalogue record for this book
is available from the British Library

Library of Congress Control Number: 2011931014

MIX
Paper from
responsible sources
FSC www.fsc.org FSC® C018575

ISBN 978 0 85793 752 0

Printed and bound by MPG Books Group, UK

Contents

List of Tables

List of Figures

Acknowledgements

This book makes use of revised and rearranged forms of several previously published papers, in addition to unpublished papers. The published papers are Creedy (2005, 2007, 2008, 2009, 2010a, 2010b, 2010c, 2010d, 2011), Creedy and Gemmell (2007), Creedy and Hérault (2011) and Creedy and Moslehi (2011). I am grateful for permission to use these papers here, and should again like to thank the referees for their constructive comments on earlier versions.

Part I

Introduction

Chapter 1

Introduction and Outline

This book is concerned with the thorny question of tax design. Its emphasis is on the issues and problems involved in choosing a tax and transfer structure. Rather than examining the details of particular systems or countries, the following chapters discuss broad problems which can be illustrated using relatively simple models.[1] However, it is well known that even the simplest possible tax structure – a basic untaxed and unconditional transfer payment combined with a proportional tax in a population where individuals differ only in their income-earning ability – presents substantial complexities.

Part II of the book is concerned with the link between economic theory and tax policy. Chapter 2, from which the title of the book is taken, discusses the question of why it is so difficult to design a tax and transfer structure which receives widespread support. It considers the numerous elements involved, such as the information needed, the modelling problems, the constraints on choices and, above all, the range of objectives and value judgements held by different judges. The crucial role of value judgements plays a substantial part in subsequent chapters. The link between economic theory and tax policy is examined further in chapter 3, stressing that there is

[1]For detailed examinations of particular tax structures, a valuable role can be played by behavioural tax microsimulation models. These have been discussed in other books by the author and colleagues; see Creedy *et al.* (2002), Creedy and Kalb (2006) and Buddelmeyer, Creedy and Kalb (2007).

no such thing as a value-free economic argument in favour of any particular structure. It explains how economic theory can nevertheless help to gain a clearer understanding of the interdependencies and relationships involved in tax design.

Part III is devoted to the analysis of particular simple tax and transfer structures, and alternative approaches to the choice of tax rates within those systems. Chapter 4 considers the general problem of selecting the tax rate in a linear tax structure, or basic income–flat tax system. This tax system is in many ways the 'workhorse' of tax analyses. The chapter discusses positive and normative aspects of the choice, covering both majority voting and optimal tax frameworks. The former turns on the choice of a single individual who holds the balance of power, while the latter depends on the maximisation of a social welfare function representing the value judgements of an independent judge. In general, explicit solutions are not available, even for simple assumptions about individuals' behaviour and the structure of the population. However, the chapter shows that some basic relationships can be established. Chapter 5 then considers explicit solutions in the voting and optimal tax models, again for the simple linear income tax, and using an assumption that individuals have Cobb–Douglas preferences defined in terms of net income and leisure. This chapter also discusses stochastic voting in addition to simple majority voting, and shows that there is an analytical correspondence with the optimal tax framework.

Chapter 6 turns to the consideration of an alternative to the linear tax structure, the loglinear income tax. This form has received relatively little attention in the literature, but has a number of convenient properties for tax analyses. It is found that this structure can give rise to particularly simple labour supply behaviour, when combined with Cobb–Douglas preferences. Again, majority voting and optimal tax outcomes are examined.

The next three chapters in Part III are devoted to the analysis of particular features of income tax systems which depart from the simple forms.

Unlike the stylised forms of linear and loglinear taxes, many actual structures have a tax-free threshold in the income tax structure. Chapter 7 considers the role of a tax-free threshold and examines the likely implications of modifications to an existing structure. Chapter 8 turns to the analysis of an in-work payment with an hours threshold, and its potential labour supply effect. This type of structure has been introduced in a number of countries in an attempt to encourage increased labour force participation by low-wage workers. However, chapter 8 shows that the implications of such a system, which introduces further nonlinearities into individuals' budget constraints, are not straightforward. Finally, chapter 9 turns to the question of identifying welfare-improving income tax reforms in practical structures having multiple rates and thresholds. Rather than trying to identify an optimal structure, the more limited objective is considered of making an adjustment to an existing system in a way which increases the value of a specified social welfare function. This involves the use of a behavioural microsimulation model.

The crucial role of value judgements, summarised by a social welfare function and in particular its implied elasticity of marginal valuation, is stressed in earlier chapters. Chapter 10, the final chapter in Part III, turns to the discussion of a number of studies which have attempted to 'measure' the elasticity of marginal valuation in a variety of contexts. The various models and underlying assumptions are examined. The fundamental point made in the chapter is a reminder of a long-recognised (but often forgotten) point that there is no way to move from an observation of what 'is' to what 'should be'.

Part IV of the book is concerned with tax revenue and its variations. Chapter 11 discusses the concept of the tax revenue elasticity, that is the elasticity of revenue with respect to income, at the individual and aggregate levels. This concept plays a central role in the analysis of fiscal drag, arising from the failure to adjust tax threshold for inflation. Chapter 12 examines the concept of the elasticity of taxable income, which attempts to measure in one elasticity all behavioural responses of taxable income to an increase in a marginal tax rate. The assumptions required for the use of such an elasticity, and its role in obtaining measures of the excess burden of income taxation, are considered in detail. Chapter 13 then turns to consideration of the way in which these two elasticities combine to generate an elasticity of tax revenue (again at individual and aggregate levels) in response to an increase in a marginal tax rate. Finally, chapter 14 presents a diagrammatic treatment of tax revenue in a multi-rate income tax structure, involving the well-known Lorenz curve of income distribution.

Part V turns to an examination, not of tax structures, but of two wide-ranging reviews of tax structures which have recently been produced. Chapter 15 discusses the report by the Tax Working Group in New Zealand, conducted under the aegis of the Centre for Accounting Governance and Taxation Research at Victoria University of Wellington. Chapter 16 is concerned with the large-scale review produced by a group of economists connected with the Institute of Fiscal Studies in London. These chapters examine the strengths and, in some cases, weaknesses of the reviews, while recognising the ambitious and difficult nature of such exercises. In discussing the various issues, it is perhaps not surprising that attention is again directed towards the arguments presented in chapter 2, which highlighted the 'tax and transfer tensions' which are inevitable in tax policy debates. In view of the many tensions involved, it is argued that economists can make a valuable contribution to rational policy debate by clarifying the nature of the interdependencies and relationships involved, and attempting to obtain orders of magnitude regarding a range of relevant summary measures and behavioural responses.

Part II

Theory and Policy

Chapter 2

Tax and Transfer Tensions

This chapter is concerned with the question of why it is so difficult to design a direct tax and transfer system having widespread support and longevity. Tax structures, particularly their transfer components, are regularly revised and public debates over reforms are typically heated. It is perhaps not surprising that the topic is prominent in debates: taxes affect everyone and transfer expenditure is now a very large proportion of total government expenditure. Furthermore, tax changes inevitably involve losers as well as gainers.

Attempts to clarify the main tensions involved in tax planning and to explain why consensus is unlikely ever to be achieved could follow two broad paths. First, 'positive' analyses attempt to explain the determinants of actual choices. This may involve the examination of public choice mechanisms and voting behaviour. It may also involve the analysis of bureaucratic behaviour, or the characteristics of politicians who need to compromise and do not necessarily act in disinterested ways. Interesting historical comparisons could, for example, be explored.

Secondly, a 'normative' approach could be followed. Instead of attempting to explain actual behaviour, this involves welfare economics which essentially investigates the implications of adopting particular value judgements. It explores the tax and transfer structure that would arise from specified basic values, and of course there is unlikely to be a consensus regarding such values. Value judgements are inevitable in the design and evaluation of tax structures: there is no such thing as a value-free optimal structure. The wide range of elements means that there is considerable scope for conflicting objectives, which are not simply different but imply mutually inconsistent policies. Although views about the role of a tax and transfer system vary substantially, in debates the basic value judgements which influence policy recommendations are seldom made explicit.

However, normative analyses cannot avoid the positive treatment of individuals' behaviour. Taxes and transfers affect the behaviour of individuals and families in ways that are not easy to predict, but which impose severe constraints on the ability of governments to achieve their objectives. For example, attempts to redistribute income using progressive taxes are restricted by adverse incentive effects on both low-income and high-income groups. Attempts to help one group of individuals often have unintended consequences for other groups. In short, incentives matter and it is necessary to have some idea of how behaviour is likely to change when the incentive structure changes. These reactions and interdependencies are of course of special interest to economists.

The present chapter follows the second path of attempting to clarify the role of value judgements in designing tax and transfer systems. There are really two types of tension, arising from conflicting values and from the practical constraints on policy arising largely from the government's budget constraint. Section 2.1 begins by producing what is essentially a taxonomy, which decomposes the elements into a range of components where value judgements are required and where constraints are imposed on the ability of governments to pursue these aims. This allows the role of a wide range of value judgements and the specifically economic components to be separated. Then section 2.2 looks at some simple forms of tax structure to illustrate how a range of problems and conflicts can arise.

2.1 Elements of the Problem

This section discusses the wide range of aspects of tax design where value judgements are relevant and where constraints are imposed on governments. A framework, or taxonomy, is produced allowing the various aspects to be decomposed.

2.1.1 Some Initial Considerations

Governments have the basic power to tax as part of their constitution, but the kind of tax and transfer system chosen depends on broad attitudes to a range of aspects relating to the role of the state. These attitudes include the following.

The tax structure is influenced by views regarding the extent to which governments may intervene in people's lives. Tax administration involves obtaining private information. It may, for example, also involve forcing people to take particular jobs. Attitudes towards these aspects are influenced by views regarding certain basic freedoms or rights. A related issue here is the level of government chosen to carry out necessary administration.

The ways in which individual responsibilities are perceived are important. For example, unemployment has variously been judged as a failing of individuals, or alternatively as a 'problem of industry'. This affects the extent to which people are categorised as being 'deserving poor' or 'non-deserving poor'.

The nature of a tax and transfer system adopted will depend on a range of paternalistic judgements. For example, some judges may prefer to provide benefits (such as rent assistance, food stamps and so on) which are linked to certain specific goods. Or, the view may be taken that people should make minimum savings for retirement in the form of a special income-related contribution in addition to income taxation.

An important factor is the view taken of intra-family intra- and inter-generational transfers versus a state system of support involving compulsory taxation. This has been particularly relevant in the context of aged care and disability care, where there have been substantial changes in attitudes over time.

A choice must be made regarding those eligible for the receipt of transfers, or payment of taxes. This may involve the choice of a social insurance type of system whereby unemployment and sickness benefits and pensions are available only to those who have a history of tax (or 'national insurance' contributions). Alternatively, eligibility may be related to nationality or residence requirements.

A judgement must be made regarding the tax base. This may be some concept of income, consumption or wealth. The decision here is influenced by views regarding the main aims of the tax system, and often a variety of tax bases are used. A comprehensive income concept involves the awkward treatment of unrealised capital gains and the coverage of such a tax.

2.1.2 Alternative Basic Aims

It is very hard to obtain a precise specification of attitudes towards the basic aims of a tax and transfer system. However, the following broad aims may be distinguished.

The view may be taken that poverty alleviation is the only or main aim of a transfer system. But even within this choice there are further difficult decisions, including the specification of a poverty line and whether this is regarded in relative or absolute terms. Also the measurement of poverty is not straightforward. The most commonly used measure is a head count measure, but some judges may prefer to allow for the depth of poverty and inequality among those considered to be in poverty. Using the headcount measure the most effective way to reduce poverty, given a certain amount of money to spend, would be to deal first with those nearest to the poverty line.

Even among those whose main concern is poverty alleviation, there can be substantial disagreement. For example, in the 19th century, poverty was seen by many people as the only legitimate concern, but the poverty line was set at a low subsistence level, with emphasis on avoiding adverse incentive effects, using the concept of 'less eligibility'. However, with a Rawlsian type of maximin approach, arising from extreme aversion to inequality, the objective is to raise the minimum level as high as possible, without any regard to the wider effects on the rest of the income distribution.

Concern may be with redistribution more broadly defined. Again, the measurement of inequality is far from straightforward, involving complex value judgements. For example, popular measures such as the Gini and Atkinson inequality measures are based on very different value judgements. The Gini is based on pairwise comparisons among individuals and involves judgements regarding fairness, while the Atkinson measure is linked to an additive Paretian welfare or evaluation function satisfying the 'principle of transfers' and involves wastefulness of inequality. The principle of transfers is the value judgement according to which a transfer from a richer to a poorer person, without changing their ranks, is considered an improvement. In practice these measures do not necessarily rank distributions in the same way. If redistribution as a major aim is combined with a desire to provide a social insurance type of scheme, with sickness, unemployment and pensions based purely on membership of a labour market category, the compulsory risk pooling with heterogeneous individuals produces some redistribution which is very hard to isolate from more systematic forms.

Some judges attach priority to other objectives, such as shifting some people into work, or increasing the labour supply of those working few hours. Alternatively, they may wish to encourage things like investment in education. Judges may have differing attitudes towards the family.

2.1.3 Constraints on Policy Choices

Although the government has the power to tax, there are severe constraints on its ability to raise revenue and to control the number of those claiming benefits. These aspects give rise to what are generally referred to as adverse incentive and moral hazard problems. The following features are relevant.

A tax and transfer system inevitably involves a reduction in labour supply, leading to lower revenue and more benefit recipients. In the low-income ranges there is a reduced incentive to participate in the labour market, and in the higher-income range there is an incentive to reduce working hours. Similarly, transfer systems affect retirement incentives, as well as those affecting saving for retirement. There are usually adverse incentive effects on non-target groups: for example, an attempt to shift some people into work or induce others to work longer hours may reduce the incentives of higher-income recipients, whose tax rates are increased by the need to raise additional tax revenue.

Incentive effects apply to many areas other than simply the supply of working hours or effort. Tax structures can affect the choice between employment and self-employment, educational choices, the incentive to shift from income to capital gains, and risk taking. The attempt to increase retirement incomes, for example through a compulsory superannuation contribution scheme, may reduce other forms of private savings. Other incentive effects include family and household formation, fertility decisions and of course internal and international migration.

The incentive and moral hazard effect imposes severe constraints on the ability to redistribute income or alleviate poverty. There is indeed some limit to the revenue which can be raised by any tax structure. This may itself depend not only on the method of raising revenue but on non-transfer expenditure. For example, labour supply may be affected by tax-financed expenditure on education and health, or infrastructure projects. Constraints also include basic perceptions of taxable capacity, the willingness to impose conditions on benefit recipients or impose structures to obtain private information, the ability and willingness to monitor the behaviour of benefit recipients, and a tolerance of 'waste' (in terms of administration costs, or transfers that are higher than 'necessary' or otherwise not well targeted). Unfortunately, relatively little is known about the orders of magnitude of these effects.

In considering the important role of incentive effects, it must of course be recognised that many individuals may be at corner solutions, an essential characteristic of which is that small changes (to say a person's net wage) are not sufficient to induce a movement away from the corner. Indeed, the highly nonlinear budget constraints which arise from income taxes with progressive rate structures and income thresholds, and means testing with benefit abatement rates, give rise to a wide range of potential labour supply responses at different ranges of the constraint. At certain corners, individuals may display 'sticky' behaviour in the face of net wage changes (resulting from tax changes), while in other ranges a very small net wage change can induce a large discrete change in labour supply.

The existence of such constraints implies that the attempt to achieve some stated aim in devising an ideal tax structure must be formulated as a constrained optimisation problem. That is, some evaluation function, which attaches weights to certain objectives such as equity and efficiency (appropriately defined), is maximised subject to at least a government budget constraint. This formed the starting point of the modern theory of optimal taxation. In this way tax policy is seen as a branch of welfare economics.

The discussion is typically in the context of the design of a tax and transfer system. However, in practice decisions relate to policy changes or reforms to an existing system, inherited from the past. Individuals will have made plans on the basis of an existing system, so any changes which may be regarded by judges as a movement towards a better system will involve unanticipated gains or losses for many people. Furthermore, administrative structures may be in place which are difficult to change in the short run. The nature of the losses and gains, along with the administrative costs of change, will generally impose further constraints on policy reforms. It is clearly important to have detailed information on the characteristics of those individuals who may experience significant losses from a reform. These considerations may be said to impose a bias towards the status quo. The emphasis of the literature on optimal taxation has been predominantly on fundamental design features, rather than with optimal tax *reform*.

In the optimal tax literature, the major constraint considered is the government's budget constraint, influenced by the kind of incentive effects mentioned above. This ignores potentially very important administrative costs. For example, means testing usually imposes high administrative costs, and gives rise to complexities and unanticipated ambiguities in the interpretation of regulations. The modern public economics literature, with its emphasis on 'second best' welfare economics, has undoubtedly neglected the extremely important and wide range of problems associated with the administration of tax structures, particularly where a range of agencies is involved.

2.1.4 Conceptual Choices

Mention was made above of the difficulties of defining and measuring concepts such as poverty and inequality. But even before such problems can be tackled, it is first necessary to make a number of fundamental conceptual choices. These can be described briefly as the 'what, when and who' of the study.

The choice of what to measure concerns the concept that is often called the welfare metric. This may be consumption, some income measure, or a broader measure such as utility (or money metric utility) which allows for the benefits of leisure time. A distinction can be made between approaches that are 'welfarist', in that policies are judged in terms of things that are thought to matter directly to the individuals concerned, and those which are 'non-welfarist'. The latter includes, for example, concern for an income-based measure of poverty or a specified number of working hours.

A choice must be made regarding the appropriate time period of measurement: should income or consumption be measured in weekly or annual terms, or over a longer time period? The chosen time period may differ depending on whether the concern is primarily about poverty or inequality. For poverty, a short period may be chosen, whereas for inequality, a judge may be more concerned with longer time periods. In the latter case, transitory variations are not considered important, and here a distinction between consumption and income also becomes less important. The pattern of systematic and transitory variations in income or consumption over time becomes important, particularly with a progressive rate structure in which more variable incomes pay higher amounts of tax than steady income streams having the same total. In examining redistribution it is not easy to separate intra-generational and inter-generational income transfers, since many transfers may involve income shifting over periods of the life cycle as well as transfers between individuals. The redistribution arising from risk pooling in an insurance scheme may be viewed quite differently from more systematic forms of redistribution, and much of the apparent redistribution among individuals is effectively shifting income between stages of the life cycle.

A decision must be made regarding the basic unit of analysis. This may be the individual, the household or some other concept. In selecting a unit, regard must also be made to the treatment of income and consumption sharing within families and households. This involves the choice of adult equivalence scales, where (without further direct evidence) an assumption is usually made of equal sharing, so that each person is given, say, income per adult equivalent. The choice of scales also cannot avoid value judgements. Sometimes concern may be with a subset of individuals, such as children. It is also possible to select the equivalent adult as the unit of analysis. Indeed the choice of individuals or equivalent adults as units arises from quite different value judgements. With the latter, the income concept and the unit of analysis are treated consistently, ensuring that each individual's contribution to inequality and poverty depends on the demographic structure of the household to which they belong. An adult in a one-person household for example will 'count for one', whereas the same adult in a multi-adult household will count for 'less than one'. This approach also satisfies the basic equity principle, associated with the principle of transfers, such that a transfer of income from a poorer to a relatively richer household, which leaves the position of the richer household unchanged, causes inequality to rise. The fulfilment of this principle enables Lorenz curve analyses to be conducted from the resulting distribution. Using the individual as the basic unit of analysis assigns to each of the individuals in a household the total household income per adult equivalent person. Every individual effectively 'counts for one', irrespective of the demographic nature of the household to which they belong. This approach consequently has the property of anonymity, in that inequality and poverty measures remain unchanged when one individual in the population is replaced by another individual who has the same living standard but belongs to a different demographically structured household. The individual unit of analysis does not in general satisfy the principle of transfers.

2.1.5 Measurement and Modelling Problems

Having made decisions regarding basic aims and concepts, many problems remain regarding the evaluation of policies. There is much room for disagreement over likely orders of magnitude involved, even among those judges with similar value judgements. Some of these problems are listed here.

Many economic variables are not easily measured. For example, given the role of durable goods, consumption over a specified period cannot be directly measured, unlike expenditure. The extent to which income or consumption is actually shared in households is seldom known, and some goods are 'public' within households but 'private' between households. Also income, wealth and unrealised capital gains are notoriously difficult to measure. These measurement problems are increased when a longer period is considered relevant, given the short time-frame used by most surveys.

Despite the importance attached to the incentive effects of taxes, modelling these responses presents huge challenges. The various potential responses (concerning savings, labour supply, the form of income, employment status, education, household formation, fertility and so on) all present their own modelling, data and estimation difficulties. Furthermore, some highly innovative tax reforms may be so far from previous experience that the prediction of responses is particularly awkward. In addition the degree to which individuals fully take up benefits to which they are formally entitled is not known. The availability of data, and their limitations, play an important role in understanding these responses.

Responses to administrative changes, for example involving the severity to which various rules are interpreted by tax and benefit officers, are also extremely difficult to predict but may be important. Also, rules may be interpreted in different ways in different administrative offices. Any ambiguity in the framing of rules can thus lead to inconsistencies.

In view of the measurement problems, reliance must inevitably be placed on assumptions and guesses about orders of magnitude, and these can be expected to differ even among those judges with similar value judgements. In particular, views about tax incidence are important, but difficult to quantify precisely, with the consequence that tax shifting is typically neglected in policy design.

2.2 Some Simplified Comparisons

It may be thought that, given explicit statements regarding the aims and incentive effects of taxes and transfers, it would be possible in principle to derive an optimal structure, using the methods of constrained maximisation. However, even for extremely simple specifications of the economic environment in simple economic models, and fully specified value judgements, this problem is largely intractable and very few clear results can be derived. Numerical methods of solution can be used, but the results are unable to provide clear practical policy guidance given the simplicity of the models. However, they have helped to emphasise the role of incentive effects and the resulting constraints on income redistribution, and may even have influenced the widespread flattening of rate structures through reductions in top marginal rates.

The present section therefore takes an indirect approach. That is, specifies the form of tax and transfer system and examines how it performs with respect to a range of criteria. A number of important features are demonstrated using simple diagrams.

In practice there are of course many types of transfer payment or benefit, some of which have overlapping qualifying conditions, and some benefits are taxable while others are not. They are often administered by different agencies, which can lead to unintended consequences for overall tax rates and can produce jumps and discontinuities in the relationship between net (after-tax and transfer) and gross (pre-tax and transfer) income. However, to highlight basic tensions it is useful to consider simplified forms of tax structure. The present section examines some of these tensions within a simple framework where only individuals are relevant (the existence of families and households is ignored) and it is assumed that all individuals have no non-income differences which matter (that is, they have no special needs relating to individual characteristics). All difficulties relating to the income concept are also ignored.

2.2.1 The Rate Structure

A full description of any tax and transfer structure is provided by the way in which marginal and average effective tax rates vary over the range of relevant incomes. A progressive structure is one for which there is an increasing average rate over all incomes: this does not require marginal rate progression (an increasing marginal rate). The degree of progressivity depends on the income distribution as well as the tax structure.

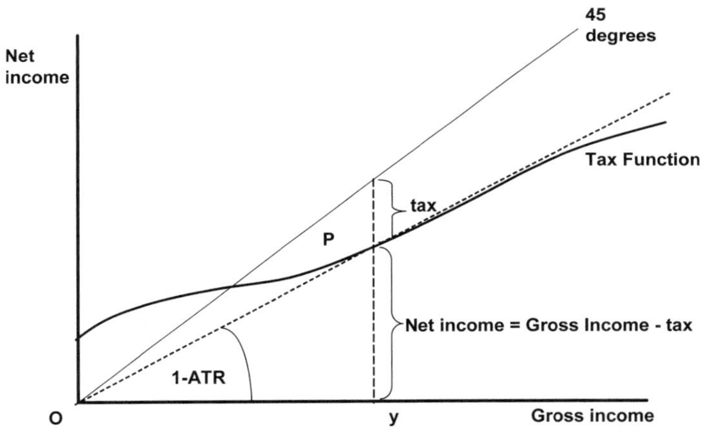

Figure 2.1: A General Tax Function

Figure 2.1 shows a general tax function in terms of the relationship between net and gross income, z and y respectively. The 45 degree line represents the absence of a tax or transfer. If the tax paid (which may of course be negative since it includes transfers) is represented by $T(y)$, then $z = y - T(y)$ and the average tax rate (ATR) at any point is given by $ATR = T(y)/y$. Hence $1 - T(y)/y = (y - T(y))/y = z/y$ and the slope of a line from the origin to a point on the schedule, at say P in Figure 2.1, is a measure of $1 - ATR$. The marginal tax rate (MTR) is given by $MTR = dT(y)/dy$ and so the slope of the tax function at the point is equal to $1 - MTR$. Redistribution is influenced by the average rate schedule while incentives are reflected in the marginal rate schedule.

2.2.2 The Basic Income–Flat Tax

The simplest possible type of tax structure is represented by a straight line in this type of diagram. Suppose there is a proportional income tax applied to all (non-transfer) income; this is shown in Figure 2.2. In addition each individual receives an unconditional transfer payment, or basic income, b. This shifts the tax schedule to the line BC. This simple structure goes under a variety of names, depending partly on how the administration of the scheme is described, but the clearest description is of a 'basic income–flat tax', or BI–FT.

The marginal tax rate, t, is constant along the whole of the range BC, but the average tax rate is initially negative until the break-even level of income, y_B, is reached. The two rates are illustrated in Figure 2.3.

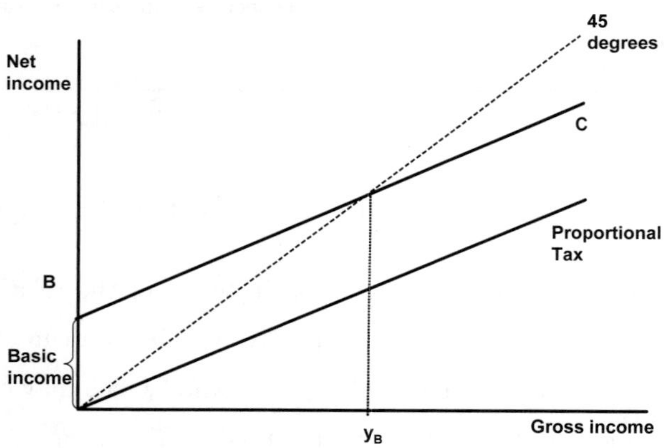

Figure 2.2: The Basic Income and Flat Tax (BI–FT)

This kind of tax structure is clearly capable of being highly redistributive

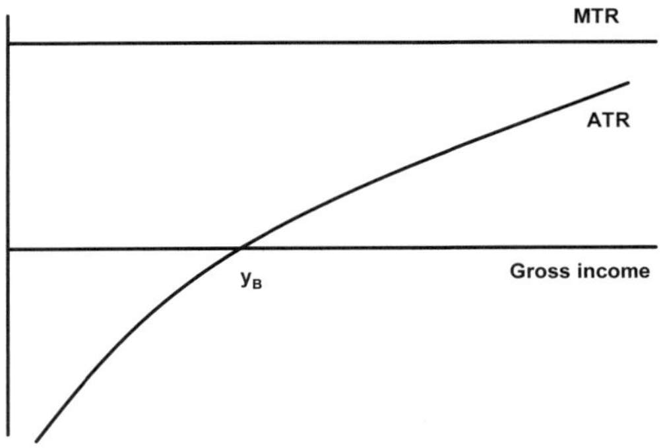

Figure 2.3: Marginal and Average Tax Rates with BI–FT

despite the constant marginal tax rate. The existence of a basic income makes it possible for some individuals to decide not to participate in paid employment (if they otherwise face a very low wage rate). The argument sometimes made that a basic income is unfair because the rich as well as the poor receive the same transfer payment carries no weight, because what matters is the profile of the average tax rate generated by the combined effect of the tax and transfer system.

It is not possible to select values of b and t independently. This is because of the existence of the government budget constraint, whereby income tax revenue must be sufficient to pay for the transfer payments made to each person. It can be seen that the tax rate must be equal to the ratio of the basic income to arithmetic mean income, bearing in mind that mean income is also affected by the tax parameters through incentive effects. Thus for a basic income of, say, one half of average income, it is necessary to have a marginal tax rate of 50 per cent, and if the basic income is a proportion, 0.3, of average income, the tax rate must be 0.30.

The BI–FT clearly has many advantages of simplicity, but the question arises of whether it is actually consistent with any particular set of value judgements and properties of the population. Early studies in the 'optimal tax' tradition, based on the (constrained) maximisation of an evaluation function defined in terms of individuals' utilities (viewed as functions of leisure and net income), and which involved a trade-off between equity and efficiency, did indeed produce a tax structure that is approximately linear. The 'welfarist' objective clearly tolerates the existence of non-workers and is concerned with inequality rather than an income-based poverty measure. However, further analysis has shown that the result is not robust when some assumptions, for example concerning the basic distribution of wage rates in the population and the type and degree of inequality aversion of the judge, are relaxed.

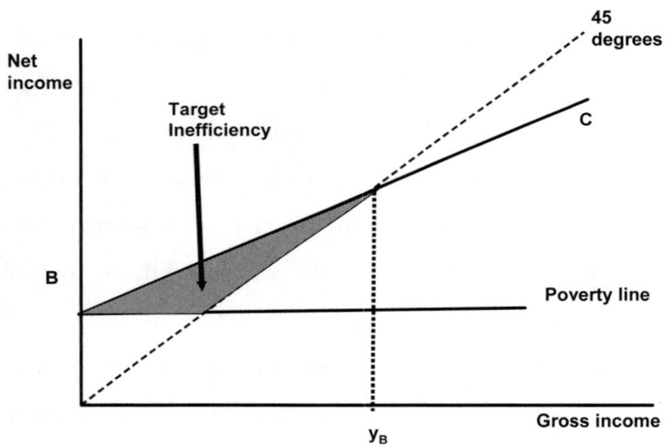

Figure 2.4: Target Inefficiency of Transfers

Those people who regard poverty alleviation as the main objective of a transfer system are critical of the BI–FT because, if b is set at the agreed poverty line, the unconditional basic income pays many individuals amounts which are regarded as excessive. This is illustrated in Figure 2.4, where the shaded area represents a degree of 'target inefficiency'. That is, if the objective is to prevent people falling below b, these transfers need not be paid and the tax rate can be much lower.

2.2.3 Means-Tested Benefits

A tax structure which deals only with poverty alleviation (that is, has a 'non-welfarist' objective) is shown in Figure 2.5, and this is referred to as a minimum income guarantee. This requires an income tax structure with a tax-free threshold, along with means testing of the transfer payment. The tax-free threshold must have a particular relationship with the guaranteed minimum income and the income tax rate, if discontinuities in the tax schedule, ABC, are to be avoided. The implied tax rates are shown in Figure 2.6, where the means testing implies that all those below the threshold income of y_T face a marginal rate of 1. The marginal tax rate above y_T can be lower than in the BI–FT having the basic income equal to the guaranteed minimum. However, the existence of a marginal tax rate of 1 over a large range of income generates a strong work disincentive. Those in favour of the minimum income guarantee argue that it is better to have a very high marginal rate applied to as small a number of people as possible, as this enables the marginal rate facing middle- and higher-income people to be correspondingly lower.

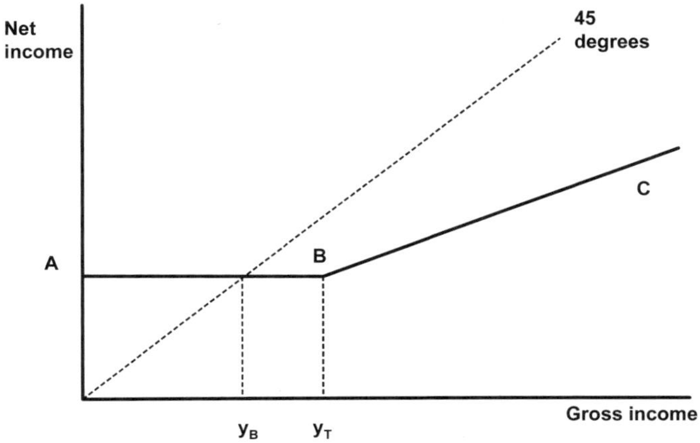

Figure 2.5: A Minimum Income Guarantee

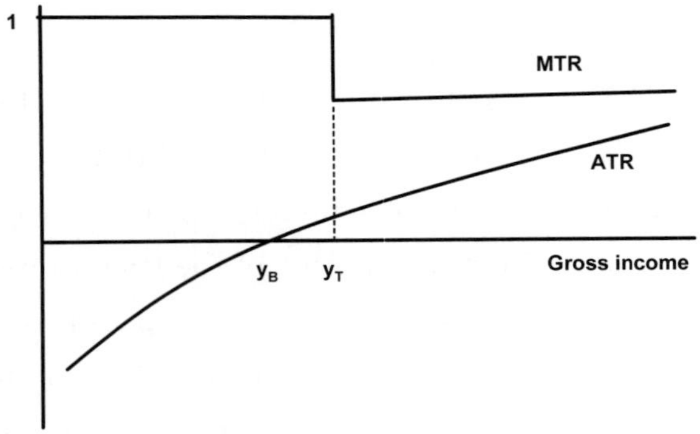

Figure 2.6: Marginal and Average Tax Rates with MIG

This point highlights a particular tension in tax policy design. The extreme adverse incentives created by the minimum income guarantee may be mitigated to some extent by reducing the marginal tax rate applied to benefit recipients. This is achieved by reducing the benefit abatement, or taper, rate applied to the means-tested transfer payment below 100 per cent. The result is shown in Figure 2.7 as a modified minimum income guarantee, where it is assumed that the tax and transfer parameters are such that the two linear segments of the relationship between net and gross income meet at the single point, B.

This reduces the marginal tax rate facing benefit recipients, but it does not unequivocally lead to an overall increase in labour supply. This is because the reduced means testing means that more people receive benefits: hence an additional group of medium income-earners face an increase in their effective marginal tax rate. Hence the attempt to improve the labour supply incentives of one group of people cannot avoid reducing the incentives facing another group. The reduced means testing is also likely to require a change in the marginal rate for those who only pay income tax, in view of the government's budget constraint. It is not possible to say, a priori, which direction the rate is likely to move.

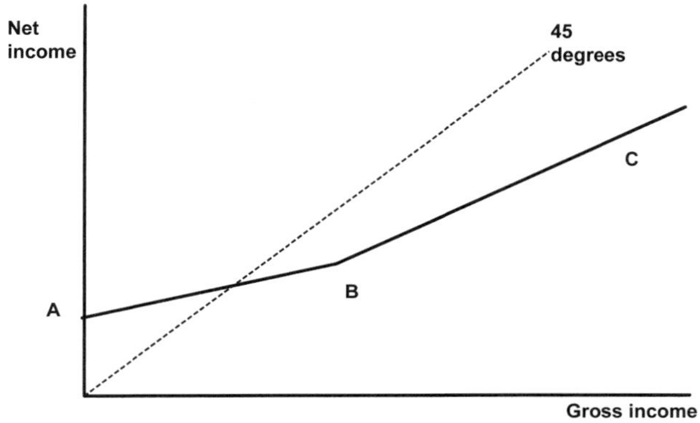

Figure 2.7: A Modified Minimum Income Guarantee

Some judges in recent years have attached importance to the desire to induce individuals to work for a specified minimum number of hours per week, using a substantial increase in a transfer payment at that hours level. This is achieved using a form of in-work payment, where there is a discontinuity (in the form of a sudden upward shift) in the net income available to individuals. But the gross income level at which this arises varies among individuals because it is related to a work hours level, rather than an income threshold. Notwithstanding the problems of monitoring hours levels and dealing with the variability in the time worked by casual workers during each week, such a scheme may indeed succeed in raising the labour supply of some groups of lower-wage individuals. But it inevitably reduces the labour supply of higher-income earners above the threshold, for which the effective marginal tax rate is higher than otherwise. This form of non-welfarist objective is thus highly likely to conflict with other aims of a tax and transfer system.

2.3 Conclusion

This chapter has considered the question of why consensus regarding the design of a tax and transfer scheme is unlikely to be reached. It was shown that a large number of value judgements are involved. These judgements involve not only the basic aims of a tax system, but a wide range of component elements. Many of these views are mutually inconsistent. Also, considerable information is needed about individuals' behaviour and characteristics, and in the absence of reliable empirical evidence, planners often have quite different perceptions about orders of magnitude.

By examining very simple structures, the chapter illustrated the difficulties of balancing different objectives. A desire to be generous to those individuals who face very low wage rates (or are unable to work for various reasons) inevitably means that the number of benefit recipients increases and the tax required to raise revenue has adverse incentive effects on other individuals. Benefits and tax rates cannot be increased without limit. Means testing of benefits may be introduced in order to restrict the number of eligible recipients, avoid providing benefits to middle- and high-income groups, and avoid a high tax rate being imposed on those groups. But it damages the incentives facing the poor: this is sometimes referred to as the poverty trap. However, an attempt to reduce the severity of means testing by reducing taper or benefit abatement rates must inevitably raise the marginal tax rate facing those middle-income individuals who become eligible. A careful balancing act is therefore needed, making an equilibrium highly elusive.

The question naturally arises of how economists can contribute to debates on tax reforms. Regarding different value judgements, the important point is one made long ago in a book by the famous economist Lionel Robbins (1935) that economists should investigate the implications of adopting clearly stated value judgements, rather than attempting to impose (in a professional capacity) their own values.

There is of course a need to continue to develop methods of modelling the incentive effects of different tax structures, in ways which accommodate the considerable heterogeneity which exists among individuals. In considering the types of model which would be of value for economists to develop, it is always worth bearing in mind that all models have their limitations. It is not possible to construct a single model capable of handling all types of personal tax problem and all kinds of potential responses to taxes. Sometimes, depending on the context, smaller and more restrictive models can be useful in highlighting important interdependencies. In other contexts, larger models are needed. In practical policy design, it is argued that a valuable role can be played by behavioural microsimulation models, while at the same time being aware of their limitations. One substantial advantage is that such models can be used to examine the potential effects of proposed policy changes, and can highlight the precise nature of the distribution of gains and losses. They can thus be used to contribute to practical policy debates regarding reforms, rather than concentrating on ideal structures which suppose that policy makers have not inherited an existing system and administrative structure.

In reporting results of analyses of the potential effects of tax policy changes, there is clearly a need to provide a wide range of summary measures, bearing in mind the various criteria used by different judges to evaluate policies. In fact a valuable role can be played by negative results here: that is, it may be far from obvious until numerical values are produced that certain objectives are mutually inconsistent. By considering a wide range of detailed and summary results from policy simulations, it is possible to articulate views about value judgements as well as appreciating the role of incentives. In this way economists can provide the kind of information which allows readers to form their own conclusions, and can thereby contribute towards rational policy debate rather than the exchange of prejudices.

Chapter 3

Income Tax Structure: Theory and Policy

If asked for practical advice about taxation, economists for many years would have referred to Adam Smith's (1776) famous four maxims. These were contribution according to ability to pay (there was some ambiguity here as to whether Smith held a benefit view or a sacrifice view), certainty, convenience and efficiency – the latter including administrative costs, distortions to activity, and the 'vexation and oppression' involved. While the list of such criteria was extended and clarified,[1] in the discussion of ability to pay it is clear that there was no acceptance of a redistributive role.[2] An explicit preference for equality of treatment via proportional taxation was made most clear in the often quoted remark by McCulloch, the author of the most extensive and systematic treatment of public finance in the classical literature. McCulloch (1845, p. 147) argued that:

> The moment you abandon the cardinal principle of exacting from all individuals the same proportion of their income or of their

[1] In particular it was extended by Lord Overstone, who suggested that a tax should be productive, computable, divisible, frugal, non-interferent, unannoyant, equal, popular and uncorruptive. This classification influenced Norman, who added 'unevasibility'. Norman's approach was dominated by his utilitarian view of sacrifice in an ability to pay context; see O'Brien (2009).

[2] Later explorations of the concept of 'equal sacrifice', as discussed for example by J.S. Mill (1848), left some ambiguity here, but see below.

> property, you are at sea without rudder or compass, and there is no amount of injustice and folly you may not commit.

The appropriate tax rate is thus determined by the independently given revenue requirement. The income tax structure at the time had a tax-free threshold and there were no transfer payments, but the 'degressive' rate structure meant that it was proportional for higher-income recipients.

The main change in the approach to taxation came from the later integration of public finance into the general area of welfare economics, which was itself a major concomitant of the successful introduction of a utility maximising approach to exchange in the 1870s. However, the most systematic early developments came from Cohen Stuart (1889) and Edgeworth (1897) in investigating the broad implications for progressivity of the utility maximising principle, in the context of the minimisation of the total disutility from taxation – ignoring any possible benefits. With the criterion of minimising total sacrifice, progression arises from decreasing marginal utility, but with equal absolute sacrifice it depends on the precise behaviour of the marginal utility of income. Even here, taking a 'classical utilitarian' perspective, there was no explicit independent role for redistribution: the maximand was strictly considered to be *total* utility.

This movement reached its ultimate conclusion in the optimal tax literature, beginning virtually a century after the initial introduction of a utility analysis into economics.[3] The utilitarian and mathematical analyses of Edgeworth were extended by allowing, in particular, for labour supply incentive effects of taxes and transfers, and including a range of specifications of the objectives of taxation, thus introducing an explicit redistributive role. In this final development, most of the important criteria suggested by Smith and others were quietly ignored. The relevant branch of welfare economics

[3] And indeed that analysis, at its inception, included the utility treatment of labour supply behaviour, by Jevons (1871). It arises from the emphasis on exchange, that is, selling labour in return for consumer goods.

into which optimal tax theory falls is the theory of the second best, in view of the fact that the government is unable to tax individuals' ability endowments and instead taxes their incomes. Sometimes stress is placed on asymmetric information aspects, in that the government cannot observe ability levels. However, the maximisation of a social welfare function itself presupposes a huge amount of information (including net incomes, hours levels and resulting utilities of all individuals).

In drawing on this branch of modern economic theory to provide policy advice regarding tax structures, a number of serious difficulties immediately arise. Tax models have a way of getting very complicated very quickly. For example, for the simplest possible tax and transfer structure – the linear income tax – with individuals differing only by productivity, the government budget constraint is nonlinear in the tax parameters if there are some nonworkers. Many interdependencies are usually involved and while economists are specially trained to identify such inter-relations, clear views can only be obtained by abstracting from many realistic features. Indeed, many of the strong results from tax analyses (for example, certain equivalence results concerning uniform direct and indirect taxes in general equilibrium models) are best interpreted as demonstrating that in fact they are most unlikely to apply in practice.[4] Furthermore, value judgements are inevitably involved because virtually every tax and transfer has distributional implications, and ultimately what matters is not the equity effect of a single tax considered in isolation, but the overall impact of a wide range of taxes and transfer payments (the latter being a relatively modern development). Many economic analyses are specially designed to give insights into the nature of the interdependencies involved.

[4] A further example is the result that indirect taxes are not necessary if preferences are separable between goods and leisure (marginal rates of substitution between goods do not vary with the wage rate).

The possible effects of taxes are often expressed in terms of measures for which it is extremely difficult to obtain empirical counterparts. Insofar as these models provide policy advice, this is often expressed in broad terms and is of a negative nature. As Edgeworth suggested when discussing income taxation and the concept of minimum sacrifice:

> Yet the premises, however inadequate to the deduction of a definite formula, may suffice for a certain negative conclusion. The ground which will not serve as the foundation of the elaborate edifice designed may yet be solid enough to support a battering-ram capable of being directed against simpler edifices in the neighbourhood. (1925, ii, p. 261)

It is important to understand why clear results may not be achieved, or why intuitively appealing results may not be reliable. But patience in the face of such limited results requires a taxonomic turn of mind that is more congenial to economists than those who need to provide direct policy advice or support. The more realistic the model, the more it has to be restricted to highly specific questions. For a general discussion of types of tax model, see Creedy (2001a).

The theory of optimal income taxation provides an interesting case study. It can be argued that analyses in this tradition have generated valuable insights into the highly complex relationships involved. They have clarified what early investigators referred to as 'the grammar of arguments' and there was no pretence that they were designed as guidance for practical policy advice. The results are largely – as in so many other cases – of a negative nature. Nevertheless, it is possible that the substantial changes in the personal income tax structures of many countries over the last 30 years – in particular, reductions in the number of marginal tax rates and the degree of rate progression – have been influenced by the optimal tax literature.[5] Care must be taken in making such statements. Establishing a clear rationale for each policy action is of course far from straightforward, and the social welfare functions which play a fundamental role in optimal tax theory seldom represent the varied objectives of politicians.[6]

In view of these problems, the aims of this chapter are modest. It begins in section 3.1 by briefly discussing the role of rules of thumb in policy advice, in particular the rule concerning broad bases and low rates, and the adherence to it in New Zealand. Section 3.2 then considers the simplest possible tax and transfer system, the linear income tax, as a way of illustrating why optimal tax models quickly become intractable. Insights from optimal tax modelling regarding the tax rate schedule are then discussed briefly in section 3.3. Optimal tax modelling typically relies on small simulation models in which there is negligible population heterogeneity. However, practical policy advice regarding the effects of alternative tax structures can be provided with the use of behavioural microsimulation models in which the full extent of population heterogeneity is represented along with all the details of highly complex tax and transfer systems (compared with the simple stylised forms used in optimal tax analyses). Nevertheless, when using such models it is important to be aware of their limitations. In particular, they deal only with the supply side of the labour market and, despite modelling labour supply, have no genuine dynamic element. Furthermore, they deal only with financial incentive effects rather than administrative behaviour and monitoring features designed to reduce moral hazard. On behavioural modelling, see Creedy and Kalb (2006). While it does not seem practicable to use such models to pro-

[5]For an empirical study of changes in income tax structures in many countries, see Peter *et al.* (2007). They show how the flattening of rate structures spread from higher- to lower-income countries, and document the use of flat-rate systems in post-communist countries since the mid-1990s.

[6]Indeed, there are familiar theories about the ways in which politicians may wish to exploit the lack of transparency of complex tax structures.

duce optimal nonlinear structures, a method of examining marginal reforms is proposed and illustrated using a simple model in section 3.4.

In the absence of direct policy advice from economic theory, more partial arguments are discussed in subsequent sections. These regard things to keep in mind with nonlinear personal tax structures. In view of recent and planned changes to the New Zealand income tax structure, special attention is given to the role and effectiveness of a top marginal tax rate at higher income levels, in revenue raising and generating redistribution and progressivity. Section 3.5 examines the effect of a top rate on selected progressivity measures. Examples are given in section 3.6 of the variety of welfare effects arising from the introduction of a top marginal tax rate.

3.1 A Rule of Thumb

There are some basic principles which are worth keeping in mind in thinking about tax structures. These include points such that: there is a difference between legal and economic incidence and taxes can be shifted in various ways (including tax capitalisation); large efficiency costs (in the form of excess burdens) can arise even when taxes appear to have little effect on behaviour; incentives matter. These points differ from the kind of maxim proposed by Smith (1776), in that here the emphasis is on the link from theoretical insights to specific policy advice. This list could easily be extended, but still does not provide strong positive advice. However, many economists (particularly those working in treasury departments) take as a starting point the basic principle that the best taxes are those having a broad base and low tax rate. As a simple rule of thumb, this is not a statement derived from a set of fundamental or universal principles, or axioms. It is meant only as a guiding aim which, though not precise, does have valuable content. Departures from the rule require a special case to be made. A broad base, which is obtained by allowing few exemptions and deductions, is of course required in order to achieve a low tax rate, for a given revenue objective. In turn, the need for low rates is generally seen in terms of the efficiency costs of taxation, where appeal is made to the long-established result that the excess burden of a tax is approximately proportional to the square of the tax rate.[7]

Of course, it is not straightforward to explain concepts such as excess burden to politicians, or to persuade them of the importance of the principle of tax capitalisation or of incentive effects. These latter effects influence another term in the excess burden approximation, the compensated demand elasticity – whether of consumption goods or leisure. The confusion between Marshallian and Hicksian (compensated) responses is also common in this context. Nevertheless it is important to continue to stress these concepts and to argue that particular policies require a trade-off to be made in terms of a balance of the perceived benefits of a tax policy against the estimated efficiency costs. It is necessary to make explicit the value judgements involved and the nature of the trade-off between gains and losses. This leads to the concept of the social welfare function which is central to optimal tax theory.

The New Zealand tax system typically scores relatively well when applying the basic broad base–low rate rule of thumb. For example, the goods and services tax, GST, has few exemptions and a single rate, whereas many other countries exempt (or zero rate) goods such as food, and apply a higher rate to 'luxury' goods. Attempts to justify exemptions are usually made on equity grounds: household budget shares for those goods are typically higher for households with low total expenditure. But this kind of selectivity has poor target efficiency qualities, the rich after all do spend more on the same goods, and there are also good administrative arguments for uniformity. These administrative arguments have less force in the context of developing economies. The spurious argument is often used that indirect taxes are regressive because high-income households save more, but this is

[7]For an indirect tax, the approximation is one half of the product of expenditure on the good, the compensated demand elasticity and the square of the tax rate.

easily dismissed. On the role of exemptions, see Creedy (2001b). Furthermore, the information needed for the imposition of an optimal non-uniform indirect structure is unlikely to be available and equity objectives can be achieved using direct taxes and transfers (which relate directly to the characteristics of the individuals involved). Exceptions are of course made in the case of excises, such as those imposed on tobacco, alcohol and petrol, which are imposed for a variety of paternalistic and externality arguments (along with revenue-raising qualities). These appear to have little overall redistributive effect, but excess burdens on some household types can be quite large; on excise taxes in New Zealand, see Creedy and Sleeman (2006).

Regarding the income tax, New Zealand has no tax-free threshold and has not (for the employed) a wide range of deductions relating to various expenses, as in many countries, such as Australia where base erosion seems endemic. This all produces in New Zealand a higher tax base and helps to keep income tax rates lower than otherwise. When making comparisons it is necessary to keep in mind that there are no separate social insurance contributions in New Zealand, as in many other countries. However, in viewing the base, New Zealand cannot be said to have a comprehensive income tax: in particular, most capital gains are not taxed.

The broad base–low rate rule of thumb suggests, through the excess burden relationship with the tax rate, a preference for a flattish income tax rate structure, although of course this does not allow for redistribution objectives and associated trade-offs which may lead to modifications. In New Zealand there are means-tested transfer payments which produce very high effective marginal tax rates for lower-income earners. Furthermore, the abatement (that is, taper, or benefit withdrawal) range for some transfers extends far up the income ranges, so that effective tax rates are significantly above the marginal income tax rates. Furthermore, a higher top marginal income tax rate was reintroduced, after being eliminated in the 1980s reforms which had substantially flattened the income tax rate structure.

A top marginal tax rate is typically introduced on the grounds that it is needed for reducing inequality. However, it is well known that tax rate progression is not needed for progressivity – indeed a linear tax (basic income with flat tax, or BI–FT) is highly redistributive, such that many individuals face a negative average rate, and the average rate is increasing over the whole income range. Furthermore, the top rate may (though not always, if the top threshold is relatively low) produce little extra revenue. The argument is also sometimes made that the labour supply elasticity, especially for higher-income prime-age males, is low so that the incentive effects of a top rate are negligible. However, labour supply behaviour is much too complicated to be described by a single elasticity. Further, even if the observed elasticity were low or zero, this could still coexist with large welfare costs and high excess burdens because it is the Hicksian elasticity that matters. Section 3.6 below returns to this issue.

3.2 The Linear Income Tax

It seems useful, though at first sight perhaps perverse, to begin by ignoring the fundamental question of the optimal *form* of an income tax and transfer system, and to concentrate instead on the narrower question of determining the optimal tax rate in the simplest possible kind of modelling framework, namely a linear structure. There is thus only one policy variable, the tax rate, that can be chosen independently, while the other decision variable, the universal or basic income, is determined via the government's budget constraint (discussed in more detail below). Indeed, this type of system is the basic 'workhorse' of optimal tax analysis, on which a number of variants have been built. It serves to demonstrate that the simplest system – it would indeed be impossible to imagine a simpler redistributive tax and economic environment to examine – is very far from being straightforward.

The framework is entirely static, involving a single period partial equilibrium model. Individuals can vary their hours of work continuously without constraint, at a fixed gross wage rate. Each individual's ability level, which determines the wage rate, is fixed and there are no other sources of income other than the untaxed transfer payment and earnings. Apart from the exogenous endowment of ability, there is an endowment of time (normalised to unity) which is divided between work and leisure. Individuals are considered to maximise utility, which depends only on an index of the consumption of marketed goods and services (where the price index is normalised to unity) and the proportion of time spent working. Apart from differences in abilities, individuals are assumed to be identical: they have the same utility functions and have no non-income characteristics which influence judgements regarding, for example, special needs (hence the basic income can be the same for all individuals). Of course, population heterogeneity is a fundamental feature of the real world and plays a crucial role in actual tax policy design (and is discussed further below). As mentioned earlier, the aim here is to demonstrate how awkward even the simplest unrealistic model is. The introduction of taste differences raises the potential for 'incentive compatibility' problems.

The framework is thus designed to be the simplest possible model for considering the elements involved in the trade-off between equity and efficiency considerations in setting the parameters of the simplest possible tax and transfer system. It is indeed trivially simple – and yet it turns out to give rise to substantial complexities. One simplification – the concentration on one form of government expenditure – is perhaps worth stressing here, particularly in view of the fact that one important lesson from a welfare economics perspective is that what matters is the overall effect of a multi-tax, multi-expenditure system, rather than the effects of each component taken in isolation. Any revenue collected for non-transfer purposes is considered simply to disappear into a 'black hole', rather than being devoted to activities such as the production of public goods, or education and health services, which would in principle affect individuals' utilities. Furthermore, such expenditure would be expected to affect individuals' productivities and thus their wage rates. The extension of an optimal tax approach to the analysis of the *composition* of government expenditure, as well as its magnitude, in this framework presents further complexities which cannot be discussed here, but which of course cannot be ignored in practical discussions.

The cornerstone of the analysis is the government's budget constraint, showing the relationship between the basic income, b, and the tax rate, t, needed to finance it. This is illustrated in Figure 3.1, where a minimum tax rate, $t_{\min}$, is needed to finance the non-transfer expenditure. If the tax is below this rate, the system requires the use of a negative basic income, that is a poll tax, to raise the non-transfer revenue. The constraint reflects a tension between 'rate' and 'base' effects of an increase in t: an increase in the rate produces a higher revenue with an unchanged total income (the base), but the base falls because of adverse incentive effects. This supposes that the substitution effect – arising from the cheaper price of leisure – outweighs the income effect of the change in the net wage. Initially the 'tax rate' effect dominates the 'tax base' effect, but at some point, where the percentage increase in the tax rate is exactly matched by the percentage reduction in total income, total revenue (and thus b) reaches a maximum. If $\bar{y}$ denotes average income and R is non-transfer revenue per head, the budget constraint is:

$$b = t\bar{y} - R \tag{3.1}$$

Hence, $\frac{d(b+R)}{dt} = \bar{y} + t\frac{d\bar{y}}{dt}$ and:

$$\frac{t}{(b+R)}\frac{d\,(b+R)}{dt} = 1 + \frac{t}{\bar{y}}\frac{d\bar{y}}{dt} \tag{3.2}$$

Thus the budget constraint becomes flat when the elasticity, $\frac{t}{\bar{y}}\frac{d\bar{y}}{dt} = -1$. This point is clearly reached before t reaches unity.

Although the equation of the budget constraint looks superficially simple, to move from (3.1) to a relationship between b and t is not simple because

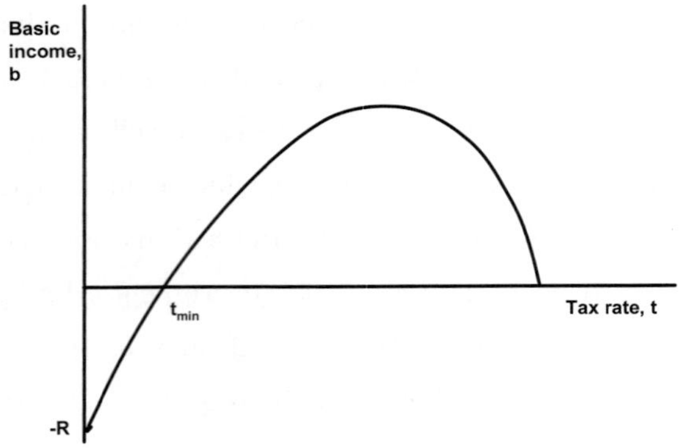

Figure 3.1: The Government's Budget Constraint

$\bar{y}$ is a function of the tax parameters, the preferences of individuals and the form of the distribution of wage rates, w. Unless strong assumptions are made regarding utility functions and the wage rate distribution, (3.1) is nonlinear.[8]

The choice of t (and consequently of b) must obviously be somewhere along the government's constraint. The issue thus arises of the choice of decision mechanism. The crucial point about the optimal tax framework is that tax choices are considered to be made by a single individual – variously referred to as a policy maker or decision maker or independent judge – who is entirely disinterested, that is, does not have a personal interest in the outcome. Hence a social welfare, or social evaluation, function is maximised, representing the value judgements of the decision maker. The welfare function is *not* regarded as representing any kind of aggregation of the views of members of the population.

The role of optimal tax analysis is therefore, from the very outset, to

[8]Suppose hours worked, expressed as a function of the gross wage, are $h(w) = 0$ for $w \leq w_m$ and $h > 0$ for $w > w_m$. Then if $F(w)$ is the distribution function of wage rates, arithmetic mean earnings are $\bar{y} = \int_{w_m} wh(w)\,dF(w)$. Even in the special case where $h(w)$ is linear in w (which arises if preferences are Cobb–Douglas), the threshold wage, w_m, is itself a function of preferences and the tax parameters.

examine the implications of adopting particular value judgements. Even if the model were not so unrealistic, no professional economist could state, on the basis of an optimal tax analysis, that, for example, the tax rate should be set at $t = x$. Furthermore, the addition of the words 'in order to maximise the welfare of society' at the end of that sentence would be meaningless, given the concept of the welfare function used. The approach can say only, for example, that for the value judgements made explicit in the evaluation function used, the optimal rate turns out to be $t = x$.

Clearly, a vast range of welfare functions could potentially be examined. In the majority of analyses, the implications of adopting a 'welfarist' evaluation function are examined: this means that welfare, W, is considered (where it is also individualistic) to depend on the variables that are of importance for the individuals themselves, that is, their utility levels. Hence, with n individuals $W = W(U_1, ...U_n)$.[9] Each individual is maximising utility, subject to the tax parameters chosen, so indirect utility for each person, V_i, can be written as $V_i(t, b)$ where the other parameters (such as those of the direct utility function) have been suppressed. Hence, in principle, it is possible to think of the welfare function being abbreviated into an expression in terms of the decision variables t and b, and this in turn gives rise to social indifference curves. These can be represented in Figure 3.1 as upward-sloping convex indifference curves, the nature of which depends on, among other things, the judge's attitude towards inequality.[10] If the judge has extreme aversion to inequality, concern is only to maximise the welfare of the poorest person and indifference curves are horizontal. Such a judge would select the tax rate at which the budget constraint reaches a peak, that is for which the

[9]The optimal rate depends also on the cardinalisation of utility used in the social welfare function, which is not surprising as any monotonic transformation is equivalent to attaching different weights to utility at different levels. When individuals have relevant non-income characteristics (concerning the size and composition of their household) further value judgements are required in relation to the use of adult equivalent scales and the income unit.

[10]In fact, they may not be convex, but the discussion here is not affected.

elasticity, $\frac{t}{\bar{y}}\frac{d\bar{y}}{dt}$, equals -1. The downward-sloping section of the constraint is thus irrelevant. As inequality aversion falls, and the judge places relatively greater emphasis on efficiency considerations, the indifference curves become steeper (a given increase in t must be accompanied by a higher increase in b to compensate) and the optimal tax rate falls. However, an indifference to inequality – as in the case of classical utilitarian judges – does not necessarily produce vertical indifference curves. The optimal rate is likely to produce a positive b and may also involve the existence of some non-workers.

Any information that an increase in an existing tax rate is likely to produce a reduction in total revenue clearly suggests that, whatever the inequality aversion of the judge, the rate is too high. Non-transfer government revenue also plays a role. With zero net revenue, the optimal linear rate is expected to fall as the elasticity of substitution between net income (consumption) and leisure rises, because the substitution effect of a tax rise is likely to be larger (so the budget constraint is flatter). But with positive net revenue, the fall in the optimal rate is eventually reversed as the elasticity of substitution rises. This is because the minimum rate needed to finance the non-transfer revenue increases as the elasticity rises.

So far, the results are quite general. Anyone asking for specific advice about the optimal rate to impose in a linear tax structure would not welcome the information simply that the first-order conditions imply a tangency between the budget constraint and the highest social indifference curve. More structure must be imposed, but even with simple forms for the social welfare function (such as the widely used iso-elastic case of constant relative inequality aversion), the common utility functions and the wage rate distribution, closed-form solutions are not available.[11] Numerical simulation results, involving iterative methods to solve for the basic income which can be financed with any given tax rate, are therefore ubiquitous in the optimal tax literature.

[11]Special cases of explicit solutions have been produced, some of them involving quasi-linear utility functions: see chapter 5.

The tangency solution view of first-order conditions for social welfare maximisation therefore provides limited insights. Starting from the same conditions, an alternative approach, which exploits duality theory, can be used to show that the optimal linear tax must satisfy the following condition, first given by Tuomala (1985):[12]

$$1 - \frac{\tilde{y}}{\bar{y}} = \left|\eta_{\bar{y},t}\right| \tag{3.3}$$

where $\left|\eta_{\bar{y},t}\right|$ represents the absolute value of the elasticity of average earnings with respect to the tax rate, and has already been discussed in the context of the shape of the government budget constraint. The term $\tilde{y}$ is a welfare-weighted average of earnings, where the weights are equal to $v_i / \sum_{i=1}^{n} v_i$, with $v_i = \frac{\partial W}{\partial V_i}\frac{\partial V_i}{\partial b}$. The latter is the weight attached by the social welfare function to an addition to person i's income (from an increase in the basic income).

The left hand side represents the proportional difference between the welfare-weighted mean of earnings and the arithmetic mean, which can be interpreted as a measure of the inequality of gross earnings. For example, extreme inequality aversion on the part of the judge would attach the highest value of 1 to this inequality measure, whatever the statistical earnings differences, and as seen above $\left|\eta_{\bar{y},t}\right| = 1$ represents the highest point of the government budget constraint. This might be thought to provide further insights in view of the fact that both sides of the equality in (3.3) deal with earnings, which are clear empirically relevant counterparts, unlike some other components of the model. Discussion can proceed in terms of a diagram showing the profiles of each side of the equation as t varies, and the way in which they, and hence their point of intersection, are likely to shift as basic assumptions are changed. However, this expression does not provide a closed-form solution. Even the welfare weights, v_i, depend in general on the tax parameters.

[12] See chapter 4 for further details.

The optimal policy perspective of choice by an independent decision maker clearly differs from public choice models which consider particular aggregation mechanisms, such as majority voting. The first problem in considering voting schemes is that individuals' preferences over t are not in general single peaked. However, some interesting comparisons can be made between the different approaches. For example, in the simple majority-voting framework, a voting equilibrium is known to exist, despite the existence of double-peaked preferences regarding the tax rate, if there is 'hierarchical adherence', such that the ordering of individuals by their income is independent of the tax rate. In this case the median voter theorem can be invoked and the median here is the person with median wage. Equation (3.3) applies also in this case, except that the welfare-weighted mean, $\tilde{y}$, is replaced by the median. In the case of stochastic voting, the voting equilibrium is generated by maximisation of a function that may appear to look something like a social welfare function, involving the weighted arithmetic mean of utilities, or the weighted geometric mean, depending on the precise details. Again, unless special assumptions are made, interior solutions are not available.

The absence of closed-form solutions for this, the simplest possible model of a population group and a tax structure, is not of course the property that limits its value in providing policy advice. A wide range of simulation analyses can easily be carried out. The problem is that it is so far removed from reality, in order to illustrate as simply as possible the nature of the trade-offs involved and the underlying structure of such models, as to be useless as a practical tool. It was never intended to provide such a tool. However, its very simplicity serves to demonstrate that more realistic models are likely to be completely intractable, which raises the question of how to proceed. Before considering this question, the following section turns to the initial question raised and ignored in starting from a linear tax – that of the form of optimal tax function.

3.3 Optimal Tax Structures

In view of the difficulties of examining even the simplest structure, it cannot be expected that a more general analysis of the optimal rate structure would generate clear results. The optimal tax problem, which in general asks what tax structure maximises a specified evaluation, or social welfare function, is known from the work of Mirrlees (1971) to give rise to a problem in the calculus of variations. In view of the nonlinearities involved, solutions generally require numerical simulation methods, unless strong simplifying assumptions are made: explicit solutions are discussed in chapter 5 below. Unfortunately, it turns out that there are few general results available – the optimal structure depends on the nature of the social welfare function examined as well as the wage rate distribution and the nature of preferences. Earlier work suggested that, for a range of assumptions, the optimal structure is approximately linear.

But in fact it is not difficult to produce models in which different tax structures are optimal. A small selection of examples includes those discussed by Diamond (1988), Chang (1994), Hashimzade and Myles (2004), Myles (1999), Saez (2001) and Tuomala (2006). A basic issue relates to the social welfare function itself. Much of the literature is welfarist in that the welfare function is specified as some function of (indirect) utilities, that is, terms which matter to individuals. But since the fundamental aim is to consider the implications of adopting alternative value judgements, other non-welfarist forms cannot be ruled out. For example, social welfare may be based solely on an income-based measure of poverty. These can give quite different results. For further discussion see Kanbur, Keen and Tuomala (1994) and for a broader treatment of non-welfarist objectives, see Kanbur, Pirttilä and Tuomala (2004). Non-welfarist objects may go further than simply attaching no value to leisure, in that they may prefer to encourage labour supply (whereas in a welfarist approach the existence of non-workers is acceptable in an optimal structure): see, for example, Besley and Coate (1992).

Hence the general treatment of optimal tax structures yields very few clear results. For other reviews of policy implications of optimal tax theory see, for example, Stern (1984), Heady (1993), Tuomala (1995) and Bradbury (1999). For a more critical discussion, see Slemrod (1990). The most unambiguous results can in fact easily be established. First, any range where the marginal tax rate is greater than 100 per cent is clearly irrelevant. Consider Figure 3.2, which shows a tax function in a diagram with net income on the vertical and gross income on the horizontal axis. This displays a range AB where the marginal tax rate (equal to 1 minus the slope of the tax schedule) is greater than 100 per cent. It is clear that this range is irrelevant, since indifference curves relating net income and gross earnings are upward sloping and convex: an increase in gross earnings involves an increase in hours worked, which must be compensated by an increase in net income (consumption). An example of a preferred position, for a particular wage rate, is shown as the tangency between the tax function and the indifference curve. Hence AB can be replaced by a marginal tax rate of unity, showing that the maximum rate is 1. It can also be shown that negative marginal tax rates (in contrast with average tax rates) can be ruled out: however, this is not true of a social welfare function based on income-poverty, where a negative marginal rate can result for the lowest earners.

A further result states that the marginal tax rate on the highest income should be zero. In Figure 3.3 consider the tax function AB, where the person with the highest wage rate reaches a tangency position at C. If the tax function is changed to ACD, where CD is parallel to the 45 degree line, the individual then faces a zero marginal rate on any extra income earned. This induces a movement to a new tangency on a higher indifference curve. The total tax revenue is unchanged and no one else is affected: hence the richest person is better off and the non-zero top marginal rate cannot have been optimal, for any Paretian welfare function. However, this result is of

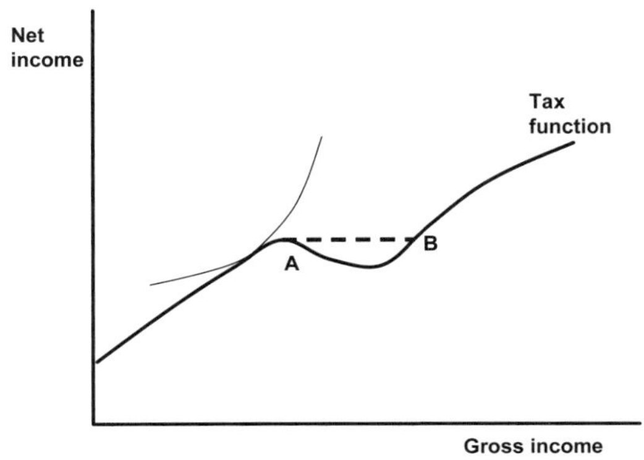

Figure 3.2: Maximum Tax Rate

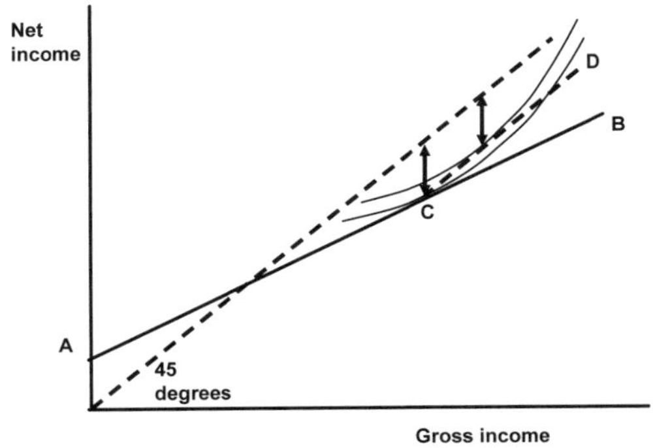

Figure 3.3: Tax Rate on Top Income

no practical relevance as there is no way to determine just where the rate should become zero.

One approach has been to consider piecewise-linear tax functions with just two or three rates. This allows for consideration of the question of whether marginal tax rates should be higher for those with relatively low earnings. Such higher marginal rates arise from the means testing of transfer payments. The resulting non-convexity of budget sets facing individuals can give rise to complex labour supply behaviour, as discussed below. Means testing is preferred by those who advocate target efficiency as the criterion by which schemes should be judged. Numerical analyses using welfarist social welfare functions show that in a very wide range of situations, the evaluation function is increased by a shift to lower taper rates and a flatter rate schedule. See, for examples, simulation results reported in Creedy (1998b) and for wide-ranging discussions of means testing, see also Atkinson (1995) and Bradbury (1999). Results inevitably involve special cases in highly simplified models with little of the considerable population heterogeneity that is observed in practice. They therefore cannot provide a strong basis for policy advice. Indeed, assumptions giving rise to means testing in an optimal structure are given in Diamond (1998). An emphasis on 'workfare', designed largely to encourage positive labour supply, rather than 'welfare', can also lead to high marginal rates imposed on low earners, as shown by Besley and Coate (1992).

Despite the dearth of general results, the optimal tax literature does support a broad argument for relatively low rates (the second part of the broad base–low rate rule of thumb), even with high inequality aversion, especially compared with the top rates operating in many countries in the 1970s. A small degree of substitution between leisure and net income imposes strong constraints on the government's ability to redistribute income. In the linear tax case, non-transfer government revenue also plays a role. With zero net revenue, the optimal linear rate falls as the elasticity of substitution (between consumption and leisure) rises. With positive net revenue, the optimal rate falls and then rises as the elasticity rises (because the minimum rate needed to finance the non-transfer revenue rises as the elasticity rises). As suggested earlier, the finding that, even in simplified models, optimal rates are not high may perhaps have had some influence on policy since the late 1970s when the very high top marginal rates existing in some countries started to be reduced.

A behavioural tax microsimulation model, which encapsulates the actual degree of population heterogeneity and most of the detail of actual tax and transfer systems, does not provide a convenient vehicle for producing an optimal tax structure. However, its advantage of providing information about changes in taxes may be exploited to examine the optimal direction of reforms. That is, such a model may be used to explore the directions of small changes in tax parameters which improve a specified social welfare function. An illustration of the kind of analysis which would be possible, but using a much simpler model, is provided in the following section.

3.4 Marginal Income Tax Reform

Consider the more realistic problem of how to move towards an optimal structure by a process of marginal tax reform. This has previously been examined in the context of indirect taxation, involving fixed incomes but differential taxation on a range of goods, where x_{ji} is the consumption of the ith taxable good by the jth household, and t_i is the unit tax on good i.[13] A standard result shows that an increase in social welfare, W, resulting from a change in the ith tax rate is:

$$\frac{\partial W}{\partial t_i} = -\sum_{j=1}^{n} v_j x_{ji} \tag{3.4}$$

where v_j is the social value of additional consumption by household j. Furthermore, aggregate tax revenue, R, from indirect taxes on K goods is given

[13] On marginal indirect tax reform see, for example, Ahmed and Stern (1984), Madden (1996) and Creedy (1999). See also chapter 9 below.

by:

$$R = \sum_{j=1}^{n} \sum_{k=1}^{K} t_k x_{jk} \tag{3.5}$$

and $\frac{\partial R}{\partial t_i}$ can be expressed in terms of (Marshallian) demand elasticities, at observed consumption levels, and expenditures. It is then possible to obtain values of the ratio, $-\frac{\partial W}{\partial t_i} / \frac{\partial R}{\partial t_i}$, the marginal welfare cost of raising tax rate i, for each good and thus to determine the required direction of changes, since an optimal system is characterised by an equi-marginal condition.

In considering income tax structures, a similar type of approach could be adopted to examine marginal adjustments to a piecewise-linear system. The social welfare function W is in this case a function of a set of marginal income tax rates and income thresholds (as well as summarising the value judgements involved). Similarly, total net revenue, R, is a function of the same set of tax parameters. It can be shown that if t_i now represents the i marginal rate, and y_j is person j's earnings, a similar result to that given above holds, whereby $\frac{\partial W}{\partial t_i} = -\sum_{j=1}^{n} v_j y_j$. For any piecewise-linear tax function, the tax paid by household j, $T(y_j)$, can be expressed as:

$$T(y_j) = t_k (y_j - a'_k) \tag{3.6}$$

where y_j falls into the kth tax bracket and a'_k is a function of all the thresholds (denoted $a_1, ..., a_K$) and marginal rates. The total tax revenue raised by those in the kth bracket, T_k, is thus:

$$T_k = t_k \sum_{j=1}^{n} (y_j - a'_k) \tag{3.7}$$

It would be possible to combine this kind of approach with a number of simplifying assumptions regarding elasticities of earnings with respect to tax rates and the proportions of earnings and people above a top rate, to consider, say, whether (for a given set of tax thresholds) a top marginal rate should be reduced or increased. For an extensive discussion on the use of elasticities to derive optimal tax rates, with emphasis on the choice of a top tax rate, and references to earlier literature, see Saez (2001). This appears to be an attractive route because, unlike the usual approach to optimal tax modelling, the conditions can be expressed in terms of (what appear to be) empirically observable counterparts such as elasticities. However, given the considerable complexities introduced by nonlinear budget constraints – unlike the consumption tax case where linear pricing is a reasonable assumption – any clear results need strong assumptions and could only be regarded as illustrative rather than of practical relevance. Nonlinear budget sets make it difficult to generalise regarding labour supply responses and welfare changes even for workers with similar preferences and with relatively simple tax structures. In practice, populations display considerable heterogeneity in preferences and household circumstances, and tax and transfer structures are extremely complex.

However, given a behavioural tax microsimulation model, there is no need to make simplifying assumptions about elasticities of earnings with respect to tax rates. The full extent of heterogeneity can be captured in behavioural microsimulation models. Such models could not realistically be used to produce an optimal tax structure, even for a clearly specified social welfare function. But for marginal reforms, the required changes, from an initial actual tax structure, could be obtained numerically. Starting from the actual tax structure, and considering small changes in a range of tax parameters, it is possible to use a microsimulation model to obtain values of welfare and revenue changes, denoted ΔW and ΔR respectively, for each tax parameter in turn. The marginal welfare costs, that is the change in welfare per dollar of extra revenue, $\Delta W/\Delta R$, should be similar for all tax parameters in an optimal system and so the direction of an optimal reform is indicated by relative orders of magnitude of these ratios.

In the absence of a New Zealand behavioural microsimulation model, the present section illustrates – nevertheless using a very simple model – the way

Table 3.1: Hypothetical Tax Structure

	Singles			Couples with children		
	Threshold	t_i	μ_i	Threshold	t_i	μ_i
1	0	0.15	150	0	0.15	300
2	200	0.25	170	200	0.85	440
3	650	0.35	235	450	0.25	170
4	1000	0.40	285	650	0.55	365
5	–	–		1000	0.60	415
6	–	–		1400	0.40	135

in which such a model could be used to examine optimal marginal income tax reforms. The first stage in illustrating the approach is to specify a hypothetical population. Two sets of populations were examined – single individuals with no dependants and workers in couple households with children (each couple is in fact modelled as if there is just one potential worker). The tax and transfer structure for each group is fully specified by a set of income thresholds and marginal rates, t_i, which apply above those thresholds, giving rise to a piecewise-linear budget line relating net income and hours of work. Each linear section, i, has a slope equal to the net wage $w = w_g(1 - t_i)$, where w_g is the gross wage rate, and when extended to the intercept where hours of work are zero, a non-wage virtual income of μ_i.

Each group is considered to face the tax and transfer structures shown in Table 13.1. In the table, the tax rates and income thresholds (expressed in terms of weekly income) are given, along with the μ_i. Only μ_1 is in fact specified and the other information is used to produce the other virtual incomes; for example, it can be shown that, for $i = 2, ..., n$, $\mu_i = \mu_{i-1} + y_i(t_i - t_{i-1})$. These effective tax schedules are chosen to be similar to those in New Zealand, although the marginal rate of 0.85 applied after \$200 is less than the very high rate of almost 100 per cent which actually applies as a result of means testing. The extension of means-tested benefits to higher-income ranges means that for couples with children, the marginal tax rate actually drops from 0.60 to 0.40 at a weekly income of $1,400. Calculation of labour supply must allow for the possibility of multiple local optima.

The population heterogeneity in each case is such that the joint distribution of wage rates and preference parameters (α, the coefficient on net income) in Cobb–Douglas utility functions is jointly lognormal, with a correlation of -0.75. The arithmetic mean of α is set at 0.75 for the case of both singles and couple workers, while the mean of log-wages is 2.7 and 3.0 for singles and couples respectively. The variance of logarithms of α is 0.10 for singles and 0.15 for couple workers. These values were chosen following experimentation in which the distributions of earnings (for simulated populations of 10,000 in each case) were similar to those for New Zealand in terms of the pattern of modes and antimodes. Suppose that the social welfare function, W, for each group takes the familiar additive individualistic Paretean form and is expressed as a function of utilities, U_j, with an inequality aversion coefficient of $\varepsilon = 0.5$:

$$W = \frac{1}{1-\varepsilon} \sum_{j=1}^{n} U_j^{1-\varepsilon} \tag{3.8}$$

A feature of optimal tax models is that results depend on the cardinalisation of utility functions used. The use of money metric utility, with current 'prices' as reference prices, was suggested by Creedy (1998b). The calculation of a social welfare function using money metric utility in a behavioural microsimulation model based on discrete hours random utility modelling of labour supply is examined by Creedy, Hérault and Kalb (2011).

Tables 3.2 and 3.3 show marginal changes for each marginal tax rate, for single individuals and workers in couple households. The change in each marginal tax rate involved a reduction of 0.02, that is two percentage points, with thresholds unchanged. Each table shows the welfare and revenue changes, along with the ratios $\Delta W/\Delta R$, and the elasticities of welfare with respect to revenue, $\eta_{W,R}$. In the case of couples, it can be seen that a reduction in the 5th marginal rate of two percentage points actually leads to an increase in tax revenue: this marginal rate is in practice affected by both means testing of transfers and the top marginal income tax rate.

Table 3.2: Marginal Tax Reforms: Singles

k	ΔW	ΔR	$\Delta W/\Delta R$	$\eta_{W,R}$
1	1.1974	−4.5569	−0.2628	−0.0646
2	1.9103	−7.9664	−0.2398	−0.0589
3	0.5746	−2.4185	−0.2376	−0.0584
4	0.3560	−0.6511	−0.5467	−0.1343

Table 3.3: Marginal Tax Reforms: Couples

k	ΔW	ΔR	$\Delta W/\Delta R$	$\eta_{W,R}$
1	1.1489	−5.6348	−0.2039	−0.0930
2	0.9349	−2.6391	−0.3543	−0.1616
3	0.7277	−2.3056	−0.3156	−0.1440
4	0.7248	−1.7888	−0.4052	−0.1848
5	0.3486	0.2484	1.4032	0.6400
6	0.3950	−0.6345	−0.6225	−0.2839

In these illustrative examples, the optimal reform is clear: a reduction in the top income tax rate produces the greatest payoff in terms of social welfare. Such illustrative exercises cannot be used as a basis for policy advice in practice, but they do highlight the way in which a behavioural microsimulation model could be exploited.

3.5 Redistribution and Progressivity

It has been mentioned that a common argument for applying a higher marginal tax rate to 'top incomes' is that it is needed for redistribution and progressivity. But the effects of a tax structure cannot be evaluated by looking at the marginal rate structure alone, as they depend fundamentally on the nature of the income distribution. This section provides some illustrative calculations of the effects of income tax structures under different income distributions. It is therefore concerned more with statistical issues than economic theory insights.

Consider the effect of income taxation alone. Table 3.4 shows thresholds and rates in New Zealand for the years 2006–7 and 2008–9. The rate structures are similar (except for the lowest rate) but thresholds are higher in 2008–9, reflecting the growth of incomes.

Table 3.4: New Zealand Income Tax Structures

2006–7		2008–9	
Threshold	Tax rate	Threshold	Tax rate
0	0.15	0	0.125
9,500	0.21	14,000	0.21
38,000	0.33	40,000	0.33
60,000	0.39	70,000	0.39

On the assumption that pre-tax incomes are lognormally distributed as $\Lambda(\mu, \sigma^2)$ where μ and σ^2 are the mean and variance of logarithms, suppose $\sigma^2 = 0.8$.[14] This gives a Gini inequality measure of 0.4589, and an Atkinson inequality measure (with inequality aversion of 0.5) of 0.1775.[15] Tables 3.5 and 3.6 report, for alternative values of μ, summary measures of the distribution of pre- and post-tax income. The upper part of each table shows the results for the actual structure and the lower part gives results obtained without the top marginal rate. The variable $\bar{x}$ is arithmetic mean pre-tax income, while G, K, L and g measure respectively the Gini inequality of post-tax income, the Kakwani measure of tax progressivity, the reduction in the Gini measure when moving from pre- to post-tax incomes (that is, the Reynolds–Smolensky measure of redistribution) and the overall effective tax ratio; on these measures see, for example, Creedy (1996).

[14] This is obviously a simplifying assumption for illustrative purposes. In view of the New Zealand tax and benefit structure, a further (small) mode is generated at the lower end of the distribution of taxable income, and other small modes and antimodes appear as a result of labour supply effects discussed above.

[15] Creedy *et al.* (2010) report average gross taxable income for 2006/7 of $33,503 with $G = 0.464$ and $g = 0.23$. The average annual 'wage' in this year was $46,000.

As expected, the tax structure (with or without a top rate) is more progressive and more redistributive as $\bar{x}$ increases, since more people are in the higher marginal rate ranges (though clearly this effect is reduced when the top rate of 0.39 is eliminated). However, for any given value of $\bar{x}$, the changes resulting from the elimination of the top marginal rate are very small. For example, considering the changes in the Gini measures of post-tax income, these are only affected at the third decimal place. The progressivity measures change by less than 0.01, and the effects on revenue, measured by g, involve reductions of less than one percentage point.

Table 3.5: 2006–7 Tax Structure

Income tax only						Income tax with MIG			
μ	$\bar{x}$	G	K	L	g	$y_m = 12k$		$y_m = 15k$	
						G	g	G	g
With top marginal tax rate									
9.8	26903	.4389	.1031	.0300	.226	.3373	.152	.2875	.101
10.0	32860	.4351	.1079	.0338	.239	.3669	.194	.3269	.160
10.2	40134	.4318	.1101	.0372	.252	.3885	.226	.3582	.204
10.3	44356	.4304	.1101	.0386	.259	.3966	.240	.3710	.222
Without top marginal tax rate									
9.8	26903	.4436	.0906	.0253	.218	.3425	.145	.2927	.094
10.0	32860	.4415	.0924	.0274	.229	.3737	.184	.3340	.150
10.2	40134	.4400	.0919	.0289	.239	.3971	.213	.3672	.191
10.3	44356	.4395	.0908	.0294	.245	.4062	.225	.3809	.207

For comparison, the right hand side of each table shows the effect on the Gini inequality measure of post-tax income and the overall average tax rate of introducing a minimum income guarantee (MIG), whereby those with after-tax income below y_m have their income brought up to y_m. Such transfer payments clearly have a much larger effect than marginal rate progression applied to the higher-income ranges.

Table 3.6: 2008–9 Tax Structure

Income tax only						Income tax with MIG			
μ	$\bar{x}$	G	K	L	g	$y_m = 12k$		$y_m = 15k$	
						G	g	G	g
With top marginal tax rate									
9.8	26903	.4355	.1302	.0334	.204	.3402	.134	.2923	.086
10.0	32860	.4316	.1332	.0373	.219	.3682	.177	.3303	.145
10.2	40134	.4281	.1333	.0408	.234	.3884	.210	.3600	.189
10.3	44356	.4267	.1321	.0422	.242	.3958	.224	.3721	.207
Without top marginal tax rate									
9.8	26903	.4391	.1201	.0298	.199	.3441	.129	.2963	.081
10.0	32860	.4367	.1204	.0322	.212	.3736	.169	.3358	.137
10.2	40134	.4350	.1177	.0339	.224	.3955	.199	.3673	.179
10.3	44356	.4345	.1153	.0344	.230	.4039	.212	.3803	.195

3.6 Welfare and a Top Marginal Rate

This section illustrates the variety of welfare changes arising from the introduction of a top marginal tax rate. It demonstrates that, even for individuals with similar tastes, welfare effects can vary substantially. Welfare changes are defined in terms of the individual's expenditure function, which is usually written as $E(w, U)$: it represents the minimum income needed to achieve a specified utility level, U, at a net wage, w. The approach used here is the standard method of obtaining welfare changes, which is sufficient for illustrative purposes.[16] The income involved in the expenditure function is in this context a 'full income' measure, M, defined as follows. If T is the maximum number of hours available for work, $M = wT + \mu$, where μ is virtual non-wage income, that is, the value of net income for zero hours of work (for the relevant section of the budget constraint). The expenditure function is thus written as $M(w, U)$ rather than $E(w, U)$ and is obtained by inverting the indirect utility function.

[16] However, Creedy and Kalb (2005) showed how such changes really need to consider the complete range of the nonlinear budget constraint facing each individual.

A change to the tax and transfer system may arise from changes in the effective marginal rates, the number of thresholds (and therefore nonlinear segments of the budget constraint) or the gross income thresholds. This may (but need not necessarily) change the individual's optimal labour supply and produce a change in the endogenous net or virtual wage rate and virtual income. The welfare effect of such a tax change is complicated by the fact that a change in either the net or virtual wage affects both the price of leisure and the value of full (or virtual) income. It is therefore useful to decompose the welfare effect into the price and income effects.

Consider a change in the tax system such that the net wage and full income for an individual change from w^0 and M^0 to w^1 and M^1. The equivalent variation can be decomposed as follows: and:

$$\begin{aligned} EV &= \left\{M^1 - M\left(w^0, U^1\right)\right\} + \left\{M^0 - M^1\right\} \\ &= EV_{\Delta w} + EV_{\Delta M} \end{aligned} \quad (3.9)$$

where the terms $EV_{\Delta w}$ and $EV_{\Delta M}$ relate respectively to the components arising from the reduction in the price of leisure over the range covered by the top rate and the fall in full income. Thus, $EV_{\Delta w}$ measures the welfare gain because leisure hours have become less costly in terms of after-tax income foregone, and $EV_{\Delta M}$ captures the loss in full income via the reduced net wage, w, associated with the tax increase. The terms in (3.9) are defined so that a positive value indicates a reduction in welfare, while a negative value implies a welfare gain. The absolute value of the first term in curly brackets in the above expressions corresponds to an area to the left of a Hicksian (compensated) leisure demand curve between appropriate 'prices' of leisure.

Examples of labour supply and welfare changes for hypothetical single individuals are shown in Table 3.7. The tax change examined involves a movement from the appropriate structure without a top marginal rate to the one with such a rate, indicated in Table 13.1: the terms sn and cn indicate either tangency or corner solutions on segment n or corner n of the corresponding piecewise-linear budget constraint. Each individual is assumed to have Cobb–Douglas preferences, with a coefficient on net income of $\alpha = 0.75$. The only difference between the individuals relates to their gross wage rates. Of course, many individuals – those who are not affected by the tax change – experience no welfare changes.

Table 3.7: Examples of Single Individuals

	Initial structure		With top rate		Welfare change			Tax
w_g	h	Pos^n	h	Pos^n	$EV_{\Delta w}$	$EV_{\Delta M}$	EV	change
18.4	55.09	s3	54.35	c4	−11.63	11.80	0.17	−4.77
25.0	56.38	s3	55.25	s4	−30.02	50.00	19.98	9.14
30.0	56.99	s3	56.04	s4	−34.87	70.00	35.13	24.14

Table 3.8: Examples of Couples with Children

	Initial structure		With top rate		Welfare change: ΔW			Tax
w_g	h	Pos^n	h	Pos^n	$EV_{\Delta w}$	$EV_{\Delta M}$	EV	change
22.6	45.23	s4	44.25	c5	−14.11	14.31	0.20	−12.25
25.0	51.89	s4	49.62	s5	−36.31	50.00	13.69	−19.10
28.2	54.61	s5	53.61	s6	−36.18	62.80	26.62	15.69
30.0	58.91	s5	58.12	s6	−31.83	70.00	38.17	28.94

The hypothetical individual with a gross wage of \$18.4 per hour reduces labour supply from 55.09 hours per week (on the fourth section of the initial relevant budget constraint) to 54.35 hours, which is at the corner solution introduced by the addition of the top marginal rate. The reduction in hours worked is small, at less than one hour, and the welfare change of $EV = 0.17$ is small, though the change in tax paid is actually negative (the individual is on the wrong side of the Laffer curve). However, the person with an hourly wage of \$25 also reduces labour supply by less than one hour but has $EV = 19.98$, composed of a marginal excess burden of \$10.85, and additional tax of \$9.14, implying a marginal welfare cost of \$1.19 – that is, an excess burden per dollar of extra revenue of over a dollar. The higher wage of \$30 results in a similarly small labour supply response, a much higher excess burden, but a smaller marginal welfare cost.

Table 3.8 shows hours and welfare changes for hypothetical workers in couple households with children, for the same tax change. In this case the absence of the top marginal rate (of 0.40) means that the initial effective rate structure has rates of 0.15, 0.85, 0.25, 0.55 and 0.35 applying above thresholds of 0, 200, 450, 650 and 1400. The worker with a wage of \$22.6 per hour actually has, before the tax change, tangency positions on segments 2 and 4, but the latter is the global maximum. The tax change gives rise to a move to the new corner solution (though the sub-optimal tangency on segment 2 is clearly unchanged). This gives rise to a small labour supply reduction, a small welfare loss, but again a tax reduction, so that again the wrong side of the Laffer curve is relevant. For the two higher wages of \$28.2 and \$30 per hour, the marginal excess burdens are similar, at \$10.93 and \$9.23 respectively, but the marginal welfare costs are \$0.70 and \$0.31 respectively.

These hypothetical examples demonstrate that it is very difficult to generalise about welfare changes, even for individuals with similar preferences. They all display small hours responses but substantial variations in marginal excess burdens and marginal welfare costs.

3.7 Conclusions

This chapter has considered, within a limited compass, the extent to which economic theory can offer specific policy advice regarding income tax structures. Ultimately, it was seen that many of the results are negative or too broad to offer direct policy guidance. Indeed, much of the theory has clarified instead just why it is very difficult to produce clear cut arguments. In providing policy advice, the point inevitably arises that the role of the economist is to examine the implications of adopting alternative value judgements

– and there are few results which do not depend in some way on the ultimate objectives of a tax system.

The extensive optimal tax literature does not provide, and was never expected to provide, clear guidance, but instead has clarified the precise way in which the optimal tax system depends on a wide range of factors, some of which relate to value judgements while others concern behavioural responses or basic conditions, such as abilities, which display considerable heterogeneity in practice. Clarifying just how certain conclusions rely on strong, and perhaps unrealistic, assumptions is of course part of the role of economists, yet it is understandable that this can provoke impatience in others.

In looking for practical advice, it appears that a more piecemeal approach must be used. That is, it is necessary to consider in turn a number of features, or their implications for particular specified outcomes, rather than hoping to produce a general rule. This chapter has discussed just a few of those factors, mainly in the context of the role of a top marginal income tax rate. Illustrative numerical examples were provided, showing the kind of calculation which may be made. In particular, it was suggested how a behavioural microsimulation model could be used to examine marginal reforms.

With reference to the statement made by McCulloch (1845), quoted in the introduction, economists might argue that the 'cardinal principle' of proportionality involves an unstated value judgement, and that there is now a better understanding of just why a simple 'compass' is not available (in view of the many measurement problems), and a better understanding of constraints imposed on any 'rudder' (or policy instrument) in attempting to achieve a policy objective. However, his argument does provide a reminder that any policy advice must be extremely tentative and will (given sufficient courage) often take the form of explaining (given the propensity of politicians to tinker with tax structures) just why a stated objective cannot be achieved by a particular policy initiative.

Part III

Tax Functions and Choices

Chapter 4

The Linear Tax Function

The purpose of this chapter is to provide a review of some of the problems involved in modelling the choice of tax rate in simple tax and transfer systems. The subject may be divided into two broad strands, positive and normative in nature. The positive line attempts to model policy choices and to investigate to what extent they can be explained as the outcome of voting behaviour. It combines modelling and empirical work. The normative line investigates the policy implications of adopting alternative value judgements. It typically uses modelling methods to examine choices implied by the maximisation of a social welfare function representing the views of a single decision maker.[1]

Special attention is given below to the simplest possible progressive tax structure, one having an unconditional transfer payment (or basic income) and a proportional income tax (or flat tax).[2] The combined effect is to generate an increasing average tax rate over the whole range of income and therefore a high degree of progressivity, even though the system has a constant marginal tax rate (and thus a non-progressive rate scale). This system may be administered in several ways (depending for example on whether in-

[1] It is often suggested that determination of the optimal tax is an exercise in 'second best' policy, since a first-best tax is one imposed on the unobservable basic endowment of ability.

[2] The following discussion considers income units for which income is the only tax-relevant variable, so that no transfers for special needs arise and income unit size and composition are irrelevant.

dividuals simultaneously pay tax and receive a benefit, or whether the net tax, which may be positive or negative, is assessed for each person), giving rise to different descriptions. But the terms 'linear income tax' or 'BI/FT' seem to be the least ambiguous.

The linear tax involves just two tax policy parameters, the basic income and the tax rate. However, the government faces a budget constraint whereby the tax raised must be sufficient to finance the transfer payment and any other non-transfer expenditure. Hence, it is possible to choose the level of only one parameter independently. Having selected the tax rate, a value of the basic income is implied. This structure therefore appears to offer a very simple policy choice: only the single income tax rate needs to be set, assuming that the non-transfer expenditure needs have already been decided.

If individuals' labour supplies, and hence their incomes, are fixed independently of the tax system, consideration of this choice is also simple. For example, complete equality could be achieved by setting a tax rate of 1 and sharing all the revenue equally, after covering non-transfer needs.[3] If the tax were to be decided democratically using majority voting, the relatively rich would vote for the minimum tax consistent with raising non-transfer expenditure while the poor would vote for the maximum feasible tax rate of 1. But of course in practice labour supply incentives are important: they impose severe restrictions on the ability of governments to redistribute income. The question then arises of what insights can be obtained about the choice of tax rate, given explicit statements about the decision-making process and information about individuals' preferences and their productivities. As mentioned earlier, the decision may for example be made as a result of a democratic vote, or it may be imposed by a government (seen as a single decision maker) holding a particular set of value judgements. The power to tax – to impose a non-voluntary imposition – is seen as a fundamental characteristic of gov-

[3]This assumes that the rich cannot vote for a poll tax (a negative basic income) to finance non-transfer expenditure.

ernments.

It is simple to describe in principle the mechanics of modelling tax choices in the context of the linear income tax where just one policy dimension is involved and heterogeneity only of abilities, and thus wage rates, is assumed to exist. The indirect utility function of each individual is obtained (by substituting optimal values into the direct utility function), and by using the government's budget constraint (relating the basic income to the tax rate) these are expressed in terms of the tax rate only (along with preference parameters of course). Using the median voter theorem, the majority-voting equilibrium is found by maximising the median voter's indirect utility with respect to the tax rate. To examine optimal policies the indirect utilities are substituted into a social welfare function, which is maximised with respect to the tax rate. Both are in principle unconstrained maximisation problems involving one variable. However, the resulting first-order condition usually turns out to be highly nonlinear. It is very difficult to produce analytical solutions, even with extremely simple models: see chapter 5 below. The technical literature is therefore extensive and usually involves the use of numerical solution methods to examine a range of assumptions.

Conceptually, the problem can also be stated simply in terms of the tangency of indifference curves (either of the median voter or the social decision maker) with a government budget constraint. But it is difficult to take such purely diagrammatic insights much further. Nevertheless some useful insights can be obtained for the linear tax structure using some basic algebra and related diagrams, as shown below. It is possible to highlight the kind of information which would be required to determine the tax rate – either in positive or normative contexts – and about the potential limits to redistribution imposed by the existence of incentive effects. The emphasis here is on two summary measures, those of earnings inequality and the elasticity of average earnings with respect to the tax rate. The properties of tax choices expressed in terms of these concepts can guide intuition regarding comparative static parameter changes.

Section 4.1 begins by describing the linear tax structure and examining the form of the government's budget constraint. Individuals' preferences regarding the choice of tax rate, subject to that constraint, are considered in section 4.2. Majority-voting outcomes and optimal tax decisions are then examined in sections 4.3 and 4.4 respectively.

4.1 The Tax System

This section describes the simple linear tax model and considers the resulting constraints faced by individuals and the government.

4.1.1 Individuals

Suppose earnings from employment, y_i, for $i = 1, ..., n$ individuals, are the only form of income, other than transfer payments. The linear income tax involves a flat-rate tax at the rate, t, along with an unconditional (non means tested) transfer payment of b per person. Hence the tax paid, $T(y_i)$, is:

$$T(y_i) = ty_i - b \tag{4.1}$$

and net income, z_i, is:

$$z_i = (1 - t)\, y_i + b \tag{4.2}$$

If $t > 0$ and $b > 0$ the tax is progressive.[4] The progressive nature of this type of structure can be seen from Figure 4.1, which shows an increasing average tax rate over the whole income range.

4.1.2 The Government's Budget Constraint

In addition to financing transfer payments from the income tax, suppose the government needs to collect net revenue of R per person. In the following

[4]However, if $b < 0$ the transfer payment is instead a poll tax. This arises if the tax rate is not high enough to finance non-transfer expenditure.

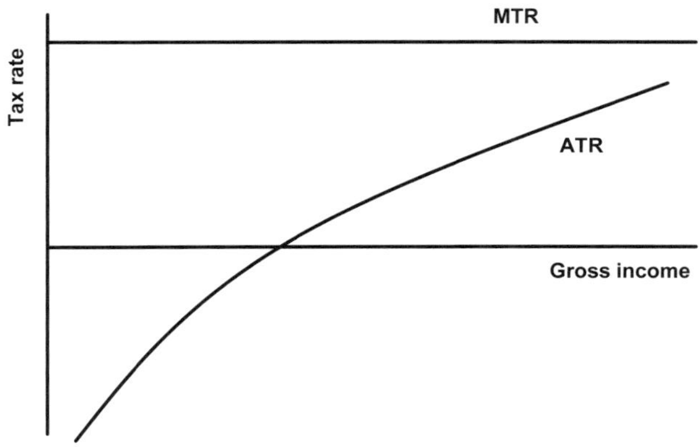

Figure 4.1: Average and Marginal Tax Rates in the Linear Income Tax Structure

analysis it is assumed that any expenditure arising from this revenue does not affect individuals' utilities. The government therefore faces a budget constraint of the form $nR + nb = t\sum_{i=1}^{n} y_i$, or:

$$R = t\bar{y} - b \tag{4.3}$$

Here $\bar{y}$ is arithmetic mean gross earnings, which depends on all the tax parameters as well as the distribution of wage rates and individuals' preferences. Holding R constant means that there is only one degree of freedom in the choice of t and b. The general form of the government's budget constraint, for fixed R, is shown in Figure 4.2. When $t = 0$, $b = -R$. So long as the tax rate exceeds $t_{\min}$, the linear tax structure is progressive.

The slope of the budget line, giving the variation in b as t varies, keeping R fixed, can be obtained by totally differentiating the budget constraint in (4.3) and setting $dR = 0$. Hence:

$$dR = \left(\bar{y} + t\frac{\partial \bar{y}}{\partial t}\right) dt + \left(t\frac{\partial \bar{y}}{\partial b} - 1\right) db \tag{4.4}$$

and:

$$\left.\frac{db}{dt}\right|_R = \frac{\bar{y} + t\frac{\partial \bar{y}}{\partial t}}{1 - t\frac{\partial \bar{y}}{\partial b}} \tag{4.5}$$

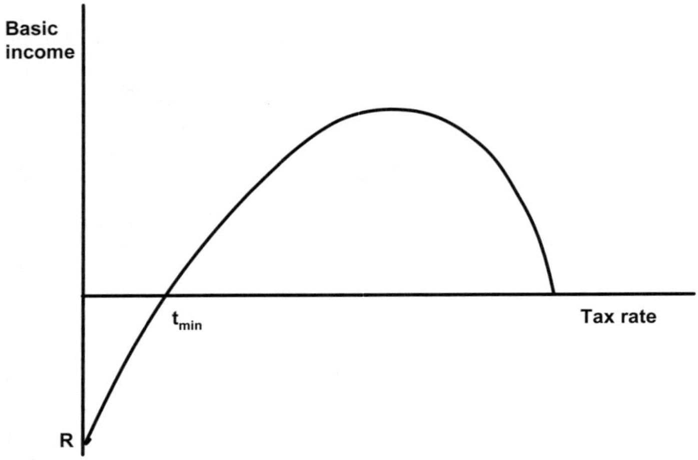

Figure 4.2: The Government Budget Constraint

The variation in average gross earnings as tax parameters vary can be obtained by totally differentiating, so that:

$$d\bar{y} = \frac{\partial \bar{y}}{\partial t}dt + \frac{\partial \bar{y}}{\partial b}db \tag{4.6}$$

and:

$$\left.\frac{d\bar{y}}{dt}\right|_R = \frac{\partial \bar{y}}{\partial t} + \left(\frac{\partial \bar{y}}{\partial b}\right) \left.\frac{db}{dt}\right|_R \tag{4.7}$$

This result could easily be converted into an expression involving elasticities. Hence the elasticity of $\bar{y}$ with respect to t depends on the partial elasticities of $\bar{y}$ with respect to t and b, along with the elasticity of b with respect to t along the government budget constraint.

4.2 Individual Behaviour

The aim of this section is to characterise an individual's preferred position on the government's budget constraint relating b and t. First, individual utility maximisation involving consumption and labour supply choices is considered in order to generate the indirect utility function expressed in terms of the tax parameters. Then the tax preferences of individuals are examined, depending on their earnings. The results are entirely general in that they do not depend on the form of utility functions or the distribution of wage rates.

4.2.1 Utility Maximisation

Let c_i and ℓ_i denote the consumption and labour supply of individual i, who faces a pre-tax wage rate of w_i, for $i = 1, ..., n$. Gross earnings are thus $y_i = w_i \ell_i$. The price of consumption is normalised to 1 and as the model is static, so that no savings are made, consumption and net income are equal; hence $c_i = z_i$.

Each individual maximises $U(c_i, \ell_i)$ subject to the budget constraint:

$$c_i = (1 - t) y_i + b \tag{4.8}$$

Suppose also that each individual is endowed with one unit of time, which may be divided between leisure and work. The effective price of leisure is the net wage. Full income, M_i, defined as the maximum income which can be obtained by devoting all available time to working, is thus:

$$M_i = w_i (1 - t) + b \tag{4.9}$$

The usual approach thus considers each individual as effectively obtaining full income and then purchasing consumption and leisure at prices 1 and $w_i (1 - t)$ respectively. Substituting the optimal values in the direct utility function gives the indirect utility function in terms of the net wage and full income, $V(w_i (1 - t), M_i)$: for present purposes this can be written more succinctly as $V(t, b)$.

4.2.2 Individual Tax Preferences

Consider each individual's preferences over the tax rate. Non-transfer expenditure is assumed to be set exogenously, so the government's budget constraint implies a value of b for any t. Hence only the latter can be selected independently. The choice must be over the tax rate, because there are two values of t corresponding to any given b, whereas choice of t gives rise to a unique b. Diagrammatically, each individual's indirect utility function $V(t, b)$ defines a set of indifference curves in Figure 4.2. If the individual works, an increase in t must be compensated by an increase in the basic income, b, so indifference curves are upward sloping from left to right. An individual's preferred position on the government budget constraint is therefore characterised by a tangency between an indifference curve and the constraint. The slope of the budget constraint is given in equation (4.5). The slope of indifference curves is given in the usual way, by setting the total differential of V equal to zero, so that:

$$dV = \frac{\partial V}{\partial t}dt + \frac{\partial V}{\partial b}db \tag{4.10}$$

and when $dV = 0$:

$$\left.\frac{db}{dt}\right|_V = -\frac{\partial V/\partial t}{\partial V/\partial b} \tag{4.11}$$

At this point, it is useful to employ a standard result from duality theory. In general for an indirect utility function of the form $V(p, m)$, for goods demanded, x_i, at prices, p_i, and a budget of m, Roy's Identity gives the Marshallian demands as $x_i = -(\partial V/dp_i)/(\partial V/dm)$. In the present context, this means that labour supply, ℓ_i, can be expressed as:

$$\begin{aligned} \ell_i &= \frac{\partial V/\partial (w_i(1-t))}{\partial V/\partial M_i} \\ &= -\frac{1}{w_i}\frac{\partial V/\partial t}{\partial V/\partial b} \end{aligned} \tag{4.12}$$

In the first line of this expression, the minus sign in the standard form of Roy's Identity has been deleted because the variable in question is the amount supplied, not demanded. Hence:[5]

$$y_i = -\frac{\partial V/\partial t}{\partial V/\partial b} \tag{4.13}$$

[5] This insight is found in Tuomala (1985).

It should of course be remembered that y_i is not fixed, but depends on the nature of preferences as well as the tax parameters. In (4.13), $\partial V/\partial t < 0$ and $\partial V/\partial b > 0$, so that the right hand side is positive. Combining (4.13) and (4.11), the slope of an individual's indifference curve, relating to preferences regarding b and t, at any point is thus:[6]

$$\left.\frac{db}{dt}\right|_V = y_i \tag{4.14}$$

At the tangency position, equating the slope of the indifference curve with the slope of the government's budget constraint, the term $\left.\frac{db}{dt}\right|_R$ in (4.5) is equated to $\left.\frac{db}{dt}\right|_V = y_i$ from (4.14). The individual's preferred combination of tax parameters therefore satisfies:

$$y_i = \frac{\bar{y} + t\frac{\partial \bar{y}}{\partial t}}{1 - t\frac{\partial \bar{y}}{\partial b}} \tag{4.15}$$

which can be rearranged to produce the following form:

$$y_i - \bar{y} = t\left(\frac{\partial \bar{y}}{\partial t} + y_i\frac{\partial \bar{y}}{\partial b}\right) \tag{4.16}$$

Using equation (4.7), and remembering that at the tangency, $\left.\frac{db}{dt}\right|_R = \left.\frac{db}{dt}\right|_V = y_i$, the term in brackets on the right hand side of (4.16) can be replaced by $\left.\frac{d\bar{y}}{dt}\right|_R$, so that:

$$y_i - \bar{y} = t\left.\frac{d\bar{y}}{dt}\right|_R \tag{4.17}$$

and dividing by $\bar{y}$ gives:

$$1 - \frac{y_i}{\bar{y}} = -\frac{t}{\bar{y}}\left.\frac{d\bar{y}}{dt}\right|_R = \left|\eta_{\bar{y},t}\right| \tag{4.18}$$

[6] This may be compared with the simple case where there are no labour supply incentive effects. In the fixed income case, individual net income, z_i, is given by $z_i = (1-t)\,y_i + b$. The individual is thus treated as selecting the tax structure which maximises net income. The indifference curves, from $dz_i = -y_i dt + db = 0$, are thus straight lines with $\left.\frac{db}{dt}\right|_{z_i} = y_i$. Furthermore, the government's budget constraint is a straight line with a slope equal to the (fixed) mean income of $\bar{y}$. Hence, as discussed in the introduction, all those with $y_i < \bar{y}$ prefer the maximum tax rate of unity.

where $\left|\eta_{\bar{y},t}\right|$ represents the absolute value of the elasticity of average earnings with respect to the tax rate. This equality characterises individual i's preferred tax rate.

However, the expression in (4.18) applies only to individuals for whom $y_i < \bar{y}$, for which tangency solutions on the government's budget constraint apply. An individual with $y_i > \bar{y}$ has indifference curves (relating b and t) with a slope, y_i, that exceeds the slope of the government's budget constraints. Hence the optimal position for such an individual is a corner solution at $t = t_{\min}$.

4.3 Majority Choice of Tax Rate

Having considered individuals' preferred tax rates, in terms of their preferred position on the government's budget line, this section examines majority voting over the tax rate. The context is therefore one of voting over a single-dimensional issue: voting simultaneously over more than one issue raises further complexities not examined here.[7] First, it is necessary to establish a feature of the model whereby individuals can be ranked in ascending order by their gross incomes in precisely the same way, independently of the tax rate. The majority outcome, corresponding to the preferences of the median voter, is then examined. Numerical examples are used to demonstrate comparative static properties of the result.

4.3.1 Individual Ranks

An important property of the present model is that the ranking of individuals by their gross earnings, which (as shown in the previous section) determines their preferred position on the government's budget constraint, and thus choice of tax rate, is not affected by the tax parameters. This condition of unchanged ranks is known as 'hierarchical adherence' or 'agent monotonicity'.

[7] On difficulties raised by multidimensional voting, see Mueller (2003, pp. 87–92).

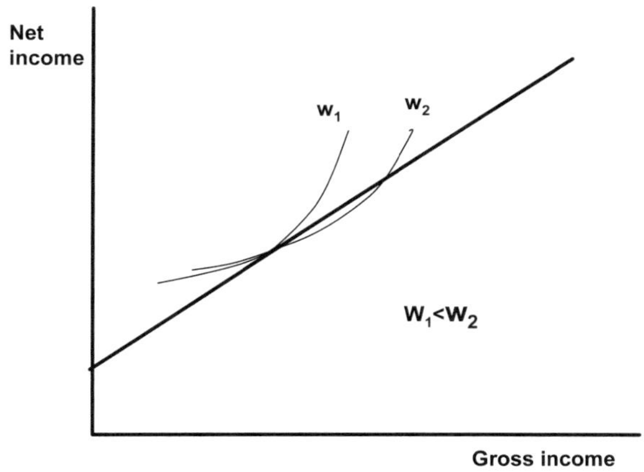

Figure 4.3: Hierarchical Adherence with Single Crossing Indifference Curves

This property is guaranteed if a 'single crossing' condition applies to individuals' indifference curves defined in terms of gross and net income; see Gans and Smart (1996). This is illustrated in Figure 4.3, which has gross earnings on the horizontal axis and net income on the vertical axis. The tax function, with a slope of $1 - t$, is shown as a straight line and the preferred position of person 1 is shown as the tangency of indifference curve w_1 with the tax function. This determines labour supply (and hence gross earnings) and consumption (net income). An individual with a higher wage, w_2, must have an indifference curve that is flatter than that associated with w_1 (at the tangency position) because any given increase in gross earnings can be obtained by working a smaller number of extra hours. Hence a given increase in gross earnings (a reduction in leisure) does not need to be compensated by as high an increase in net income as for the person with the lower wage rate. The person with the higher wage rate therefore reaches a tangency to the right of that of the person with the lower wage. This must apply for all linear tax functions, whatever their slope. Those with relatively high w necessarily have relatively high y.

4.3.2 The Median Voter

Consider the majority choice of the tax rate, for given R. It is well known that single-peaked preferences guarantee a voting equilibrium in which the median voter dominates. The median voter unambiguously holds the balance of power, and coalitions would not be formed between those on either side of the median. In the present framework, single-peakedness arises if the relationship between V and t is concave, so that $d^2V/dt^2 > 0$. With positive marginal utility and a concave relationship between b and t, single-peakedness is guaranteed if the individual always works, that is, if w_i exceeds the minimum wage, w_L, necessary to avoid the corner solution where $\ell_i = 0$. Hence if all $w_i > w_L$, combined with the fact that the ranks of individuals are independent of the tax system, the median voter can unambiguously be identified with the median wage, w_m, and hence the median earnings, y_m.

If there are individuals who do not work, that is if $w_i < w_L$ for some i, their preferences are not single peaked. Remembering that w_L depends on the tax rate, such an individual may work when t is very low and suffer from increases in t. However, once the tax rate is sufficiently high for them to stop working altogether, they prefer t to rise further because they desire only the highest possible transfer payment and are not themselves directly affected by further increases in t. Roberts (1977) showed that there is nevertheless a majority-voting equilibrium, so long as the ranks of individuals are independent of the tax system. This condition has already been established above.[8]

Having demonstrated that the median voter theorem applies in this case, it can be seen from (4.18) that substitution of y_m for y_i shows that the

[8]The existence of a majority-voting equilibrium in the case of a tax-free threshold is demonstrated by Creedy and Francois (1993), who also show that in a multi-period context hierarchical adherence is not sufficient to guarantee an equilibrium.

majority choice satisfies the condition:

$$1 - \frac{y_m}{\bar{y}} = \left|\eta_{\bar{y},t}\right| \tag{4.19}$$

The left hand side of this expression can be interpreted as a measure of the inequality of earnings: it is the proportional difference between the median and the arithmetic mean gross earnings. It is assumed that the wage rate distribution is positively skewed, so that the median wage is less than the arithmetic mean. While this condition is simply stated and has terms with convenient interpretations, it does not of course provide a 'closed form' solution for the majority choice of tax rate. The simplicity of this condition disguises considerable complexity, since $\bar{y}$ and $\eta_{\bar{y},t}$ depend on the complete wage rate distribution and the tax parameters.

4.3.3 Illustrative Examples

It is useful to consider how the terms in (4.19) are likely to vary with t. This can be achieved using numerical examples based on specific assumptions regarding the wage rate distribution and utility functions. Suppose that individuals have constant elasticity of substitution (CES) utility functions, which can be written as:

$$U = \left\{\alpha c^{-\rho} + (1-\alpha)(1-\ell)^{-\rho}\right\}^{-1/\rho} \tag{4.20}$$

where the endowment of time is normalised to unity, so that $1-\ell$ is leisure, and the elasticity of substitution, θ, is equal to $1/(1+\rho)$. Define Ψ as:

$$\Psi = \left\{\alpha^{\theta} + w\left(\frac{1-\alpha}{w(1-t)}\right)^{\theta}\right\}^{-1} \tag{4.21}$$

It can be shown that interior solutions for labour supply and consumption are:

$$\ell = 1 - \Psi M\left(\frac{1-\alpha}{w(1-t)}\right)^{\theta} \tag{4.22}$$

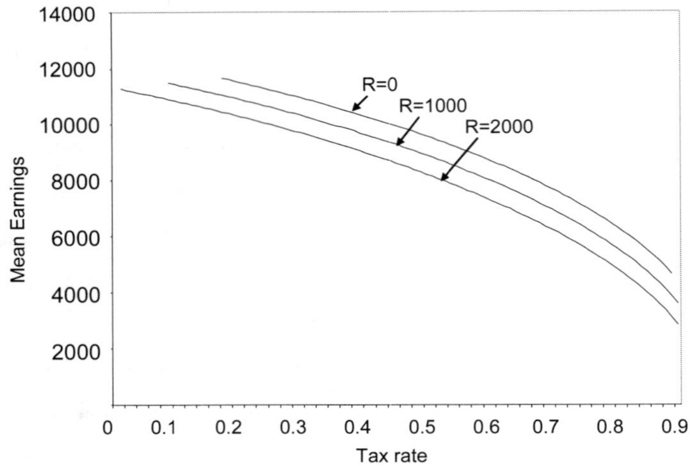

Figure 4.4: Mean Earnings

and:[9]

$$c = \Psi M \alpha^{\theta} \tag{4.23}$$

where, as above, M is full income given by $w_i(1-t)+b$. Equation (4.22) applies only for wage rates in excess of a minimum, w_L, for which $\ell = 1$. Suppose that wage rates are lognormally distributed as $\Lambda(w|\mu, \sigma^2)$. A simulated population of individuals' wages can therefore be obtained by selecting random values from this lognormal distribution. For given preference parameters (common to all individuals) it is possible to find the value of b which satisfies the government's budget constraint, for given values of t and R, using a process of trial and error.[10]

Figure 4.4 shows the variation in arithmetic mean gross income, $\bar{y}$, with

[9] The expenditure function, expressed in terms of full income, is found to be $E(w,U) = U\Psi^{-1}\alpha^{\sigma/\rho}\left\{1+w^{1-\sigma}\left(\frac{1-\alpha}{\alpha}\right)^{\sigma}\right\}^{\sigma/(1-\sigma)}$.

[10] This involves using a trial value of b and solving each individual's labour supply decision. The resulting total values of tax revenue and expenditure can be checked. If revenue exceeds expenditure, the value of b is increased and the process is repeated until convergence is reached. For further discussion of such iterative methods, see Creedy (1996).

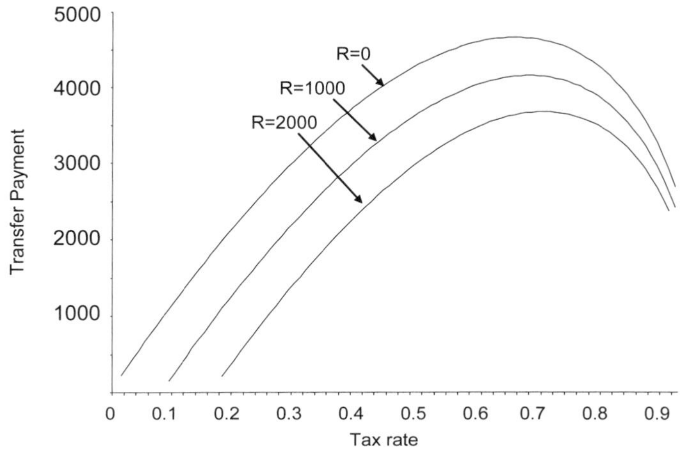

Figure 4.5: Government Budget Constraint

the marginal tax rate, t, for three different values of non-transfer expenditure, R. These results are for a wage rate distribution, $\Lambda\left(w \mid 10, 0.5\right)$, and $\alpha = 0.98$ with $\theta = 0.7$.[11] Clearly, average income decreases as the tax rate increases. The profile for the smaller level of non-transfer expenditure is higher because, for a given tax rate, the transfer payment must be smaller so that labour supply is higher. The corresponding government budget constraints showing the variation in b as t increases are shown in Figure 4.5, again for three values of non-transfer expenditure. When the tax rate increases from low levels, the 'tax rate effect' on total revenue, and hence b, is greater than the 'tax base effect' arising from the adverse incentive effects. However, after a certain point the reduction in the tax base outweighs the effect of the increasing tax rate, and the transfer payment falls as t rises.

The profiles of $1 - \frac{y_m}{\bar{y}}$ and $\left|\eta_{\bar{y},t}\right|$, for the three R values, are illustrated in Figure 4.6 for variations in the tax rate, t. Both profiles are upward sloping as

[11] On the choice of parameter values in the CES case, see Creedy (1996, pp. 136–139). For example, the choice cannot be made independently of the units of measurement of wages.

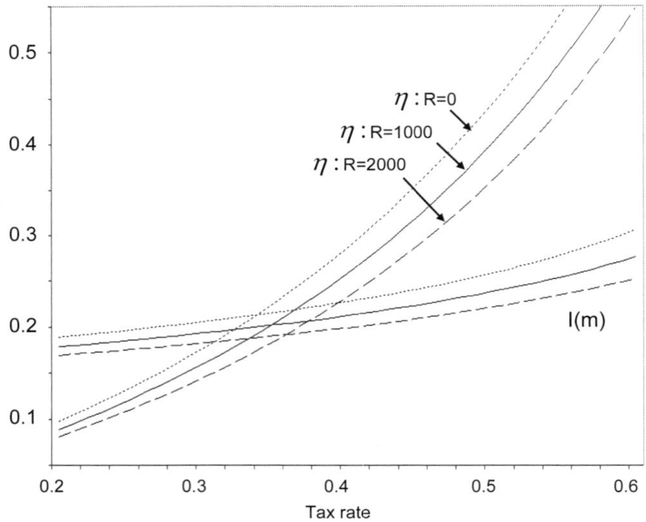

Figure 4.6: Median Voter Outcomes

both the absolute elasticity of $\bar{y}$ with respect to t, and the inequality of gross earnings, in this case expressed in the form, $1-\frac{y_m}{\bar{y}}$, rise with t. However, the (absolute) elasticity rises faster than inequality and there is consequently a single equilibrium position. The majority choice of tax rate can thus be read from the appropriate point of intersection of the two profiles. Increasing R shifts the profile of $1-\frac{y_m}{\bar{y}}$ and that of $\left|\eta_{\bar{y},t}\right|$ downwards. In the examples shown here, the shift in the latter profile is relatively larger. Hence the median voter's choice of t increases.

The effect of an increase in inequality can be examined by varying the assumed value of the variance of logarithms of w. A higher variance implies a lower value of $w_m/\bar{w}$ and thus of $y_m/\bar{y}$, for any given tax rate.[12] An increase in wage rate inequality resulting from an increase in σ^2 has the effect of shifting the profile of $\left|\eta_{\bar{y},t}\right|$ downwards slightly. That is, it produces a small

[12]It can be shown that in a lognormal distribution with variance of logarithms equal to σ^2, the ratio $w_m/\bar{w} = \exp\left(-\sigma^2/2\right)$.

reduction in the absolute elasticity for any given tax rate. However, it clearly produces an upward shift in the profile of $1 - \frac{y_m}{\bar{y}}$, since $y_m/\bar{y}$ is lower for any given tax rate. Both of these effects imply an unequivocal increase in the majority-voting equilibrium tax rate. The increase is smaller, the smaller is the effect on $\left|\eta_{\bar{y},t}\right|$. This suggests that higher inequality (associated with the higher skewness of the distribution of earnings) produces a majority vote for a higher tax rate, and thus a more redistributive (and progressive) tax structure.[13]

4.4 Optimal Taxation

This section turns to the normative analysis of tax rate choices, where emphasis is on examination of the implications of adopting particular value judgements, summarised by a social welfare function. It is shown in subsection 4.4.1 that the condition satisfied by the optimal linear tax is very similar to that obtained for the majority-voting outcome. The difference is that the inequality measure on the left hand side of $1 - \frac{y_m}{\bar{y}} = \left|\eta_{\bar{y},t}\right|$ is replaced by one in which the median voter's earnings are replaced by a weighted average of earnings. Illustrative examples are then presented in subsection 4.4.2.

4.4.1 A Social Welfare Function

Suppose the aim of the government is to maximise a social welfare function of the form $W = W(V_1, ..., V_n)$. This function of individual (indirect) utilities can be regarded, since each V_i depends on the tax parameters, as a function of t and b. It therefore gives a set of 'social indifference curves' in Figure 4.2. The choice of optimal tax rate is thus represented as a tangency of a social

[13]Empirical studies of the relationship between inequality and redistributive taxation have found mixed results; see, for example, Borck (2007). This simple majority-voting model abstracts from numerous practical factors (the role of parties, political influence, voter participation, uncertainty and so on) as well as dynamic considerations.

indifference curve with the government budget constraint.[14] The slope of an indifference curve is given by:

$$\left.\frac{db}{dt}\right|_W = -\frac{\partial W/\partial t}{\partial W/\partial b} \tag{4.24}$$

where:

$$\frac{\partial W}{\partial t} = \sum_{i=1}^{n} \frac{\partial W}{\partial V_i}\frac{\partial V_i}{\partial t} \tag{4.25}$$

and:

$$\frac{\partial W}{\partial b} = \sum_{i=1}^{n} \frac{\partial W}{\partial V_i}\frac{\partial V_i}{\partial b} \tag{4.26}$$

The term $\frac{\partial W}{\partial V_i}\frac{\partial V_i}{\partial b} = v_i$ is the 'welfare weight' attached by the social welfare function to an addition to person i's income (from an increase in the basic income). Furthermore, using (4.13):

$$\sum_{i=1}^{n} \frac{\partial W}{\partial V_i}\frac{\partial V_i}{\partial t} = \sum_{i=1}^{n}\left(\frac{\partial W}{\partial V_i}\frac{\partial V_i}{\partial b}\right)\left(\frac{\partial V_i/\partial t}{\partial V_i/\partial b}\right) = -\sum_{i=1}^{n} v_i y_i \tag{4.27}$$

Thus:

$$\left.\frac{db}{dt}\right|_W = \sum_{i=1}^{n}\left(\frac{v_i}{\sum_{i=1}^{n} v_i}\right) y_i \tag{4.28}$$

The right hand side of this expression is a weighted average of the y_is, which can be denoted $\widetilde{y}$. Hence equating the slopes of the social indifference curve and the government budget constraint gives:

$$\widetilde{y} = \frac{\overline{y} + t\frac{\partial \overline{y}}{\partial t}}{1 - t\frac{\partial \overline{y}}{\partial b}} \tag{4.29}$$

The optimal tax rate therefore satisfies the same kind of condition as the majority-voting outcome, but with median earnings replaced by $\widetilde{y}$, so that:

$$1 - \frac{\widetilde{y}}{\overline{y}} = \left|\eta_{\overline{y},t}\right| \tag{4.30}$$

[14] An alternative route to the following result, used by Tuomala (1985), involves using the Lagrangian, $L = W + \lambda\left(t\overline{y} - b - R\right)$. The first-order conditions for maximisation, $\frac{\partial L}{\partial t} = 0$ and $\frac{\partial L}{\partial b} = 0$, give, in addition to the budget constraint, the two equations $\sum_{i=1}^{n} \frac{\partial W}{\partial V_i}\frac{\partial V_i}{\partial t} = -\lambda\left(\overline{y} + t\frac{\partial \overline{y}}{\partial t}\right)$ and $\sum_{i=1}^{n} \frac{\partial W}{\partial V_i}\frac{\partial V_i}{\partial b} = \lambda\left(1 - t\frac{\partial \overline{y}}{\partial b}\right)$. Dividing these two conditions therefore reproduces the result below.

The left hand side of this expression, as with (4.19), defines an inequality measure, this time involving the proportional difference between the weighted average earnings and the unweighted average earnings, where the weights depend on the form of the social welfare function. The optimal tax is that rate which satisfies equation (4.30).[15]

Since the majority choice and the social welfare function maxima are both described in terms of tangency solutions of a form of indifference curve along the government's budget constraint, it is perhaps not surprising that they can be expressed in fundamentally the same way. The only difference relates to the inequality measure used. Hence, if in general a measure of the inequality of earnings, taking the form of a proportional difference between average earnings and some other measure of location, is denoted by $I(y)$, the desired tax rate is the root of:

$$I(y) = \left|\eta_{\bar{y},t}\right| \tag{4.31}$$

Again, this does not provide a closed-form solution, and of course any solution must also satisfy $t > t_{\min}$ if the tax system is to be progressive. That is, if the tax does not raise sufficient revenue to finance the non-transfer expenditure, R, the shortfall must be made up by imposing a poll tax (a negative b) on each individual. But, as with majority voting, the expression in (4.30) provides a condition in terms of easily interpreted concepts.

4.4.2 Illustrative Examples

In subsection 4.3.2, profiles of $\left|\eta_{\bar{y},t}\right|$ were shown, on the assumption that utility functions display constant elasticity of substitution. Examination of optimal tax choices therefore requires corresponding values of the inequality measure, $I(y) = 1 - \frac{\tilde{y}}{\bar{y}}$ to be produced, where $\tilde{y}$ depends on the welfare

[15] This is the result given by Tuomala (1985). However, in the accompanying diagram, he draws a downward-sloping curve of $1 - \frac{\tilde{y}}{\bar{y}}$ against t. It is shown below that both the right and left hand sides of (4.30) slope upwards.

weights, v_i. Although it is possible to examine the implications of using any type of social welfare function, a convenient approach for present purposes is to specify welfare in terms of each individual's income, rather than utility.[16] Using a constant relative inequality aversion form of the welfare function, the contribution to social welfare of the ith individual is $y_i^{1-\varepsilon}/(1-\varepsilon)$, where ε is the constant relative inequality aversion coefficient. The term $\tilde{y}$ can thus be replaced by the equally distributed equivalent level of income, y_e, defined as the level of income which, if obtained by everyone, produces the same social welfare as the actual distribution. Hence, the term $I(y)$ can be replaced by Atkinson's inequality measure, A, since it is the proportional difference between arithmetic mean income and the equally distributed equivalent level and:

$$A = \frac{\bar{y} - y_e}{\bar{y}} \tag{4.32}$$

where:

$$y_e = \left\{ \frac{1}{n} \sum_{i=1}^{n} y_i^{1-\varepsilon} \right\}^{1/(1-\varepsilon)} \tag{4.33}$$

Figure 4.7 illustrates the variation in the inequality of net income and gross earnings as the tax rate increases, for a given value of $\varepsilon = 0.2$. Inequality of gross earnings increases as t rises, whereas the inequality of net income falls steadily. The relatively small decrease in the inequality of net income over a wide range of t indicates the severe constraint on the government's ability to redistribute income imposed by adverse incentive effects. Figure 4.8 illustrates the relevant profiles for $R = 1000$ and $\varepsilon = 0.8$, for two values of the variance of logarithms of wage rates. In this case the profile of $\left|\eta_{\bar{y},t}\right|$ is virtually unchanged, so the upward movement in the inequality profile clearly produces a higher choice of optimal tax rate. Hence, higher inequality is again associated with a more redistributive tax structure. Similarly, a higher value of the inequality aversion coefficient shifts only the profile of $1 - \tilde{y}/\bar{y}$ upwards, implying a higher optimal tax rate.

---

[16] The conditions under which this is consistent are discussed by Banks *et al.* (1996).

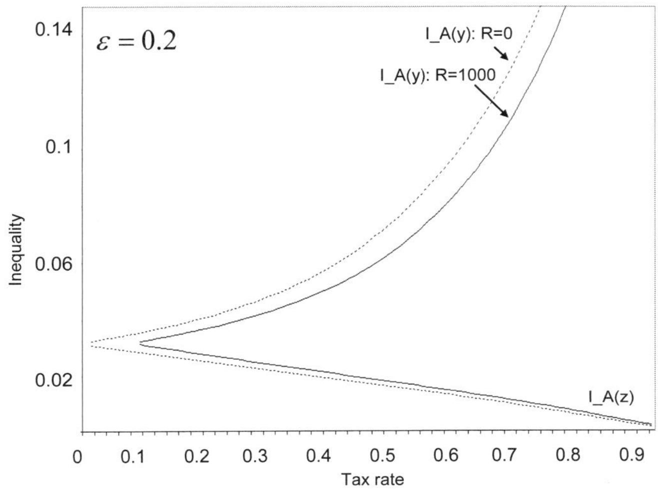

Figure 4.7: Inequality of Net Income and Gross Earnings

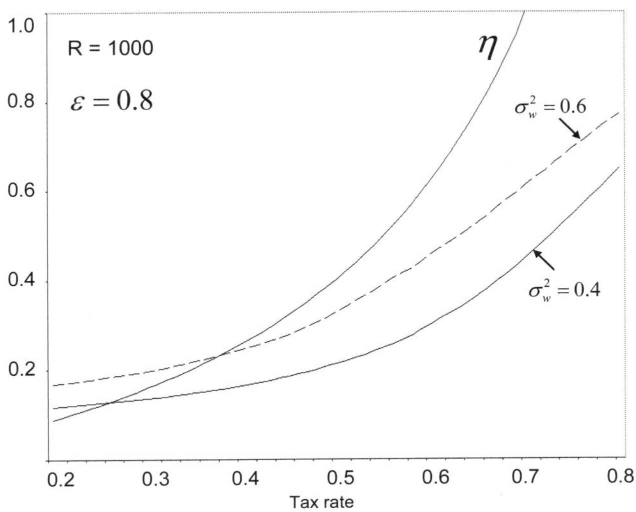

Figure 4.8: Change in Inequality of Wages

The effect of differences in the elasticity of substitution is less clear cut in this framework because it depends on the non-transfer revenue needed. If there is a pure transfer system, with $R = 0$, the optimal tax rate falls as the elasticity of substitution increases. However, if $R > 0$ the optimal rate falls as the elasticity of substitution, θ, increases from low values. But at higher values of θ, further increases actually lead to an increase in the optimal tax rate. This arises because the minimum tax rate needed to finance the non-transfer expenditure is higher for higher values of θ.

4.5 Conclusions

This chapter has considered the choice of linear income tax rate in both majority-voting and social welfare-maximising contexts. Although the basic problem in each case – of finding the most preferred tax for the median voter and the welfare-maximising tax for an independent judge or decision maker – can be simply stated, it is usually not possible to obtain explicit solutions even for simple assumptions about preferences and population heterogeneity. The present chapter has instead given special attention to a formulation of the required conditions in terms of easily interpreted magnitudes, the elasticity of average earnings with respect to the tax rate and a measure of inequality. The inequality measure takes the same basic form in each model. It is either the proportional difference between the median and arithmetic mean earnings (in the voting model) or the proportional difference between a weighted average of earnings and arithmetic mean earnings (for maximisation of a social welfare function), where the weights depend on value judgements regarding inequality aversion. The approach enables the comparative static effects of a range of parameter changes to be considered. The results were reinforced using numerical examples based on the constant elasticity of substitution utility function.

Chapter 5

Choosing a Linear Income Tax Rate

The previous chapter considered the general problem of choosing the linear income tax rate. The aim of the present chapter is to obtain explicit, or closed-form, solutions in the special case where individuals have Cobb–Douglas preferences defined over leisure and consumption. First, in the simple majority-voting model, an explicit solution is obtained for the median voter's choice or tax rate, on the simplifying assumption that all individuals work (thereby giving rise to a simple form of the government's budget constraint). Second, for maximisation of a social welfare function, which expresses the value judgements of an independent judge, an approximation to the optimal tax rate is obtained in the case where wage rates follow the lognormal distribution and there is constant relative inequality aversion. Results depend on approximating a form of welfare-weighted mean wage rate. Third, stochastic voting equilibria are considered where the tax rate arises from maximisation of a 'support function' which shares some features of certain special types of social welfare function.

From the initial work of Mirrlees (1971), numerical methods are typically used, involving a search procedure for a simulated population of individuals. The value of a specified social welfare function is computed for a range of tax rates, where for each rate the government budget constraint is solved iteratively. The approach to approximation suggested here is therefore applied to a framework that has formerly required the use of numerical simulation methods. If an optimal tax is part of a larger model, or if a quick calculation is needed for illustrative purposes, the proposed method is helpful. Furthermore, the approximation method adopted may be of interest with regard to other related problems involving the maximisation of a social welfare function.

All approaches clearly require the use of explicit assumptions regarding the nature of heterogeneity, utility functions and, importantly, the social welfare function to be maximised. Broome (1975) discussed the case of a maxi-min social welfare function involving maximisation of the basic transfer payment. Special cases of utility functions giving rise to closed-form solutions for the optimal linear tax rate are given in Atkinson and Stiglitz (1980, pp. 408–9), using a Pareto distribution of wage rates. Hindriks and Myles (2006, pp. 503–505, pp. 493–495) discuss a special case of majority voting, and two-person examples of the optimal tax rate structure, using quasi-linear preferences. A further explicit solution to an optimal tax problem, assuming that income supply functions are linear in the wage rate, is given by Deaton (1983).

First, section 5.1 derives the form of the indirect utility function. It is shown how an assumption that most individuals work, combined with Cobb–Douglas preferences, generates a convenient government budget constraint in which the transfer payment is expressed as a linear function of the tax rate and the arithmetic mean wage rate.[1] Section 5.2 examines simple majority voting over the tax rate, where a closed-form solution is produced involving the ratio of the median wage to the arithmetic mean wage. In section 5.3, an expression for the tax rate which maximises a general evaluation function is obtained involving the ratio of a weighted mean wage to the arith-

[1]The assumption that everyone works, thereby avoiding corner solutions, is common among those giving explicit solutions.

metic mean. Section 5.4 considers the evaluation function as a social welfare function, where the weighted average wage is a welfare-weighted mean. An approximation to this is derived and the performance of the approach is compared with results from a numerical method based on a large simulated population, and where full account of corner solutions is taken. Section 5.5 then examines the case of stochastic voting where probability distributions regarding the proportion of votes obtained by a party with a given agenda are relevant. This framework is less well known in the public finance literature, compared with simple majority voting where voting is deterministic. Section 5.5 briefly derives the 'support function' involved in stochastic-voting models, which can again be considered as special cases of the general evaluation function discussed in section 5.3. Brief conclusions are in Section 5.6.

5.1 Cobb–Douglas Preferences

Consider the linear income tax where there is an unconditional transfer payment per person of b and a proportional tax at the rate t. Letting c denote consumption of goods (with price equal to 1) and h leisure (with total time set to 1), utility functions take the Cobb–Douglas form, omitting subscript i:

$$U = c^{\alpha} h^{1-\alpha} \tag{5.1}$$

Full income is:

$$M = w(1-t) + b \tag{5.2}$$

and demands for consumption and leisure are:

$$c = \alpha M \tag{5.3}$$

and:

$$h = \frac{(1-\alpha) M}{w(1-t)} \tag{5.4}$$

Earnings, y, are thus:

$$y = \alpha w - \frac{(1-\alpha)\, b}{(1-t)} \tag{5.5}$$

The assumption that most individuals work allows a very convenient expression for arithmetic mean earnings to be obtained from (5.5), since:[2]

$$\bar{y} = \alpha \bar{w} - \frac{(1-\alpha)\, b}{1-t} \tag{5.6}$$

If an amount, R, of non-transfer expenditure per person is needed, the government budget constraint is:

$$b = t\bar{y} - R \tag{5.7}$$

Substituting for $\bar{y}$, the transfer payment can be expressed in terms of t as:

$$b = \frac{\alpha t \bar{w} - R}{1 + (1-\alpha)\left(\frac{t}{1-t}\right)} \tag{5.8}$$

Substituting c, h into U and using (5.8), indirect utility can be written, using $k = \alpha^{\alpha}(1-\alpha)^{1-\alpha}$, as:

$$V = \frac{kM}{\{w(1-t)\}^{1-\alpha}} \tag{5.9}$$

or:

$$V = k\{w(1-t)\}^{\alpha} A \tag{5.10}$$

with:

$$A = \left[1 + \frac{\bar{w}}{w}\left\{\frac{\alpha t - R/\bar{w}}{1-\alpha t}\right\}\right] \tag{5.11}$$

5.2 Majority Voting over the Tax Rate

First, consider majority voting over the tax rate. A majority-voting equilibrium is known to exist which is dominated by the median voter. If the

[2]Strictly, for workers their wage rates must exceed $w_{\min} = (1-\alpha)\, b / \{\alpha(1-t)\}$. If some individuals do not work, average earnings become $\overline{y} = \frac{1}{n}\sum_{w>w_{\min}}\{\alpha w_i - \theta\}$ where $\theta = b(1-\alpha)/(1-t)$. Hence $\overline{y} = \alpha\overline{w}H(w_{\min})$ where $H(w_{\min}) = \{1 - F_1(w_{\min})\} - \frac{\theta}{\alpha\overline{w}}\{1 - F(w_{\min})\}$ and $F_1(w_{\min})$ and $F(w_{\min})$ denote respectively the proportion of total wage (rates) and the proportion of people with $w < w_{\min}$.

median wage is w_m, the majority choice is the solution to $dV/dt = 0$. This gives the first-order condition:

$$\frac{\alpha A}{1-t} = \frac{dA}{dt} \tag{5.12}$$

with:

$$\frac{dA}{dt} = \left(\frac{\bar{w}}{w_m}\right) \frac{\alpha\left(1 - R/\bar{w}\right)}{\left(1-\alpha t\right)^2} \tag{5.13}$$

Rearrangement of (5.12) gives the majority choice as the appropriate root of the following quadratic:[3]

$$t^2\alpha^2\left(1-\frac{\bar{w}}{w_m}\right) + t\left[\frac{\bar{w}}{w_m}\left\{(1-\alpha)\left(1-\frac{R}{\bar{w}}\right)+2\alpha\right\} - 2\alpha\right] + \left(1-\frac{\bar{w}}{w_m}\right) = 0 \tag{5.14}$$

Using the standard result that, where $At^2 + Bt + C = 0$ the two roots are $\left\{-B \pm \sqrt{B^2 - 4AC}\right\}/2A$, it is found that the smallest root is the relevant one, as the largest root exceeds unity.

5.3 A General Evaluation Function

Consider the values of t and b which maximise an evaluation of the general form:

$$W = W\left(V_1, ..., V_n\right) \tag{5.15}$$

which is assumed to be concave in t and b. The maximum is equivalent to a tangency solution whereby the highest indifference curve is tangential to the government budget constraint.

$$\left.\frac{\partial b}{\partial t}\right|_W = \left.\frac{db}{dt}\right|_R \tag{5.16}$$

[3] Could be written as $\alpha^2t^2 - Kt + 1 = 0$ where $K = 2\alpha + (1-\alpha)\left(\frac{1-R/\bar{w}}{1-w_m/\bar{w}}\right)$, or if $\delta = R/w_m$, then $K = 1 + \alpha + (1-\delta)\left(\frac{\bar{w}}{w_m} - 1\right)^{-1}$.

5.3.1 Indifference Curves

Totally differentiating W gives:

$$dW = \left(\sum \frac{\partial W}{\partial V_i}\frac{\partial V_i}{\partial b}\right) db + \left(\sum \frac{\partial W}{\partial V_i}\frac{\partial V_i}{\partial t}\right) dt \tag{5.17}$$

and the slope of indifference curves is therefore obtained by setting $dW = 0$. Thus, defining the 'marginal value of income of person i' as:

$$v_i = \frac{\partial W}{\partial V_i}\frac{\partial V_i}{\partial b} \tag{5.18}$$

and the weights:

$$v_i' = \frac{v_i}{\sum v_i} \tag{5.19}$$

it can be seen that:

$$\left.\frac{\partial b}{\partial t}\right|_W = -\sum v_i' \frac{\partial V_i/\partial t}{\partial V_i/\partial b} \tag{5.20}$$

In general for an indirect utility function of the form $V(p, m)$, for goods demanded, x_i, at prices, p_i, and a budget of m, Roy's Identity gives the Marshallian demands as $x_i = -\left(\partial V/dp_i\right)/\left(\partial V/dm\right)$. In the present context, this means that labour supply, ℓ_i, can be expressed as:

$$\begin{aligned} \ell_i &= \frac{\partial V_i/\partial\left(w_i\left(1-t\right)\right)}{\partial V_i/\partial M_i} \\ &= -\frac{1}{w_i}\frac{\partial V_i/\partial t}{\partial V_i/\partial b} \end{aligned} \tag{5.21}$$

In the first line of this expression, the minus sign in the standard form of Roy's Identity has been deleted because the variable in question is the amount supplied, not demanded. Hence:

$$y_i = -\frac{\partial V_i/\partial t}{\partial V_i/\partial b} \tag{5.22}$$

and from above:

$$y_i = \alpha w_i - \frac{\left(1-\alpha\right)b}{\left(1-t\right)} \tag{5.23}$$

Hence:

$$\left.\frac{\partial b}{\partial t}\right|_W = \sum v_i' \left(\alpha w_i - \frac{(1-\alpha)\,b}{(1-t)}\right)$$
$$= \alpha\tilde{w} - \frac{(1-\alpha)\,b}{(1-t)} \tag{5.24}$$

where $\tilde{w} = \sum v_i' w_i$ is a weighted mean wage.

5.3.2 The Solution

Totally differentiating the budget constraint in (5.7) gives:

$$dR = \left(\bar{y} + t\frac{\partial \bar{y}}{\partial t}\right) dt + \left(t\frac{\partial \bar{y}}{\partial b} - 1\right) db \tag{5.25}$$

Hence the slope of the budget line, giving the variation in b as t varies, keeping R fixed, can be obtained by setting $dR = 0$, to give:

$$\left.\frac{db}{dt}\right|_R = \frac{\bar{y} + t\frac{\partial \bar{y}}{\partial t}}{1 - t\frac{\partial \bar{y}}{\partial b}} \tag{5.26}$$

where $\bar{y}$ is also given in (5.6) above. Hence:

$$\frac{\partial \bar{y}}{\partial t} = -\frac{(1-\alpha)\,b}{(1-t)^2} \tag{5.27}$$

$$\frac{\partial \bar{y}}{\partial b} = -\left(\frac{1-\alpha}{1-t}\right) \tag{5.28}$$

Hence substitution gives:

$$\left.\frac{db}{dt}\right|_R = \frac{\alpha\bar{w}\,(1-t) - \frac{(1-\alpha)b}{(1-t)}}{1-\alpha t} \tag{5.29}$$

Equating this with the slope of the social indifference curve in (5.24) gives:[4]

$$\tilde{w}\,(1-t)\,(1-\alpha t) - \bar{w}\,(1-t)^2 = -t\,(1-\alpha)\,b \tag{5.30}$$

[4] Tuomala (1985) uses the above duality result and an alternative rearrangement of the first-order condition (using the general terms involving $\partial\bar{y}/\partial t$ rather than evaluating them explicitly as here) to obtain an expression in terms of earnings, rather than the wage rate. He showed that the tax rate maximising W satisfies $1 - \frac{\tilde{y}}{\bar{y}} = \left|\eta_{\bar{y},t}\right|$, where $\left|\eta_{\bar{y},t}\right|$ is the absolute value of the elasticity of average income with respect to the tax rate. While this provides an interesting insight into the characteristics of the optimal tax rate, it is not helpful in providing an explicit solution.

Substituting for b from the government budget constraint gives:

$$\tilde{w}(1-\alpha t) - \bar{w}(1-t) + \frac{t(1-\alpha)(\alpha t\bar{w} - R)}{1-\alpha t} = 0 \tag{5.31}$$

and after further rearrangement:

$$t^2\alpha^2\left(1-\frac{\bar{w}}{\tilde{w}}\right) + t\left[\frac{\bar{w}}{\tilde{w}}\left\{(1-\alpha)\left(1-\frac{R}{\bar{w}}\right)+2\alpha\right\} - 2\alpha\right] + \left(1-\frac{\bar{w}}{\tilde{w}}\right) = 0 \tag{5.32}$$

Comparison with the median voter case above shows that the solution takes the same form except that w_m is replaced by the weighted mean, $\tilde{w}$. However, unlike the median voter solution which can be solved using the standard result for the roots of a quadratic, (5.32) presents difficulties because of the complexity of the term $\tilde{w}$. The following sections examine alternative forms of evaluation function, first in the context of optimal taxation and secondly in the context of stochastic voting.

5.4 The Optimal Tax

5.4.1 A Social Welfare Function

If W is considered to be a social welfare function which represents the value judgements of an independent person, the solution is the resulting optimal tax. The term, $\tilde{w}$, is then a welfare-weighted mean wage and v_i is the 'social marginal valuation of income' of person i. The weights v_i' strictly depend on the optimal tax rate itself. However, suppose W takes the widely used iso-elastic form of social welfare function:

$$W = \sum_i \frac{1}{1-\varepsilon} V_i^{1-\varepsilon} \tag{5.33}$$

Then:[5]

$$\frac{\partial W}{\partial V_i} = V_i^{-\varepsilon} \tag{5.34}$$

and using:

$$V_i = \frac{kM_i}{\{w_i(1-t)\}^{1-\alpha}} \tag{5.35}$$

differentiation gives:

$$\frac{\partial V_i}{\partial b} = \frac{k}{\{w_i(1-t)\}^{1-\alpha}} \tag{5.36}$$

so that:[6]

$$v_i = \left(\frac{k}{(1-t)^{1-\alpha}}\right)^{1-\varepsilon} \frac{M^{-\varepsilon}}{w^{(1-\alpha)(1-\varepsilon)}} \tag{5.37}$$

In order to make further progress, suppose that b is small in relation to w. Then v_i can be expressed as:

$$v_i = Kw_i^{(1-\alpha)(\varepsilon-1)-\varepsilon} \tag{5.38}$$

where $K = k^{1-\varepsilon}(1-t)^{(1-\alpha)(\varepsilon-1)-\varepsilon}$ and $\tilde{w}$ can be approximated using $\tilde{w}_A$, given by:

$$\begin{aligned} \tilde{w}_A &= \frac{\sum v_i w_i}{\sum v_i} \\ &= \frac{\frac{1}{n}\sum w_i^{1+\theta}}{\frac{1}{n}\sum w_i^{\theta}} \end{aligned} \tag{5.39}$$

with:

$$\theta = (1-\alpha)(\varepsilon-1)-\varepsilon \tag{5.40}$$

This can be further simplified using the assumption that the wage rate is lognormally distributed. Suppose w follows a lognormal distribution, $\Lambda(\mu, \sigma^2)$, with mean and variance of logarithms of μ and σ^2 respectively. Therefore the

[5] In the marginal commodity tax reform literature, where a similar term appears in the condition which establishes whether a tax rate should be increased or decreased slightly in order to move towards a welfare-maximising structure, observed income is generally substituted for the term V_i in empirical applications: see Ahmad and Stern (1991) and Banks *et al.* (1996).

[6] It is clearly possible to write $v_i = V_i^{1-\varepsilon}/M_i$ but it does not help.

median and mean income are $w_m = e^{\mu}$ and $\bar{w} = e^{\mu + \sigma^2/2}$, and the moment of order θ is given by:

$$\bar{w}_\theta = \exp(\mu\theta + \frac{\theta^2\sigma^2}{2}) \tag{5.41}$$

Hence:

$$\tilde{w}_A = \exp\left[\mu + \frac{\sigma^2}{2}(1 + 2\theta)\right] \tag{5.42}$$

Thus an approximation for $\tilde{w}$ is obtained that depends on the variance of logarithms of wages, the (common) coefficient on consumption in individuals' utility functions and the degree of relative inequality aversion of the social welfare function. Hence this result can be used to obtain the smallest root of the quadratic (5.32). From (5.42) it can also be seen that:

$$\frac{\tilde{w}_A}{\bar{w}} = \exp\left[-\sigma^2\left\{1 - \alpha\left(1 - \varepsilon\right)\right\}\right] \tag{5.43}$$

In considering optimal allocations, the results are of course not invariant with respect to monotonic transformations of utility functions. That is, results depend on the particular cardinalisation of utility used, since social welfare functions treat the utilities as cardinal in $W(V_1, ..., V_N)$: indeed, the role of the welfare function is to make value judgements regarding interpersonal comparisons of utility explicit. Subsection 5.4.3 discusses the use of a money metric utility measure, which is invariant with respect to monotonic transformations of utility, in the social welfare function.

5.4.2 Some Comparisons

It is necessary to examine whether this does indeed provide a useful approximation. This subsection reports some calculations of optimal tax rates using the above approximation for $\tilde{w}$, along with computations based on a simulated population size of 10,000, involving a systematic evaluation of the social welfare function (5.33) for a range of tax rates. All results were obtained using a mean and variance of logarithms of wages of $\mu = 10$ and $\sigma^2 = 0.5$. In the simulations, allowance was made for nonworkers (those at the corner solution where $h = 1$). The resulting government budget constraint was solved iteratively for the transfer, given a tax rate.[7] Of course, the value obtained using a simulated population cannot claim to be 'exact' since it varies slightly depending on the random draws obtained from the wage rate distribution, the population size and the accuracy specified when solving the government's budget constraint for each value of t examined.

Table 5.1: Simulated and Approximate Optimal Tax Rates

ε	α	τ_o	τ_A	$t_{\tilde{w}_A(1+0.05)}$
$R = 3000$				
0.3	0.4	0.38	0.40	0.36
0.3	0.6	0.38	0.40	0.37
0.3	0.8	0.40	0.45	0.40
0.5	0.4	0.40	0.42	0.39
0.5	0.6	0.41	0.44	0.41
0.5	0.8	0.44	0.51	0.48
0.8	0.4	0.43	0.46	0.43
0.8	0.6	0.44	0.49	0.47
0.8	0.8	0.48	0.57	0.55
$R = 0$				
0.5	0.4	0.37	0.39	0.36
0.5	0.6	0.37	0.42	0.38
0.5	0.8	0.41	0.49	0.45

Table 5.1 reports alternative values of the optimal tax rate for a range of values of inequality aversion, ε, and the exponent on consumption, α, in the utility functions. The term τ_o denotes the optimal rate using simulations while, as above, τ_A denotes the value obtained using the smallest root of the quadratic along with $\tilde{w}_A$. It can be seen that in most cases the two values differ by just a few percentage points, although the approximation overstates the optimal tax slightly, this being larger for higher values of ε and α.

In considering the steps used to obtain the approximation, this overstatement is not surprising. First, in order to simplify the government's budget

[7] This uses appropriate integrals of the lognormal wage distribution.

constraint it assumes that all individuals work. Second, in simplifying the welfare weights, the assumption that b can be neglected in the term M_i in equation (5.37) means that the weighted average attaches slightly too much weight to the lowest wage rates. Hence the value of $\tilde{w}_A$ is expected to understate the 'true' value somewhat. With this in mind, the final column of Table 5.1 reports the improvement obtained by using the above approximation, but with $\tilde{w}_A$ increased by 5 per cent in each case.

5.4.3 The Use of Money Metric Utility

This subsection considers the use of money metric utility instead of utility in the social welfare function.[8] A feature of money metric utility is that it is invariant with respect to monotonic transformations of the utility function; it represents a particular monotonic transformation of utility, for given reference prices. In general, where the direct utility function is written as $U = U(x)$, where x is a vector of consumption levels, and the indirect form is $V = V(p, y)$, where y is income (the budget) and p is a vector of prices, money metric utility (sometimes referred to as equivalent income), m_u, is defined by:

$$V(p_r, m_u) = V(p, y) \tag{5.44}$$

Let $E(p, U)$ denote the expenditure function, the minimum expenditure required to achieve utility level U at prices, p, then:

$$m_u = E(p_r, V(p, y)) \tag{5.45}$$

For example, in the two-good Cobb–Douglas case of consumption of x_1, and of x_2 of the goods at given prices p_1 and p_2 respectively, $U = x_1^{\alpha} x_2^{1-\alpha}$ and:

$$V(p, y) = y \left(\frac{\alpha}{p_1}\right)^{\alpha} \left(\frac{1-\alpha}{p_2}\right)^{1-\alpha} \tag{5.46}$$

[8]The role of this measure in optimal tax models was investigated in detail in Creedy (1998c).

Hence the expenditure function is:

$$E(p, U) = U \left(\frac{p_1}{\alpha}\right)^{\alpha} \left(\frac{p_2}{1-\alpha}\right)^{1-\alpha} \tag{5.47}$$

By substituting the right hand side of (5.46) for U in the expenditure function, the income, m_u, needed to achieve U at the set of reference prices, p_r, is:

$$m_u = y \left(\frac{p_{r1}}{p_1}\right)^{\alpha} \left(\frac{p_{r2}}{p_1}\right)^{1-\alpha} \tag{5.48}$$

In the present context of labour supply variations, suppose that reference prices are those that apply where there is no tax, so that $b = t = 0$ and full income is simply the wage rate, w. When $t > 0$, m_u for the Cobb–Douglas case is given by substituting into (5.48), so that:

$$m_u = \{w(1-t) + b\} \left(\frac{1}{1-t}\right)^{1-\alpha} \tag{5.49}$$

This result applies for tangency solutions, that is, for those who work.[9] Assuming, as above, that all individuals work, the simple form of the government's budget constraint can be used.

If the social welfare function is written as $W = \sum m_{u,i}^{1-\varepsilon} / (1-\varepsilon)$, then:

$$\frac{\partial m_u}{\partial b} = \left(\frac{1}{1-t}\right)^{1-\alpha} \tag{5.50}$$

and it can be seen that $v_i = \frac{\partial W}{\partial m_{u,i}} \frac{\partial m_{u,i}}{\partial b}$ is proportional to $\{w(1-t)+b\}^{-\varepsilon}$. Again, supposing that b is small in relation to $w(1-t)$, v_i is proportional to $w^{-\varepsilon}$ and, as before:

$$\begin{aligned} \tilde{w}_A &= \frac{\sum v_i w_i}{\sum v_i} \\ &= \frac{\frac{1}{n}\sum w_i^{1+\theta}}{\frac{1}{n}\sum w_i^{\theta}} \end{aligned} \tag{5.51}$$

[9]Those who do not work and for whom $h = 1$ receive only the unconditional transfer, a, so that the full income required to achieve utility of a^{α} at the reference prices is given by $m_u = a^{\alpha} \left(\frac{1}{\alpha}\right)^{\alpha} \left(\frac{w}{1-\alpha}\right)^{1-\alpha}$. This value applies for $w \leq a(1-\alpha) / \{\alpha(1-t)\} = w_L$.

with $\theta = -\varepsilon$. Hence using the assumption of lognormality as before:

$$\begin{aligned} \tilde{w}_A &= \exp\left\{\mu + \frac{\sigma^2}{2}(1-2\varepsilon)\right\} \\ &= \exp\left\{\mu + \frac{\sigma^2}{2}(1-\varepsilon)\right\}\exp\left(-\frac{\varepsilon\sigma^2}{2}\right) \end{aligned} \tag{5.52}$$

In Creedy (1998c) it was shown that when $\varepsilon = 1$, the optimal linear tax using money metric utility is the same as when using utility in the social welfare function. This is also confirmed using the approximation approach here: setting $\varepsilon = 1$ in both (5.52) and (5.42) gives the same value of $\tilde{w}_A = \exp(\mu - \sigma^2/2)$. For values of $\varepsilon < 1$ the money metric utility measure gives a relatively lower optimal tax rate.

The first term in (5.52) is in fact closely related to Atkinson's measure of the inequality of wage rates. Following Atkinson (1970), let w_{ede} denote the 'equally distributed equivalent' wage, representing the equal wage which gives the same welfare as the actual distribution, using a welfare function of the form $W = \frac{1}{1-\varepsilon}\sum w_i^{1-\varepsilon}$. This is the same as the above but with V or m_u replaced by w. Thus:

$$w_{ede} = \left(\frac{1}{N}\sum_{i=1}^{N} w_i^{1-\varepsilon}\right)^{\frac{1}{1-\varepsilon}} \tag{5.53}$$

Again using the lognormal properties, the median and mean income are $w_m = e^{\mu}$ and $\bar{w} = e^{\mu + \sigma^2/2}$. The term $w^{1-\varepsilon}$ has mean and variance of logarithms of $(1-\varepsilon)\mu$ and $(1-\varepsilon)^2\sigma^2$, so that:

$$w_{ede} = \exp\left((1-\varepsilon)\mu + (1-\varepsilon)^2\frac{\sigma^2}{2}\right)^{\frac{1}{1-\varepsilon}} = \exp\left(\mu + (1-\varepsilon)\frac{\sigma^2}{2}\right) \tag{5.54}$$

In view of the fact that the approximation, by neglecting b above, gives too much weight to low incomes, so that $\tilde{w}_A$ is somewhat low, an approximation to $\tilde{w}$ can be obtained from (5.52) by neglecting the final term (which is less than unity) and simply using the equally distributed equivalent wage rate, that is, by setting $\tilde{w}_A = w_{ede}$.

5.5 Stochastic Voting

This section considers stochastic voting, where it is shown that there is policy convergence whereby each party attempts to maximise a 'support function', which has superficial similarities with a social welfare function. First the derivation of the form of support function arising from this framework is given.[10] Two special cases are then examined.

5.5.1 The Basic Model

Suppose the population consists of K groups of individuals, where group k has population proportion n_k, for $k = 1, ..., K$, so that $\sum_{k=1}^{K} n_k = 1$. Within each group individuals have the same ability (that is, wage rate). Hence if there are two political parties, A and B, with associated policies, individuals within each group have the same indirect utility except for a stochastic element. Voter i in group k prefers party A if:

$$V_{k,A} > V_{k,B} + s_{i,k} + g \tag{5.55}$$

The term $s_{i,k}$ represents member i of group k's additive bias towards party B. This bias is considered to arise from factors which are not related to the policies of the parties. In addition g represents a population-wide additive bias towards party B. The $s_{i,k}$ are random variables, along with g. The introduction of random components involves a substantial change to the voting framework, compared with the deterministic model in which the probability of an individual voting for party A switches from 0 to 1, as $V_{k,A}$ switches from being less than, to greater than, $V_{k,B}$.

As the $s_{i,k}$ represent additive biases, they are centred around zero – a negative value indicates a bias towards party A. For the kth group, suppose the values of $s_{i,k}$ lie between $-s_k^*$ and $+s_k^*$. The population bias takes values between $-g^*$ and $+g^*$. Hence groups are distinguished by the range

[10] For an extensive treatment see, for example, Persson and Tabellini (2000).

of values which the bias towards party B can take, for people within the group. Members of the group have different views – these may for example be thought of in terms of strength of ideological bias or bias depending on personal characteristics of party members (unrelated to their policies).

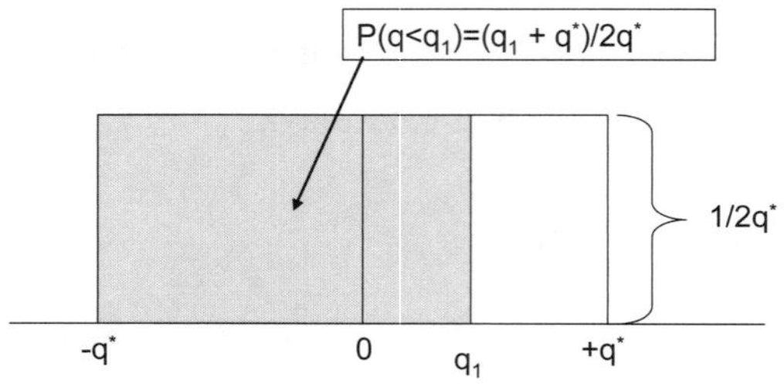

Figure 5.1: A Rectangular Distribution

Further progress is helped by giving more structure to the distributional framework. Suppose the distribution of biases within each group is assumed to be uniform within the relevant range; that is, the density functions of the variables follow rectangular distributions. Figure 5.1 illustrates a uniform or rectangular distribution of a variable, q, taking values between $-q^*$ and $+q^*$. Since the area underneath the uniform density function must be 1, the uniform density, the height of the rectangle, must equal $1/2q^*$. Furthermore, the probability of observing a value less than or equal to, say, q_1 is the shaded area to the left of q_1, so that $P(q \leq q_1) = (q_1 + q^*)/2q^*$. This property is used in what follows.

From (5.55) there is, within each group, a threshold value of $s_{i,k}$, say s'_k, such that all individuals with $s_{i,k} < s'_k$ vote for party A. This is given by:

$$s'_k = V_{k,A} - V_{k,B} - g \tag{5.56}$$

Using the above general result for rectangular distributions, the proportion of each group voting for party A, $p_{k,A}$, is equal to the proportion with $s_{i,k}$

below s'_k, and is given by:

$$\begin{aligned} p_{k,A} &= \frac{s'_k + s^*_k}{2s^*_k} \\ &= \frac{1}{2} + \frac{V_{k,A} - V_{k,B} - g}{2s^*_k} \end{aligned} \tag{5.57}$$

The proportion of individuals, over all groups, who vote for party A is the weighted sum:

$$p_A = \sum_{k=1}^{K} n_k p_{k,A} \tag{5.58}$$

Here p_A is a random variable because it is a function of the random variable g. The probability of party A winning the election, $P(A)$, is equal to the probability that $p_A \geq \frac{1}{2}$. This requires the probability that $\sum_{k=1}^{K} n_k p_{k,A} \geq \frac{1}{2}$, or:

$$P(A) = P\left[\sum_{k=1}^{K} n_k \left(\frac{1}{2} + \frac{V_{k,A} - V_{k,B} - g}{2s^*_k}\right) \geq \frac{1}{2}\right] \tag{5.59}$$

This can be rewritten as:

$$P(A) = P\left[\sum_{k=1}^{K} \frac{n_k}{s^*_k}(V_{k,A} - V_{k,B}) + \frac{1}{2}\sum_{k=1}^{K} n_k - g\sum_{k=1}^{K} \frac{n_k}{s^*_k} \geq \frac{1}{2}\right] \tag{5.60}$$

and since $\sum_{k=1}^{K} n_k = 1$, this becomes:

$$P(A) = P[g \leq g_A] \tag{5.61}$$

where:

$$g_A = \left(\frac{1}{\sum_{k=1}^{K} \frac{n_k}{s^*_k}}\right) \sum_{k=1}^{K} \frac{n_k}{s^*_k}(V_{k,A} - V_{k,B}) \tag{5.62}$$

This probability is the area of the rectangle with height $1/2g^*$ and base $g^* + g_A$, so that the probability of party A winning is:

$$P(A) = \frac{1}{2} + \frac{1}{2g^*}\left(\frac{1}{\sum_{k=1}^{K} \frac{n_k}{s^*_k}}\right) \sum_{k=1}^{K} \frac{n_k}{s^*_k}(V_{k,A} - V_{k,B}) \tag{5.63}$$

Suppose party A wishes to maximise this probability by selecting a policy, conditional on party B having selected its policy. Since $V_{k,B}$, g^*, the s^*_k and

n_k are constant, the first-order condition for a maximum is the same as that required to maximise:

$$\sum_{k=1}^{K} \left(\frac{1}{2s_k^*} \right) n_k V_{k,A} \tag{5.64}$$

This is a weighted sum of the indirect utilities, and since the densities are $1/2s_k^*$, the weights can be interpreted as the probabilities, within each group, of having a bias towards party B within the relevant range (from $-s_k^*$ to $+s_k^*$). The indirect utilities obviously depend on the policy choices, so that (in addition to the sizes of the groups) the values of $1/2s_k^*$ play an important role in the determination of party A's optimal policy. A small change in policy has a larger effect on its support by voters in group k, the larger is the density, $1/2s_k^*$ (that is, the smaller is the range of biases of members of the group). This contrasts significantly with the deterministic majority-voting framework, where only the preferences of the median voter count (provided the conditions required for the existence of an equilibrium are satisfied). For example, if higher-income groups have a more concentrated bias, compared with lower-income groups, they have a relatively larger importance in determining the policy decision of party A, despite the fact that lower-income groups may form a majority of the population (with a positively skewed income distribution). An implication is therefore that voting over a tax and transfer system may well result in less redistribution than under the basic deterministic majority-voting model.

Several further important implications follow from this. The situation facing party B is symmetric with that of A, which implies that – as each party is assumed to be trying to maximise its chances of winning the election – the policies of the two parties converge. Hence both parties can be regarded as having the same objective function:[11]

$$S = \sum_{k=1}^{K} \left(\frac{1}{s_k^*} \right) n_k V_k \tag{5.65}$$

[11] The 2 in the denominator can obviously be ignored.

where of course V_k is regarded as a function of policy variables. Letting $\eta_k = n_k/s^*_k$, then:

$$S = \sum_k \eta_k V_k \tag{5.66}$$

This common objective – or support function – therefore looks very much like a social welfare function expressed as a weighted sum (or weighted arithmetic mean) of indirect utilities. This is a form of utilitarian welfare function, except that the weights do not depend on value judgements of the decision-maker or judge whose views are represented by the social welfare, or evaluation, function. The weights are determined by the bias characteristics of the different income groups. A special case of (5.65) arises if all $s^*_k = s^*$ for all k, in which case the objective function to be maximised is exactly the same as the 'classical utilitarian' social welfare function.[12]

An alternative specification of bias in which the additive form in (5.55) is replaced by a multiplicative form, whereby what matters are the relative sizes of $V_{k,A}$ and $V_{k,B}$ rather than the absolute sizes, leads to a formulation which is additive in the logarithms. The objective function is thus expressed as a weighted geometric mean of indirect utilities, rather than a weighted arithmetic mean. This is clearly similar to the Nash maximand in a bargaining context. In the case where the bias densities are equal across groups, then a symmetric Nash solution applies.

A further important implication is that the above framework has not placed any restriction on the number of policy instruments under consideration. Hence the problems of the existence of a majority-voting equilibrium with deterministic voting do not arise. Similarly, in the case of voting over only one dimension, the single-peakedness of preferences is not relevant. However, the expression in (5.65) must be concave in policy instruments in order

[12]The utilitarian form has also been rationalised in terms of a social contract among individuals making a type of 'constitutional choice' behind a veil of ignorance, in which all outcomes are treated as being equally likely. This argument was first stated by Edgeworth (1881). A social contract arising from extreme risk aversion leads to the Rawlsian maxi–min evaluation function.

to satisfy the second-order conditions for a maximum.

5.5.2 Case 1: Additive Support Function

In the additive case discussed above, each party maximises a function taking the form:

$$W = \sum_i \eta_i V_i \tag{5.67}$$

and the voting outcome is equivalent to the maximisation of a utilitarian type of social welfare function which is a weighted sum of the V_is. Then:

$$\frac{\partial W}{\partial V_i} = \eta_i \tag{5.68}$$

and $\frac{\partial V_i}{\partial b}$ is the same as given above, so that:

$$\begin{aligned} v_i &= \frac{k\eta_i}{\{w(1-t)\}^{1-\alpha}} \\ &= \frac{k}{(1-t)^{1-\alpha}}\left(\frac{\eta_i}{w_i^{1-\alpha}}\right) \end{aligned} \tag{5.69}$$

Then:

$$\tilde{w} = \frac{\sum \eta_i w_i^{\alpha}}{\sum \eta_i w_i^{\alpha-1}} \tag{5.70}$$

In the case of no bias ($\eta_i = 1$) this can be expressed using the appropriate moments from the lognormal distribution. The voting equilibrium then coincides with the optimal tax resulting from a 'classical utilitarian' welfare function where only the sum of utilities matters. More generally, covariances are required, which means that further structure needs to be added to the model, regarding the joint distribution of s^* and w.

5.5.3 Case 2: Multiplicative Support Function

As mentioned earlier, a relative specification of bias results in a support function of the form:

$$W = \sum_i \eta_i \log V_i \tag{5.71}$$

Thus the voting outcome can be said to be equivalent to the maximisation of a social welfare function having the same form as that of the Nash bargaining solution. Hence (5.71) is sometimes referred to as a Nash social welfare function, in contrast with the additive forms discussed above, though it seems best not to conflate stochastic-voting support functions and social welfare function. In this case:

$$\frac{\partial W}{\partial V_i} = \frac{\eta_i}{V_i} \tag{5.72}$$

and using:

$$\frac{\partial V_i}{\partial b} = \frac{k}{\{w(1-t)\}^{1-\alpha}} \tag{5.73}$$

substitution gives:

$$v_i = \frac{\eta_i}{M_i} \tag{5.74}$$

The weighted average $\tilde{w}$ takes the form:

$$\tilde{w} = \frac{\sum v_i w_i}{\sum v_i} = \frac{\sum \frac{\eta_i w_i}{M_i}}{\sum \frac{\eta_i}{M_i}} \tag{5.75}$$

Suppose, as above, that b is small relative to w, so that $\tilde{w}$ can be approximated by:

$$\begin{aligned} \tilde{w} &= \frac{\sum \eta_i}{\sum \eta_i w_i^{-1}} \\ &= \frac{1}{\sum \eta_i w_i^{-1}} \end{aligned} \tag{5.76}$$

since $\sum \eta_i = 1$. As with the additive case, further progress in examining $\tilde{w}$ requires the joint distribution of s^* and w.

5.6 Conclusions

The aim of this chapter has been to consider explicit solutions regarding the choice of linear tax rate, in the case where individuals have Cobb–Douglas preferences. Alternative approaches were examined, including the simplest case, that of the median voter model, and the maximisation of some kind of evaluation function. The latter includes the standard optimal tax context and alternative specifications of stochastic-voting models.

An explicit solution to the median voter model was found to be given by the smallest root of a quadratic equation involving the ratio of the median to the arithmetic mean wage rate. In the optimal tax context, the same expression applies but the median wage is replaced by a welfare-weighted wage rate, where in general the weights depend on the tax parameters themselves. A convenient method of calculating an approximation to the optimal tax rate was suggested, making use of an assumption that the wage rate distribution is lognormal, for the ubiquitous iso-elastic social welfare function. This average depends on the degree of inequality aversion of the welfare function and the coefficient on consumption in individuals' utility functions. Calculations showed that the method performs well in comparison with standard simulation methods of computing the optimal tax rate, particularly after adjusting the welfare-weighted average wage upwards slightly. The method is easy to use, requiring just a few arithmetic steps. Cases of support functions involved in stochastic-voting models, which in formal terms resemble social welfare functions, were found to be more complex, requiring much more structure to be imposed on the model.

Chapter 6

A Loglinear Tax Function

The simple linear tax function has long been a 'workhorse' of tax analysis. Its two parameters, the unconditional basic income received by everyone and the fixed marginal (and hence average) tax rate applied to non-transfer income, are easily interpreted and the linear form often makes analysis tractable. Furthermore a basic income–flat tax structure (BI–FT) has been advocated by some policy commentators. The linear structure gives rise to fairly simple labour supply functions, when combined with conventional utility functions such as Cobb–Douglas and CES. When used in models with a government budget constraint, the loss of a degree of freedom in policy choices means that only the marginal tax rate can be chosen independently, and hence the linear tax can be incorporated into (unidimensional) majority voting and optimal tax models, although strong assumptions are often required if explicit solutions are to be available.

The aim of this chapter is to examine the use of a convenient alternative specification – a loglinear relationship between net, or after-tax, income and gross income – which has received relatively little attention in the tax literature. This can also be useful when it is required to introduce a stylised income tax function into a wider model. For example, it can provide a smooth two-parameter approximation to a multi-step schedule having a range of marginal rates between income thresholds. The loglinear form has both increasing average tax rates with income, required for progressivity, and increasing marginal tax rates with income. Studies using this form purely as an income tax function include Edgeworth (1925), Dalton (1954), Creedy (1979), Atkinson (1983), Hersoug (1984), Waterson (1985), Creedy and McDonald (1992) and Creedy and Gemmell (2006). However, a simple modification to the function allows it to cover means-tested transfer payments (negative income taxation) in addition to positive tax payments. Unlike the linear form, which has no means testing and a flat tax, the loglinear tax has income-testing of transfers and an increasing marginal tax rate. Yet when combined with commonly used utility functions, it produces relatively simple labour supply behaviour. This form has been used, for example, by Bénabou (1996) in the context of an overlapping generations model.

Section 6.1 describes the loglinear function and investigates the resulting government budget constraint. Section 6.2 then considers individual maximisation and labour supply behaviour using the simple Cobb–Douglas utility function. Majority voting is examined in section 6.3. The standard optimal tax framework, involving maximisation of a utilitarian social welfare function specified in terms of individuals' utilities, is then examined in section 6.4.

6.1 A Loglinear Tax Function

Subsection 6.1.1 describes the loglinear function and the interpretation of its two parameters. The resulting government budget constraint, which imposes a loss of a degree of freedom in policy choices, is derived in subsection 6.1.2.

6.1.1 Progressive Taxes and Transfers

Define z_i and y_i respectively as the net income and gross income of individual i. Suppose taxes and transfers are described by a loglinear tax function, with parameters $\tau < 1$ and y_b, as follows:

$$z_i = y_i^{1-\tau} y_b^{\tau} \tag{6.1}$$

The parameter, y_b, is the break-even income level at which individuals neither pay tax nor receive transfers; that is, when $y_i = y_b$, then $z_i = y_i$.[1] Figure (6.1) demonstrates the nonlinear relationship between the disposable income and gross income. An individual with income above y_b pays tax and an individual below the break-even income receives a benefit. Transfers are effectively means-tested, falling to zero at y_b.

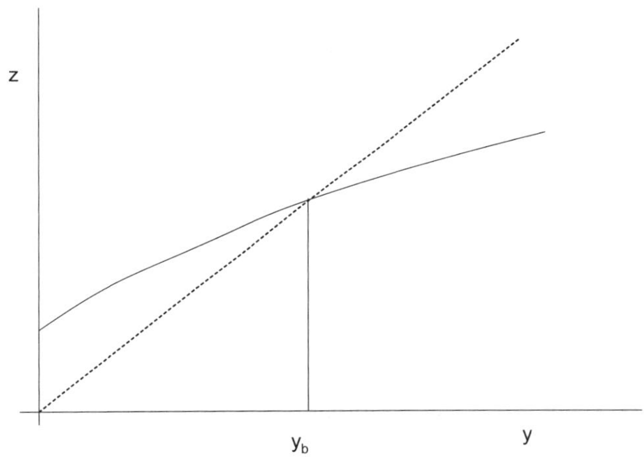

Figure 6.1: The Loglinear Tax Function

Consider the minimum level of net income, $z_{\min}$, which is obtained where gross income is equal to 1. Rewrite (6.1) in logarithm form as $\log(z_i) = (1-\tau)\log(y_i) + \tau\log(y_b)$. Hence:

$$\log\left(z_{\min}\right) = \log(z_i)\big|_{y_i=1} = \tau\log(y_b) \tag{6.2}$$

and minimum net income is equal to y_b^τ. This represents the maximum transfer payment available.

Unlike a standard piecewise-linear tax function, where fixed marginal effective tax rates apply between specified income thresholds, the 'tax rate'

[1]It would of course be possible to specify the function as $z_i = by_i^\tau$, where b represents the maximum transfer payment (available to those with $y_i = 1$). However, it is more convenient to have the break-even level more transparent, as in the specification above.

facing any particular individual is not transparent. Let $T(y)$ denote the tax paid by an individual with gross income, y, so that:

$$\begin{aligned} T(y_i) &= y - z \\ &= y - y^{1-\tau} y_b^{\tau} \end{aligned} \tag{6.3}$$

Therefore the marginal tax rate, MTR, and average tax rate, ATR, corresponding to income level, y, are respectively:

$$MTR = 1 - (1-\tau) y^{-\tau} y_b^{\tau} \tag{6.4}$$

$$ATR = 1 - y^{-\tau} y_b^{\tau} \tag{6.5}$$

The parameter, τ, is thus the marginal rate at the income level, $y = y_b$, at which the average rate is zero. A progressive tax system is defined as one in which the average tax rate increases when income increases, over the whole range of incomes. The average tax rate increases if the marginal tax rate exceeds the average tax rate, and applying this rule it can be shown that progression requires the tax parameter τ to be greater than zero, $\tau > 0$. The loglinear form may perhaps be regarded as providing a convenient smooth approximation, involving just two parameters, to a piecewise-linear function having several marginal rates and income thresholds.

6.1.2 The Government Budget Constraint

In a pure transfer system within a single-period framework with a pay-as-you-go system (which excludes borrowing or lending by the government), the government budget constraint is such that total net revenue is zero; that is, the total benefits paid to those below y_b are equal to the total tax revenue obtained from those with $y > y_b$. This means that it is not possible to set y_b and τ independently, as a degree of freedom in policy choices is lost. It is necessary to solve for y_b in terms of the parameter, τ.

At this point it is convenient to suppose there is a continuous distribution of income, with distribution function of gross income denoted by $F(y)$, with

$0 < y < \infty$. Hence the government budget constraint can be written:

$$\int_0^{y_b} \left(y^{1-\tau} y_b^{\tau} - y\right) dF(y) = \int_{y_b}^{\infty} \left(y - y^{1-\tau} y_b^{\tau}\right) dF(y) \tag{6.6}$$

Therefore:

$$\int_0^{y_b} y^{1-\tau} y_b^{\tau} dF(y) + \int_{y_b}^{\infty} y^{1-\tau} y_b^{\tau} dF(y) = \int_0^{y_b} y dF(y) + \int_{y_b}^{\infty} y dF(y) \tag{6.7}$$

Hence:

$$y_b^{\tau} \int_0^{\infty} y^{1-\tau} dF(y) = \int_0^{\infty} y dF(y) \tag{6.8}$$

The right hand side of this constraint is clearly arithmetic mean gross income, $\bar{y}$.

It is possible to solve for y_b, given any value of τ, in terms of the ratio of the first moment about the origin to the $(1-\tau)$th moment about the origin. Here it is convenient to make an explicit assumption about the form of the distribution of income. Suppose gross income is lognormally distributed with mean μ_y and variance σ_y^2. Hence $y \sim \Lambda(\mu_y, \sigma_y^2)$, and from the well-known properties of this distribution, the arithmetic mean income is equal to $\bar{y} = \exp\left(\mu_y + \sigma_y^2/2\right)$. Furthermore, $y^{1-\tau}$ is also distributed lognormally such that:

$$y^{1-\tau} \sim \Lambda\left(\left(1-\tau\right)\mu_y, \left(1-\tau\right)^2 \sigma_y^2\right) \tag{6.9}$$

Hence:

$$\int_0^{\infty} y^{1-\tau} dF(y) = \exp\left(\left(1-\tau\right)\mu_y + \frac{\sigma_y^2}{2}\left(1-\tau\right)^2\right) \tag{6.10}$$

Substituting in (6.8) gives:

$$y_b^{\tau} \exp\left(\left(1-\tau\right)\mu_y + \left(1-\tau\right)^2 \frac{\sigma_y^2}{2}\right) = \exp\left(\mu_y + \frac{\sigma_y^2}{2}\right) \tag{6.11}$$

Thus:

$$\begin{aligned} y_b^{\tau} &= \exp\left(\mu_y + \frac{\sigma_y^2}{2} - \left(1-\tau\right)\mu_y - \left(1-\tau\right)^2 \frac{\sigma_y^2}{2}\right) \\ &= \exp\left(\tau\mu_y - \frac{\tau\sigma_y^2}{2}\left(\tau - 2\right)\right) \end{aligned} \tag{6.12}$$

and:

$$\begin{aligned} y_b &= \exp\left(\mu_y + \frac{\sigma_y^2}{2} + \frac{\sigma_y^2}{2}(1-\tau)\right) \\ &= \bar{y}\exp\left(\frac{\sigma_y^2}{2}(1-\tau)\right) \end{aligned} \tag{6.13}$$

Therefore, the break-even level of income depends positively on average income and the variance of logarithms of the distribution of gross income and negatively on the tax parameter, τ.

If, instead of a pure transfer system, the tax structure has to raise net revenue of g per person in order to finance non-transfer expenditure, then g must be subtracted from the right hand side of (6.11), and the break-even income level becomes:

$$y_b = \left(1 - \frac{g}{\bar{y}}\right)^{1/\tau} \bar{y}\exp\left(\frac{\sigma_y^2}{2}(1-\tau)\right) \tag{6.14}$$

Hence if it is desired to extend the following analysis to cover the case where there is some non-transfer government expenditure per person, which does not enter individuals' utility functions, it is most convenient to express this expenditure as a fixed proportion of arithmetic mean income from employment.

6.2 Individual Maximisation

This section examines utility maximisation, by examining optimal labour supply for Cobb–Douglas direct utility functions.[2] This allows the required form of indirect utility functions to be obtained.

6.2.1 Labour Supply and Earnings

Each individual is assumed to derive utility from consumption, c, which in this static framework is equal to net income, z, and leisure, h. The total

[2]The more general constant elasticity of substitution (CES) form gives rise to a non-linear equation for optimal hours of leisure.

time available for work and leisure is normalised to one unit, so that $h \leq 1$. Then the budget constraint facing the ith individual is:

$$c_i = (w_i (1 - h_i))^{1-\tau} y_b^\tau \tag{6.15}$$

The direct utility function is assumed, for convenience, to be Cobb–Douglas, so that:

$$\begin{aligned} U_i &= c_i^\alpha h_i^{1-\alpha} \\ &= \left\{(w_i (1 - h_i))^{1-\tau} y_b^\tau\right\}^\alpha h_i^{1-\alpha} \\ &= \left\{w_i^{\alpha(1-\tau)} y_b^{\alpha\tau}\right\} (1 - h_i)^{\alpha(1-\tau)} h_i^{1-\alpha} \end{aligned} \tag{6.16}$$

Differentiating with respect to h_i gives:

$$\frac{\partial U_i}{\partial h_i} = \left(w_i^{\alpha(1-\tau)} y_b^{\alpha\tau}\right) h_i^{-\alpha} (1 - h_i)^{\alpha(1-\tau)} \left((1 - \alpha) - \alpha (1 - \tau) \frac{h_i}{1 - h_i}\right) \tag{6.17}$$

The first-order condition for utility maximisation, $\frac{\partial U_i}{\partial h_i} = 0$, therefore gives the interior solution for optimal leisure as:

$$h_i = \frac{1 - \alpha}{1 - \alpha\tau} \tag{6.18}$$

Consequently leisure, and thus labour supply, depends on only the preference parameter, α, and the tax parameter, τ, and is independent of the wage rate, w_i. In a population in which heterogeneity is reflected only in variations among individuals in the wage rate, then all individuals work the same number of hours. This contrasts strongly with the corresponding result for the linear tax function. Labour supply is always positive, under the assumption made above that $\tau < 1$. Hence, again unlike the case of the linear tax function, corner solutions with $h_i = 0$ and their associated complications do not arise.

Gross income is thus simply proportional to the wage rate for each individual, with:

$$y_i = w_i (1 - h_i) = w_i \frac{\alpha (1 - \tau)}{1 - \alpha\tau} \tag{6.19}$$

6.2.2 The Indirect Utility Function

Indirect utility, V_i, is obtained by substituting optimal leisure into the direct utility function:

$$V_i = \left\{ w_i^{\alpha(1-\tau)} y_b^{\alpha\tau} \right\} \left(\frac{\alpha(1-\tau)}{1-\alpha\tau} \right)^{\alpha(1-\tau)} \left(\frac{1-\alpha}{1-\alpha\tau} \right)^{1-\alpha} \tag{6.20}$$

Furthermore, substituting for y_b from the government budget constraint gives, for the term in curly brackets in (6.20):[3]

$$w_i^{\alpha(1-\tau)} y_b^{\alpha\tau} = w_i^{\alpha(1-\tau)} \bar{y}^{\alpha\tau} \left\{ \exp\left(\frac{\sigma_y^2}{2}(1-\tau) \right) \right\}^{\alpha\tau} \tag{6.21}$$

It is also necessary to consider the arithmetic mean gross income, $\bar{y}$, since it is also a function of the tax parameters and the wage rate distribution. Suppose the wage rate distribution is lognormally distributed as $\Lambda(\mu_w, \sigma_w^2)$. Then from (6.19), the wage rate and gross earnings distributions are related using:

$$\mu_y = \mu_w + \log \frac{\alpha(1-\tau)}{1-\alpha\tau} \tag{6.22}$$

and:

$$\sigma_y^2 = \sigma_w^2 \tag{6.23}$$

Hence, $\bar{y} = \frac{\alpha(1-\tau)}{1-\alpha\tau}\bar{w}$, in (6.21) is equal to:

$$\bar{y} = \exp\left[\mu_w + \frac{\sigma_w^2}{2} + \log \frac{\alpha(1-\tau)}{1-\alpha\tau} \right] \tag{6.24}$$

which uses the standard property of the lognormal distribution that, for example, $\bar{w} = \exp\left(\mu_w + \frac{\sigma_w^2}{2}\right)$. As expected, an increase in the tax rate reduces the average income, since:

$$\frac{\partial \bar{y}}{\partial \tau} = -\frac{\bar{w}\alpha(1-\alpha)}{(1-\alpha\tau)^2} < 0 \tag{6.25}$$

[3] In the case mentioned above where a fixed proportion $\delta = g/\bar{y}$ of revenue is raised for non-transfer purposes, the right hand side of (6.21) is simply multiplied by $(1-\delta)^\alpha$. Holding δ fixed instead of g means that this adjustment is independent of the tax rate.

and an increase in the (common) preference for consumption raises $\bar{y}$. In addition:

$$\frac{\partial^2 \bar{y}}{\partial \alpha \partial \tau} = -\frac{\bar{w}\left(1+\alpha^2\tau - 2\alpha\right)}{\left(1-\alpha\tau\right)^3} \tag{6.26}$$

which may be positive or negative. For the lognormal distribution, median income is less than the average income and from (6.13) it is clear that average income is less than break-even income level. This relationship between median, mean and break-even levels of income holds for all feasible levels of the tax parameter.

6.3 Majority Voting

This section examines the majority-voting equilibrium choice of tax parameter, τ. First, it can be shown that the indirect utility function is concave in τ, so that preferences are single peaked.[4] Hence the median voter theorem can be invoked and it is only necessary to examine the preferred value of the individual with median w, denoted w_m. It is useful to write the median voter's indirect utility function in (6.20), after substituting for y_b and $\bar{y}$, using (6.13) and (6.24). Furthermore, for the lognormal distribution, the logarithm of median income is equal to the mean of logarithms, so that $\exp\left(\mu_w\right) = w_m$. It is also most convenient to take logarithms, since the value of τ which maximises indirect utility is not affected by monotonic transformation. Then $\log V_m$ becomes:

$$\begin{aligned}\log V_m &= \alpha \log w_m + \alpha \log \alpha + (1-\alpha)\log(1-\alpha) \\ &\quad + \alpha\tau\sigma_w^2 - \frac{\alpha\tau^2\sigma_w^2}{2} + \alpha \log(1-\tau) - \log(1-\alpha\tau)\end{aligned} \tag{6.27}$$

Differentiating gives:

$$\frac{dV_m}{d\tau} = \alpha\left(1-\tau\right)\sigma_w^2 - \frac{\alpha\tau\left(1-\alpha\right)}{\left(1-\tau\right)\left(1-\alpha\tau\right)} \tag{6.28}$$

[4] This contrasts with the case of the linear tax function, where preferences can be double peaked. However, as Roberts (1977) showed, a majority-voting equilibrium exists if there is hierarchical adherence whereby the ranking of individuals does not depend on the tax rate.

Hence the median's choice of tax parameter, τ_m, is given by the solution to:

$$\sigma_w^2 = \frac{\tau_m (1-\alpha)}{(1-\tau_m)^2 (1-\alpha\tau_m)} \tag{6.29}$$

At first sight, a difference between this result for the loglinear tax function and the standard linear function is that the majority-voting equilibrium does not appear to depend on the median wage in relation to the arithmetic mean wage. However, this is subsumed in the variance of logarithms of the wage rate. Rearrangement of $\bar{w} = \exp\left(\mu_w + \frac{\sigma_w^2}{2}\right)$, and using $\mu_w = \log w_m$ gives:

$$\sigma_w^2 = 2\log\frac{\bar{w}}{w_m} \tag{6.30}$$

and (6.29) could easily be written in terms of $\frac{\bar{w}}{w_m}$. A higher variance of logarithms of wages implies greater skewness of the wage rate distribution and a larger distance between the median and arithmetic mean wage rates.

It would be possible to rewrite (6.29) as a cubic equation in τ_m, suggesting the possibility of three roots. However, writing the right hand side of (6.29) as $f(\tau) = \tau(1-\alpha)/\left\{(1-\tau)^2(1-\alpha\tau)\right\}$, it can easily be seen that $f(0) = 0$ and $f(1) = \infty$, with $df(\tau)/d\tau > 0$ and $d^2 f(\tau)/d\tau^2 > 0$. Thus $f(\tau)$ strictly increases with τ when $0 < \tau < 1$, is convex, and approaches an asymptote at $\tau = 1$. Importantly, this implies that there is a unique solution to (6.29). The comparative static properties of the model, involving the effects on the majority choice of τ of variations in α and σ_w^2, can be investigated using implicit differentiation, where (6.29) is written as $F(\tau_m, \alpha, \sigma_w^2) = 0$. It can be shown that:

$$\frac{d\tau_m}{d\alpha} = -\frac{F_a}{F_\tau} > 0 \tag{6.31}$$

and:

$$\frac{d\tau_m}{d\sigma_w^2} = -\frac{F_{\sigma_w^2}}{F_\tau} > 0 \tag{6.32}$$

The clear result that the tax parameter increases as basic wage rate inequality increases is also obtained for the linear income tax structure. Furthermore, the linear tax combined with homogeneous preferences also produces the result that the median voter's choice of tax rate increases as the preference for consumption (net income) increases. Essentially, this arises in the linear tax case because a higher preference for consumption implies higher labour supplies and hence a higher arithmetic mean taxable income and unconditional transfer: redistribution benefits the median voter, who is below the arithmetic mean, and so a higher tax rate is unambiguously chosen.[5] However, with the present loglinear tax function, the intuition is less obvious. The median voter's utility must increase as a result of a joint increase in α and τ, which satisfies the government budget constraint. Hence the median voter's choice must satisfy:

$$\frac{dV_m}{d\tau} = \frac{\partial V_m}{\partial \tau} + \frac{\partial V_m}{\partial \alpha}\frac{d\alpha}{d\tau} = 0 \tag{6.33}$$

rather than simply setting the right hand side of (6.28) equal to zero. Hence of concern is whether:

$$\left.\frac{d\tau}{d\alpha}\right|_{V_m} = -\frac{\partial V_m/\partial \alpha}{\partial V_m/\partial \tau} > 0 \tag{6.34}$$

In view of the nonlinearity of the first-order condition, reliance must be placed on the implicit differentiation above.

The nature of the solution can be illustrated further using Figure 6.2. The vertical axis shows how the right hand side of (6.39), $f(\tau)$, varies with τ, for two different values of α. It is again clear from these schedules in Figure 6.2 that the median voter's choice of τ has one feasible solution. For any given value of wage inequality, σ_w^2, the value of τ_m is thus easily obtained from the diagram. For example, if $\sigma_w^2 = 0.5$, τ_m is equal to 0.29 for $\alpha = 0.2$ and is 0.41 for $\alpha = 0.7$. Furthermore, the diagram illustrates the comparative

[5] For the linear structure, Holder (2008) has shown that if the preference for leisure varies among individuals (such that hierarchical adherence exists), a greater deviation between the median voter's preference for leisure and the average preference parameter is important. A higher median preference compared with the arithmetic mean is associated with a higher chosen tax rate. In that case, the median voter benefits by being able to have relatively more leisure and a higher degree of redistribution.

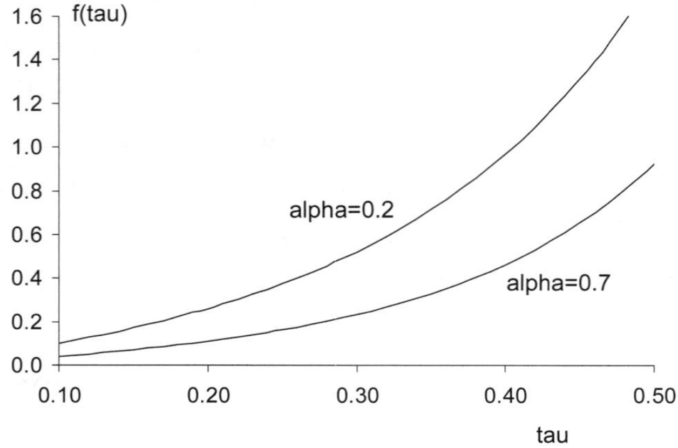

Figure 6.2: Variation in $f(\tau)$ with τ for Alternative α

static result reported above that the choice of tax parameter increases as the inequality of the wage rate distribution increases, and as the weight attached to consumption in the (common) utility function increases.

6.4 A Social Welfare Function

Consider the choice of tax rate by an independent judge or policy maker, whose value judgements can be described by an individualistic, additive and Paretean welfare, or evaluation, function, W, satisfying the principle of transfers. The welfare function is expressed in terms of individuals' (indirect) utilities, and is thus described as 'welfarist'. Aversion to inequality on the part of the judge is reflected in the degree of concavity of the weighting function, $H(V_i)$, with:[6]

$$W = \frac{1}{N} \sum_{i=1}^{N} H(V_i) \tag{6.35}$$

[6]For convenience the discrete summation over $i = 1, ..., N$ people has been used here, whereas in specifying the wage rate distribution above, a continuous form was used. This merely simplifies the notation.

In the literature on optimal linear taxation, $H(V_i)$ is usually specified as taking a constant relative inequality aversion form, $H(V_i) = V_i^{1-\varepsilon}/(1-\varepsilon)$, with ε measuring the degree of aversion. Even in the simplest of frameworks, where individuals are assumed to have identical utility functions and therefore differ only in the value of w_i, it is well known that a closed-form solution for the optimal linear tax cannot be obtained unless special (quasi-linear) utility functions are used, or various approximations are made; see Creedy (2009).

In the present context the derivation of the optimal loglinear tax rate becomes intractable except for the case where $\varepsilon = 1$, whereby $H(V_i) = \log V_i$. Hence this section concentrates on the optimal value of the tax parameter, τ, for a utilitarian social evaluation function of the form:[7]

$$W = \frac{1}{N}\sum_{i=1}^{N} \log V_i \tag{6.36}$$

Substituting V_i from (6.20) into (6.36), and remembering that $\sigma_y^2 = \sigma_w^2$, gives for a pure-transfer system:

$$\begin{aligned} W &= \log\left[\left(\frac{\alpha(1-\tau)}{1-\alpha\tau}\right)^{\alpha(1-\tau)}\left(\frac{1-\alpha}{1-\alpha\tau}\right)^{1-\alpha}\left\{\exp\left(\frac{\sigma_w^2}{2}(1-\tau)\right)\right\}^{\alpha\tau}\right] \\ &\quad +\alpha(1-\tau)\frac{1}{N}\sum_{i=1}^{N}\log w_i + \alpha\tau\bar{y} \end{aligned} \tag{6.37}$$

with $\bar{y}$ given by (6.24). Using $\frac{1}{N}\sum_{i=1}^{N}\log w_i = \mu_w$, this can be written as:

$$\begin{aligned} W &= \alpha(1-\tau)\log\alpha(1-\tau) - (1-\alpha\tau)\log(1-\alpha\tau) \\ &\quad +(1-\alpha)\log(1-\alpha) + \frac{\alpha\sigma_w^2}{2}\tau(1-\tau) \\ &\quad +\alpha\mu_w + \alpha\tau\left\{\frac{\sigma_w^2}{2} + \log\frac{\alpha(1-\tau)}{1-\alpha\tau}\right\} \end{aligned} \tag{6.38}$$

[7]Mention should also be made of the fact that the optimal rate is not invariant with respect to monotonic transformations of utility. That is, the cardinalisation of utility functions – a fundamental requirement if interpersonal comparisons are to be made – matters. Indeed the form in (6.36), with unit inequality aversion, in combination with (6.20), is equivalent to the optimal rate with zero inequality aversion and a cardinalisation of utility given by taking logarithms of the indirect utility function.

The first two lines of (6.38) correspond to the first line of (6.37), while the last line of (6.38) corresponds to the second line of (6.37). Differentiating with respect to τ, setting $dW/d\tau = 0$ and rearranging eventually gives the optimal tax parameter, τ_{SWF}, as the root of the following nonlinear equation:

$$\sigma_w^2 = \frac{\tau_{SWF}(1-\alpha)}{(1-\tau_{SWF})^2(1-\alpha\tau_{SWF})} \tag{6.39}$$

Comparison with (6.29) shows that the optimal choice, with $\varepsilon = 1$, is exactly the same as the majority-voting equilibrium, $\tau_m = \tau_{SWF}$, in this case where wage rates are lognormally distributed and preferences follow the Cobb–Douglas form.

6.5 Conclusions

This chapter has explored the use of a loglinear tax and transfer function as an alternative to the linear form that has received so much attention in the public finance literature. The loglinear function displays increasing marginal and average tax rates along with a means-tested transfer payment. It consists of two parameters, a break-even income threshold, where the average tax rate is zero, and a tax parameter. The latter is the marginal tax rate at the gross income level for which the average tax rate is zero.

When combined with Cobb–Douglas utility, the resulting labour supply is particularly simple, implying a fixed positive labour supply that is independent of the individual's wage rate. It was found that preferences regarding the tax parameter are single peaked, so that the median voter theorem can be applied. For common preferences and a lognormal wage rate distribution, the majority choice of tax parameter was found to be the unique root of a nonlinear equation involving the variance of logarithms of wages and the exponent on net income (consumption) in the utility function. As with the linear tax function, higher basic inequality is associated with a higher choice of tax parameter. Considering the optimal choice of tax parameter by an independent judge who maximises an additive social welfare function involving the sum of logarithms of (indirect) utilities, the same expression is obtained as with the median voter's choice. Hence the use of constant relative inequality aversion of unity, which implies a relatively high trade-off between equity and efficiency, coincides with the majority choice, even though the median voter is entirely selfish and has no concern for inequality.

Chapter 7

A Tax-Free Threshold

This chapter examines the role of a tax-free threshold in income tax structures. Such a threshold, below which the income tax rate is zero, is a feature of many tax systems and was initially motivated largely by equity considerations. However, this feature is not required in an integrated tax and transfer structure, such as the structures examined in chapters 4 to 6. Those countries without a tax-free threshold usually have some kind of tax rebate to deal with distributional objectives in low-income ranges. The simultaneous payment of income tax and receipt of benefits is a feature of modern tax and transfer systems which can only be avoided by raising the tax-free thresholds to a very high level. This would provide a tax cut for everyone, and so would require complementary adjustments to other features of the tax structure, if only to maintain revenue neutrality, without which alternative policies cannot be properly compared.[1]

In policy debates on tax and welfare reform, the tax-free threshold is often seen as a crucial equity component. Criticism of a lack of indexation of the threshold is accompanied by arguments in favour of raising it to a level

[1] For example, Saunders (2006, p. xxvi) argues that, 'At the same time as the top marginal rate is reduced, the tax-free threshold should be raised to a level above the welfare minimum (subsistence) level ... it would mean that all taxpayers enjoyed a substantial tax cut.' He does not mention compensating changes to other forms of revenue or expenditure along with this revenue-reducing reform, so it is unclear how this policy change would be financed and what the impact of this alternative revenue-generating process would be.

which ensures that no individual in receipt of transfer payments actually pays income tax.[2] However, in a structure with many means-tested benefits such that some benefits are not confined to the lower-income ranges, this could prove difficult to achieve. What really matters in a complex multi-tax and transfer structure is the overall redistributive effect: an early clear statement of this view was made by Hicks (1946, p. 150), who dated its realisation from the last quarter of the 19th century. Raising the threshold in order to help low-income groups actually has a low 'target efficiency' in that it involves at least the same absolute gains by those subject to higher marginal tax rates.

In order to place the debate regarding the role of the tax-free threshold in perspective, section 7.1 examines early views when income taxation was first introduced. In structures containing few – if any – transfer payments and a large number of individuals below the threshold who were considered to be at a subsistence level, and where income tax revenue formed a relatively low proportion of total tax revenue, the threshold played an important role. However, unlike current systems, the tax structure was designed to achieve proportionality at higher income levels, involving a type of rate 'degression' discussed in section 7.1. Section 7.2 considers alternative tax and transfer systems, paying attention to the need to make revenue-neutral comparisons. The role of tax rebates is examined, along with the possibility of achieving a revenue- and distribution-neutral change involving abolition of the tax-free threshold.

[2]For example, Saunders and Maley (2006, p. 113) argue that, 'The principled case for raising the threshold is that workers should be allowed to earn and retain enough money to meet their own subsistence needs before any tax is taken away from them.' However, the principle involved (whether of a basic value judgement or an efficiency criterion) is not actually mentioned. A similar argument for raising the threshold was made by Veit-Wilson (1999), who showed that in practice in the UK there had been no coordination between those responsible for tax thresholds and those responsible for setting benefit levels.

7.1 Early Views on Income Taxation

In early discussions on income tax, considerably more attention was given to the subject of differentiation by income source rather than the question of progression.[3] Indeed, the use of different tax rates according to the source of income (particularly with regard to permanent and temporary incomes) was discussed 'with a sophistry comparable only to that of later scholastic logic' (Shehab, 1953).[4] Attitudes to progression were influenced by the dominance of an 'ability to pay' view of the role of taxation, concentrating on the sacrifice made. This is in contrast with a 'benefit' or quid pro quo view according to which taxation should relate to the benefits obtained from the resulting tax-financed activity.[5] Given the huge importance for the classical economists of the concept of a subsistence level, and since there was no significant system of transfer payments (as relief to the poor involved entry to the dreaded workhouse), it is not surprising that there was virtually universal support for the idea of a tax-free income range. But, other than the acceptance of such a range, there was little acceptance of a redistributive role for income taxation.[6] Clarification of the utilitarian arguments relating to decreasing marginal utility – which imply progression only under special conditions –

[3]Five separate schedules, for different sources, operated in the UK from 1803, when the income tax was first introduced as a temporary revenue-raising measure during the Napoleonic Wars. They lasted for 150 years.

[4]In the UK, much of the discussion was associated with various Select Committees appointed by Gladstone during his long attempt to repeal the income tax reintroduced by Peel in 1842. Later, debate was stimulated by two Royal Commissions (Colwyn, 1920; Radcliffe,1955). For a survey of the history of public finance, see Creedy (1984), and for a collection of writings on taxation, see O'Brien (1999).

[5]Some people argued that these were equivalent because the state provided the protection and rights under which all incomes are obtained, while others believed that benefits were too difficult to assign.

[6]Sabine (1980, p. 130) states, 'Until 1894 its only real concession to equity was a comparatively high threshold', and Blum and Kalven (1953, p. 4) suggest that, 'it is almost unanimously agreed that some exemption keyed to at least a minimum subsistence standard of living is desirable'. It should also be remembered that tax rates were initially very low, there was no pay-as-you-go collection mechanism and income declarations were difficult to monitor.

was not provided until the work of Cohen Stuart (1889) and Edgeworth (1897).

A simple 'equal sacrifice' approach was taken, particularly by Mill (1848), in the context of an 'ability to pay' approach. He provided an early argument for the use of a single tax rate applied to all incomes measured in excess of the subsistence level, and in this he was strongly supported by McCulloch (1845).[7] This system gives rise to an increasing average tax rate for those above the threshold, so that despite a constant marginal tax rate it is progressive (and inequality reducing). However, the principle that the tax-free threshold should apply to all incomes was not actually adopted in the UK until after the Royal Commission of 1920: see Shehab (1953, pp. 93, 246) for details. The system in use for many years involved taxation of gross income above the threshold, but with a gradual 'shading in' of the tax rate until the point where a fixed rate applied.[8] Hence many higher-income taxpayers were subject to a constant marginal and average tax rate. Another similar system involves a gradual reduction in the tax-free threshold as income increases, until it is exhausted and the tax is proportional. Hence the UK system for many years was more strictly described, using the now unfamiliar term, as 'degressive' rather than progressive, because it implied a fixed average rate beyond a certain amount.[9]

As redistribution came to be accepted as a legitimate role of government, most income tax schemes not only applied a common tax-free threshold to all income levels (as well as introducing various personal allowances, often pos-

[7] The later utilitarian approaches redefined Mill's 'equal sacrifice' to mean 'equal marginal sacrifice', thus implying minimum aggregate sacrifice.

[8] This is similar to the current Australian low income tax offset, where low-income individuals in essence receive additional tax-free income, which is taken away at higher income levels by increasing the marginal tax rate.

[9] On degression, see for example Bastable (1903, pp. 316–317), de Viti de Marco (1936, pp. 289–290). Goode (1964, p. 226) refers to a 'vanishing exemption'. Cassel (1901) suggested that the tax-free threshold should actually increase as income increases, because expenditure on necessities increases, while still maintaining a structure that can be described as being progressive.

itively related to income), but also introduced a progressive (graduated) tax rate scale. This often involved a large number of marginal rates, increasing to very high levels: for an historical overview of the Australian system, see, for example, Groenewegen (1990). The income tax structure also came to exist alongside a complex range of (usually means-tested) transfer payments. The latter feature means that there is often an overlap between the tax and benefit systems, so that many benefit recipients are also liable to pay income tax. The overlap has in turn led to the introduction of tax rebates, also subject to what are variously called taper, withdrawal or abatement rates. In attempts to improve the target efficiency of tax and transfer systems, effective marginal tax rates (allowing for all tax rates and tapers) are typically highest for the low-income benefit recipients, although their average tax rates are negative.

An increase in the tax-free threshold, while moving some individuals out of the tax 'net', provides a benefit to all taxpayers so that, as a way of helping the poor, it is not well targeted. Furthermore, in a tax and transfer system consisting of a range of taxes and benefits, what matters is the overall effect rather than that of a single tax, so it is far from clear that the role of the tax-free threshold corresponds to its original one of helping low-income individuals at a subsistence level. The fact that many benefit reforms are introduced independently without full consideration of the overall effects can easily lead to unintended consequences, such as discontinuities in the relationship between gross and net income and ranges where marginal tax rates can exceed 100 per cent.

In modern tax and transfer systems it is therefore by no means unusual for individuals both to pay income tax (which for some people is partly compensated by income tax rebates) and receive benefits.[10] Given the presence

[10] Bastable (1903, p. 319) suggested that 'In any country where legal provision is made for poor relief, it would seem that to tax those at the point of minimum subsistence would be simply to drive them into the ranks of pauperism, and to take with one hand in order to give back with the other'. But there is no longer anything unusual about giving with

of income tax rebates, the need for a tax-free threshold is not as strong as formerly. The simplest tax and transfer system is an integrated 'basic income–flat tax' structure (or BI–FT) which has no role for a tax-free threshold but instead combines a universal (non-means-tested) basic income with a proportional tax applied to all income: for an extensive discussion of this option, see Atkinson (1995). Early studies of optimal income taxation actually suggested that the optimal structure is approximately linear, and this may well have contributed to the widespread flattening of structures since the early 1970s. However, the extensive literature has demonstrated that optimal structures depend crucially on the nature of population heterogeneity (in particular the wage rate distribution), on preferences and the social welfare function used to evaluate alternatives.

Despite the general movement towards flatter rate scales over the last 15 or so years, very few countries have adopted an income tax structure without a tax-free threshold. An exception is New Zealand. However, the use of personal allowances meant that there was an effective tax-free threshold from the introduction of the income tax in 1891 until 1972. There is now a relatively broad base, with a range of tax rebates for low incomes, a combination of different means-tested transfer payments and a progressive, or graduated, marginal income tax rate structure. For discussion of the tax reform changes in New Zealand, see Stevens (1990).

In Australia, no indexation took place from 2000/2001 up to 2003/2004, when the tax thresholds were increased slightly, or in 2004/2005. In 2005/2006 and 2006/2007 larger increases were introduced, particularly for the top two tax thresholds. The tax-free income threshold has not changed since 2000/2001. Before the July 2000 change, there was no indexation over a long period. Hence there have been calls to increase the tax-free threshold as a way of helping low-income groups. But, as mentioned above, such an

one hand while taking with another.

increase gives the same support to higher-rate taxpayers. The question is how might elimination of the Australian tax-free threshold be achieved with minimal impacts on lower-income groups? One alternative may be to abolish the tax-free income range and replace this with a similar amount in rebates for lower-income individuals. The remaining funds could be used to pay for a reduction in the middle-income tax rates to compensate those on middle and higher incomes (outside of the range of the new rebate) at least partly. Such a policy change could be expected to result in labour supply effects, since high-level rebates extend further up the income scale and thus lead to higher effective marginal rates for all people who have income in the extended rebate withdrawal range. In addition, higher taxes are expected for high-income groups if the increase in tax base is not sufficient to allow tax rates to be reduced by a large enough amount to compensate each individual fully for the loss of the tax-free income range.

Determining a revenue-neutral policy change that abolishes the tax-free income range is complex, as is the determination of potential labour supply responses with a range of effects working in opposite directions. A proper analysis requires a microsimulation model to evaluate the hypothetical policy options and enable full inclusion of all aspects of the reform. However, before reporting a policy simulation using a behavioural microsimulation model for Australia, the following section considers some basic aspects of integrated tax and transfer systems.

7.2 Comparison of Alternative Structures

This section considers, using a simple framework, the potential implications of a reform involving elimination of the tax-free threshold in a range of different income tax systems. In particular, it raises the question of whether a revenue-neutral and distribution-neutral reform is possible in principle, and considers potential labour supply responses and welfare implications arising from alternative reforms. This discussion assists in designing sensible policy options for investigation.

Subsection 7.2.1 discusses the case of income tax in isolation, while subsection 7.2.2 introduces transfer payments in the simplest possible system, that of a proportional income tax combined with a basic income. Variations involving means-tested benefits are then examined in subsections 7.2.3 and 7.2.4. Means-tested transfer payments form an important part of the tax structures of many countries.

7.2.1 Income Tax Only

Consider first the income tax system in isolation, and suppose that initially there is only one (positive) marginal tax rate of t and a tax-free threshold of a.[11] Hence income tax paid on an income of y, denoted $T(y)$, is given by:

$$\begin{aligned} T(y) &= t(y-a) \qquad & y > a \\ T(y) &= 0 \qquad & y \leq a \end{aligned} \tag{7.1}$$

For taxpayers, the average tax rate is $t(1 - a/y)$, which clearly increases towards t with increasing y. Marginal and average rates for this income tax structure are illustrated in Figure 7.1. This system has an increasing average tax rate and is thus progressive, for incomes over a. Overall it is inequality reducing (the inequality of post-tax is less than that of pre-tax income) so long as a is not too high.[12] It is this characteristic that provides the basic motivation for the use of a tax-free threshold. Indeed, when income tax was first introduced, there were typically no transfer payments. However, in modern systems with many different types of benefit, what matters is the overall effect, rather than the effect of a single tax in isolation.

[11] A system of personal allowances is equivalent to a tax-free threshold, though allowances may vary by household size and composition.

[12] If t is held constant and a is increased, inequality gradually falls. However, if for already high tax-free thresholds a, the threshold is further increased, very few people remain to pay tax, so that inequality increases, since the post-tax distribution again moves

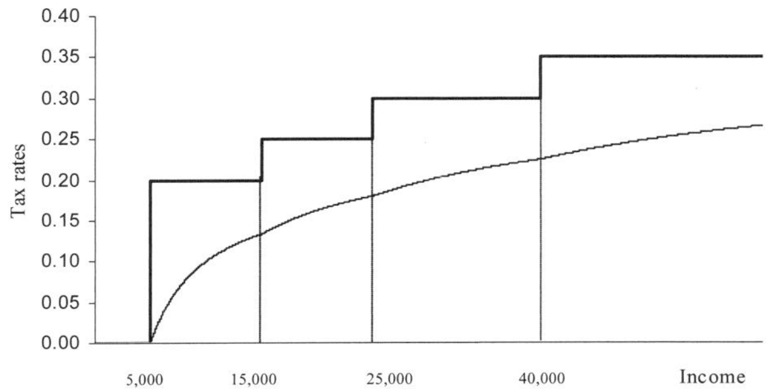

Figure 7.1: Marginal and Average Tax Rates with a Tax-Free Threshold

In fact, the income tax with a tax-free threshold shares characteristics of a combined tax and transfer scheme. This is because, for taxpayers, net (after income tax) income, z, is:

$$z = at + (1 - t)\,y \tag{7.2}$$

For $y > a$, this income tax system is equivalent to a BI–FT tax and transfer system (a linear tax) with a basic income of at and a flat tax rate t. This characteristic provides a motivation for eliminating the tax-free threshold. With a tax-free threshold, any attempt to help the very low paid taxpayers – those close to, but above, the threshold – by raising the threshold and taking them out of the 'tax net' is accompanied by a simultaneous increase in the implicit transfer given to all taxpayers. Furthermore, if there is marginal rate progression and increasing the threshold shifts all the other income tax thresholds up by the same amount as the tax-free threshold increase, then the increase is highest for the higher rate-payers. A further motivation for eliminating the tax-free threshold is that the accounting period and the unit of analysis are no longer relevant.[13]

closer to the pre-tax distribution. For inequality to fall continuously, the tax rate must be increased as a is increased.

[13]Considerable energy is involved in treating the accounting period for tax purposes as

Expected total revenue per person from the income tax, R, is:

$$R = t \int_a^\infty (y - a)\, dF(y) \tag{7.3}$$

where $F(y)$ is the distribution function of pre-tax income and $0y < \infty$. This can be written as $R = t\bar{y}G(a)$ where $\bar{y}$ is expected income $\int_0^\infty y dF(y)$ and:

$$G(a) = \{1 - F_1(a)\} - \frac{a}{\bar{y}}\{1 - F(a)\} \tag{7.4}$$

and $F_1(a)$ denotes the first moment distribution function, that is, the proportion of total income in the population obtained by those with income below a.[14] Clearly, $G(0) = 1$, and a proportional, or flat, tax raises $R = t\bar{y}$ per person.

Eliminating the tax-free threshold therefore obviously increases the revenue raised from the income tax. A revenue-neutral elimination of the threshold allows a reduction in the constant marginal tax rate, now applying over all $y > 0$, to be made. If the new rate is denoted t', then:

$$t' = tG(a) \tag{7.5}$$

However, such a change involves a move from a progressive income tax to one having a constant average rate t'. This affects the income distribution, benefiting high-income individuals relative to lower-income individuals.

Some progression can be re-introduced by the explicit introduction of a transfer payment or rebate which is given to low-income individuals, or a transfer applying over the whole range of incomes. In principle it would be possible to eliminate the tax-free threshold while retaining precisely the same relationship between gross and net income, by giving a transfer of at to all those with $y > a$, and introducing a means-tested benefit of $B(y) = ty$ for those with $y < a$. This is effectively a tax rebate which cancels the effect of

a single year, when individuals have fluctuating incomes and other circumstances during the year, and are subject to pay-as-you-go tax collection.

[14]The function $G(.)$, and extensions, has a fundamental role in the analysis of tax and transfer systems; see Creedy (1996).

the income tax. Such a change in administration would make no sense where there is no well-developed tax administration, poor monitoring of incomes, a large number of individuals in the lower-income groups, and low tax revenue. It is thus not surprising that a 'degressive' system was used in the UK for many years in order to achieve proportionality for the higher-income groups: a tax rebate (taking with one hand and giving with the other) would have been extremely cumbersome. However, in the modern context, a rebate for low-income groups is feasible as one component of a range of income transfers.

7.2.2 Basic Income–Flat Tax System

Instead of a means-tested benefit, consider the use of an unconditional basic income, that is, a BI–FT system. Suppose a non-means-tested transfer payment of b is introduced, and the flat tax rate is t^*. Net income for all individuals is thus:

$$z = b + (1 - t^*)\, y \tag{7.6}$$

This system is unambiguously progressive as total tax paid, $T(y) = t^* y - b$, and the average tax rate, $t^* - b/y$, increases over the whole range of income. The latter is initially negative, becomes zero at $y = b/t^*$ and asymptotically approaches t^* as y increases. Average and marginal rates for this structure are shown in Figure 7.2. With its negative tax for incomes below b/t^* and with its higher tax rate t^* (compared to t in the previous section), this system is clearly more progressive than the income tax alone so the reform is not distribution neutral.

To ensure that a reform, involving replacement of the income tax in subsection 7.2.1 with the linear tax, is revenue-neutral, consider total net government revenue per person. This becomes:

$$R^* = t^* \bar{y} - b \tag{7.7}$$

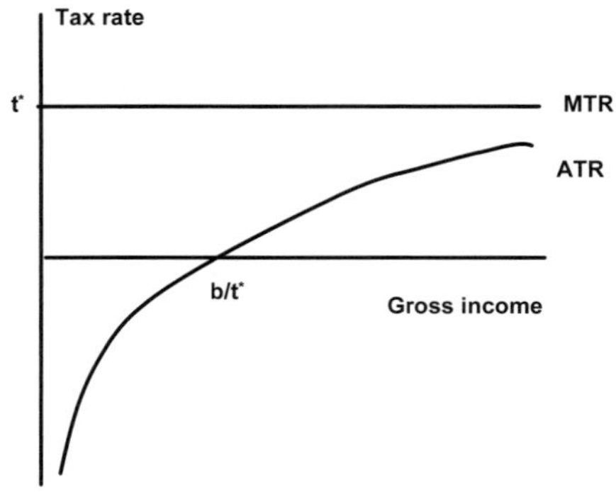

Figure 7.2: Tax Rates in the Linear Tax Structure

and the new tax rate is given by:

$$t^* = \frac{b}{\bar{y}} + tG(a) \tag{7.8}$$

Everyone receives b rather than only those above a receiving an implicit transfer of at, so it is not possible to have $b = at$ and $t = t^*$ without reducing total net revenue. Thus it is possible to have a revenue-neutral but not a distribution-neutral reform involving a move from a tax-free threshold to a basic income with a flat tax.

The above results apply for a fixed distribution of pre-tax income. However, in addition to distributional effects, the reform may also be expected to have labour supply effects. This complicates matters further; for example to remain revenue neutral, further adjustments to the tax parameters b and t^* would be required. The direction of the labour supply effects is ambiguous and needs to be determined empirically. High-income groups face a lower marginal rate if $t^* < t$, giving rise to a substitution effect, while at the same time also facing an income effect. Due to the income effect of receiving a basic income b and the higher marginal tax rate t^*, the labour supply of some of those previously having an income $y < a$ is likely to fall, in some cases to the non-participation corner of the budget constraint.

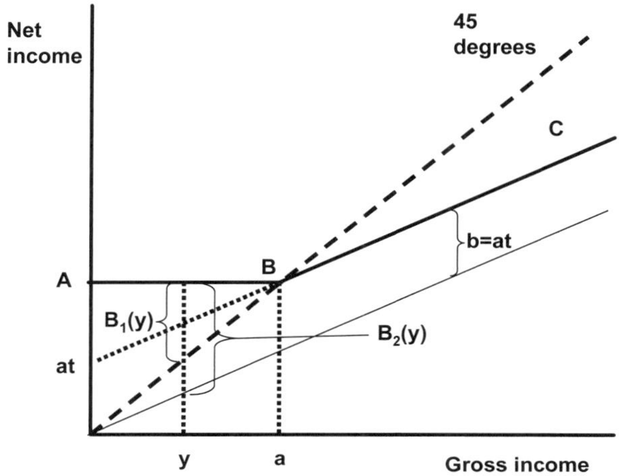

Figure 7.3: A Minimum Income Guarantee

7.2.3 Income Tax with a Minimum Income Guarantee

Consider now an income tax having a tax-free threshold of a combined with a minimum income guarantee such that all those with y below a have their net income brought up to the level a. Hence, for $y < a$, benefits are given by $B_1(y) = a - y$ and the MIG involves means testing with a taper rate of 100 per cent. The relationship between net and gross income is shown in Figure 7.3 as the line ABC.

Suppose the tax-free threshold is eliminated but the MIG still guarantees a minimum income of a for those with $y < a$. Hence for $y < a$:

$$z = y - ty + B_2(y) = a \tag{7.9}$$

and benefits are given by:

$$B_2(y) = a - (1 - t)\,y \tag{7.10}$$

Abolishing the tax-free income therefore involves a reduction in the benefit taper rate, from 1 to $1 - t$, to allow for the fact that each extra dollar of income also attracts income tax. Of course, the overall effective marginal tax rate continues to be 100 per cent. Those with $y > a$, who initially receive an implicit transfer of at while being taxed implicitly at the flat rate of t on all their income, can now be given an explicit unconditional basic income of $B(y) = b = at$.

Hence in this special case it is possible to combine the elimination of a tax-free threshold with a slight reform of the benefit structure in order to maintain precisely the same relationship between net and gross income. This involves a relatively minor change in administration in view of the fact that means testing was initially applied to low-income groups, thereby requiring an existing sophisticated tax and benefit structure. The change is revenue and distribution neutral and would simply be a change in the administrative arrangements.

However, elimination of the tax-free threshold is motivated by a desire to flatten the income tax structure and to take away the implicit transfer given to those higher-income individuals who pay tax. An alternative reform, instead of maintaining the effective status quo of the MIG with a tax-free threshold, might not introduce a basic income for taxpayers but, keeping the MIG at the level a, extend the income range over which individuals are entitled to the means-tested benefit. Suppose the tax-free threshold is eliminated, the marginal and average income tax rate applying to everyone becomes t' and the MIG is received by all those with income below y_T, where $y_T > a$. This is illustrated in Figure 7.4.

For continuity in the relationship between z and y it is required to have:

$$a = (1 - t')\, y_T \tag{7.11}$$

so that:

$$y_T = \frac{a}{1 - t'} \tag{7.12}$$

The above reform is clearly not distribution neutral. However, it can be made revenue neutral. Consider the effect on the tax rate t', needed to

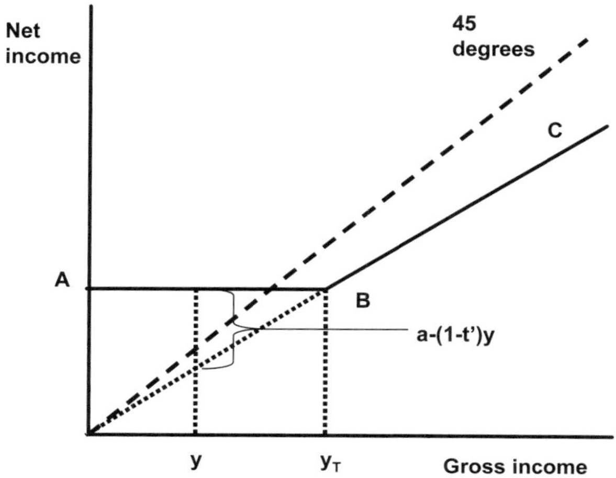

Figure 7.4: An Alternative Reform

achieve revenue neutrality given a fixed distribution of y. Under the pre-reform tax structure, suppose that non-transfer expenditure of E per person must be financed from the income tax system, in addition to the MIG. The government's budget constraint is thus:

$$E + \int_0^a (a-y)\, dF(y) = t \int_a^\infty (y-a)\, dF(y) \tag{7.13}$$

It can be shown, using the expression $G(a)$ from (7.4), that:[15]

$$t = \frac{E/\bar{y} + \{G(a) - (1 - a/\bar{y})\}}{G(a)} \tag{7.14}$$

Under the reformed system, the government's budget constraint becomes:

$$E + \int_0^{a/(1-t')} \{a - (1-t')\, y\}\, dF(y) = t'\bar{y} \tag{7.15}$$

After some rearrangement, this can be written as:

$$t' = 1 + \frac{E/\bar{y} - \left\{1 - \frac{a}{\bar{y}} F\left(\frac{a}{1-t'}\right)\right\}}{1 - F_1\left(\frac{a}{1-t'}\right)} \tag{7.16}$$

[15]When $a = 0$, and there is no MIG nor a tax-free threshold, this reduces to the simple expression, $t = E/\bar{y}$.

This expression does not provide a closed-form solution for t' as it is highly nonlinear, with terms in both integrals F and F_1 depending on t', along with their limits of integration. However, it seems likely that $t' < t$.

In practice the above results would be modified by labour supply responses to the change in the tax structure, since the expressions assume a fixed distribution of y. The extension in the range of y for which means testing applies (with a taper rate of $1-t'$) means that more lower-income individuals, who previously simply paid income tax, now receive means-tested benefits and thus face a higher marginal tax rate (since in practice $t' < 0.5$ and the taper rate exceeds the income tax rate). Hence their labour supply is likely to fall. Higher-income individuals face a lower marginal tax rate if $t' < t$, giving rise to a substitution effect in favour of higher labour supply, and simultaneously there is an income effect in the same direction because of the elimination of the implicit transfer of at. The overall effect at the population level is thus unclear.

7.2.4 A Modified Minimum Income Guarantee

In practice, tax and transfer systems do not usually have the simple MIG form examined in the previous subsection. Benefits typically have a taper rate, s, where $t < s < 1$, and a range of 'free' income before the taper begins to apply. Furthermore, the receipt of the transfer payment extends beyond $y = a$. A simplified form of tax and transfer system, referred to as a modified MIG, is shown in Figure 7.5, where the relationship between net (after-tax-and-transfer) income and gross income is shown by the piecewise-linear schedule ABCD. The diagram concentrates on the lower ranges of the income distribution. To reduce the number of parameters involved, the form illustrated assumes that the taper-free range of the benefit is the same as the tax-free range of the income tax structure, equal to a. Although in practice, tax and transfer systems are usually highly complex, with numerous overlapping benefits, each with its own threshold, the simple form shown in Figure 7.5 is a reasonable approximation, which captures the issues relevant to a more complex system.

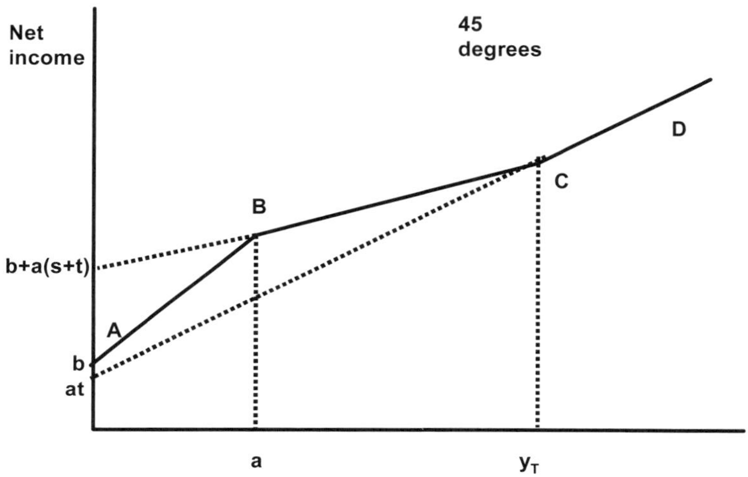

Figure 7.5: A Modified Minimum Income Guarantee

In the pre-reform situation, suppose the benefit received when $y = 0$ is equal to $B(0) = b$. As continuity is imposed on the relationship, the point B in Figure 7.5 must correspond to a net income of $z = a + b$. The segment BC, when continued to the net income axis, must have an intercept of $b + as$.[16] Furthermore, the threshold income y_T, above which the means-tested benefit is exhausted and individuals only pay income tax, is given by the constraint imposing continuity between sections BC and CD:

$$(b + as + at) + (1 - s - t)\, y_T = at + (1 - t)\, y_T \tag{7.17}$$

so that:

$$y_T = \frac{b + as}{s} \tag{7.18}$$

[16] This is because it must be the case that if q is the intercept, $a + b = q + a(1 - s)$, which can be solved for q.

For those between B and C, the net transfer, defined as the difference between their net income z and their gross income y, is given by:

$$\begin{aligned} z - y &= \{b + as + at + (1 - s - t)\, y\} - y \\ &= b - (t + s)\,(y - a) \end{aligned} \tag{7.19}$$

For this tax and transfer system the government's budget constraint is therefore given by:

$$\begin{aligned} &E + b \int_0^a dF(y) + \\ &\int_a^{(b+as)/s} \{b - (t + s)\,(y - a)\}\, dF(y) = t \int_{(b+as)/s}^{\infty} (y - a)\, dF(y) \end{aligned} \tag{7.20}$$

This is clearly highly nonlinear because s affects the limits of integration.

A reform involving the elimination of the tax-free threshold in the income tax would generate extra revenue. The latter could be used to reduce the income tax rate to t'. In addition, a tax rebate could be introduced in order to maintain the section AB. Individuals who previously paid no tax as they were below the tax-free threshold, a, would need to receive a tax rebate of $t'y$ up to a maximum of $t'a$. The tax rebate would have a taper rate s_{tr} applying above a. This taper rate can be chosen so that the tax rebate is exhausted at the same time as the benefit b at threshold y_T.[17] This reform implies that individuals with gross income between a and y_T face a higher effective marginal tax rate than before; that is, people formerly subject to the means-tested taper rate s now face an additional taper rate s_{tr} corresponding to the withdrawal of the tax rebate. This system is shown in Figure 7.6. The point C moves downward to C′ due to the introduction of the new taper rate s_{tr}, which needs to be larger than the reduction in the income tax rate. Again the reform is not completely distribution neutral. The overall effect on net income inequality is not obvious as it depends on the pre-tax income distribution.

[17] This is not a necessary constraint but it limits the number of parameters involved.

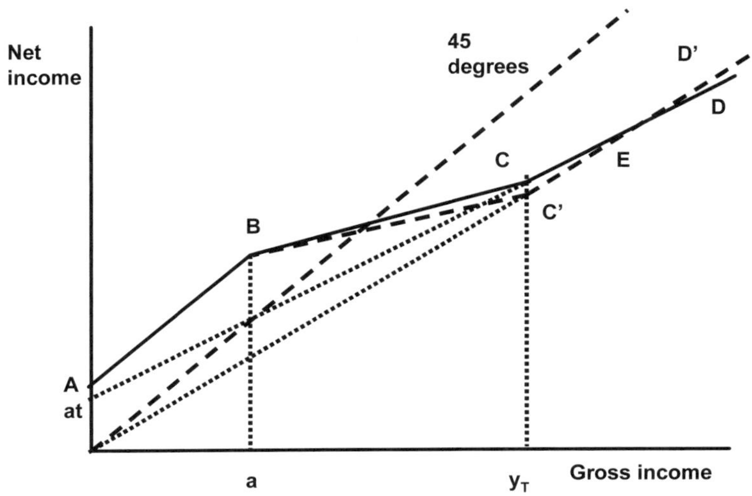

Figure 7.6: The Modified MIG Without a Tax-Free Threshold

The condition required for revenue-neutrality is complex in this case, again because of the nonlinearities involved. As mentioned above, the marginal income tax rate is changed to t' when the tax-free threshold is abolished. The continuity of the section BC′ and C′D′ requires the following condition:

$$(b + as' + at') + (1 - s' - t')\, y_T = (1 - t')\, y_T \tag{7.21}$$

where $s' = s + s_{tr}$. Hence:

$$y_T = \frac{b + as' + at'}{s'} \tag{7.22}$$

By combining equations (7.22) and (7.18), it is possible to solve for s_{tr} to ensure that both benefits and tax rebate are exhausted at the same threshold:

$$s_{tr} = \frac{sat'}{b} \tag{7.23}$$

The net transfer received by those with pre-tax income between a and y_T becomes:

$$\begin{aligned} z - y &= \{b + as' + at' + (1 - s' - t')\, y\} - y \\ &= b - (s' + t')\,(y - a) \end{aligned} \tag{7.24}$$

and this is smaller than in the pre-reform situation because $(s' + t')$ has to be larger than $(s + t)$ in order to satisfy the government budget constraint. That is, extra government revenue has to be generated by individuals on the section BE to finance the cost of the tax cut for high-income individuals on section ED$'$. Hence the new government budget constraint is:

$$E + b\int_0^a dF(y) +$$

$$\int_a^{(b+as'+at')/s'} \{b - (s' + t')(y - a)\}\, dF(y) = t' \int_{(b+as'+at')/s'}^{\infty} y dF(y) \tag{7.25}$$

Again a closed-form solution for t' is not available.

The labour supply implications of this type of piecewise-linear tax and transfer system are complex, particularly because there is an increase in the effective marginal tax rate over a range (section BC) combined with a decrease above y_T as entitlement to the means-tested benefit and tax rebate is exhausted.

Again the above results are likely to be modified by labour supply responses to the tax reform. Their overall effect is unclear *a priori* as it depends on the initial distribution of income and the balance of income and substitution effects. This reform involves a minimum of changes – adjusting t while keeping net incomes of the low-income people unchanged by introducing a tax rebate – and of course it would be possible to modify other parameters.

7.3 Conclusions

This chapter has examined the role of the tax-free income tax threshold in a complex tax and transfer system consisting of a range of taxes and benefits, each with their own taper rates and thresholds. When considering the introduction of income taxation in societies which had no significant transfer payments and with many individuals regarded as being at a subsistence level, it is not surprising that a tax-free threshold was used. However, particularly in the UK, a 'degressive' rate structure was used to produce proportionality at the higher-income levels: progressivity was not a primary objective of the tax system. Considering a range of tax and benefit systems, particularly those having benefit taper rates whereby some benefits are received by income groups other than those at the bottom of the distribution, for which a sophisticated revenue collection and benefit payment system is in place, it was suggested that a tax-free threshold is not a necessary requirement to achieve redistribution. The simultaneous payment of tax and receipt of benefits does not generate excessive difficulties. What matters is the overall effect of the system.

Chapter 8

In-Work Payment With Hours Threshold

The adverse incentive effects of traditional means-tested social transfers, arising from relatively high marginal tax rates at low hours levels and exacerbated by fixed costs of working, have led to a search for innovations designed to encourage higher labour force participation. For example, various forms of in-work benefit have been introduced. These include the US earned income tax credit, where the benefit is phased in, and the UK working tax credit, which involves a bonus payment at 16 hours and 30 hours, for families with and without children respectively.[1] An in-work payment involving an hours threshold was recently introduced in New Zealand, as part of a package of welfare reforms referred to as 'working for families'.

The effect of this kind of payment is that it introduces a discontinuity in the budget constraint at the hours threshold at which net income increases. Budget constraints often have small discontinuities arising from the difficulties of integrating a number of different types of transfer payment, and these are typically regarded as shortcomings. However, a major motivation for a jump in net income of this kind is that it is thought to provide a strong

[1] On labour supply effects of the US tax credits, see Eissa and Hoynes (1999). For a description of the UK system, see Brewer (2003); empirical studies of labour supply effects include Duncan and Giles (1996).

incentive for relatively low-wage individuals to increase their labour supply up to the threshold level. A suggested rationale for this is that individuals are expected to have longer-term benefits from such a higher attachment to the labour market, such as increased productivity and other characteristics.[2] However, the budget constraint facing the government means that relatively high benefit withdrawal, or taper, rates must apply to a range of hours above the threshold level. This can have the effect of reducing the hours worked of some individuals.

The net effect on labour supply and the income distribution of such a reform cannot therefore be predicted on a priori grounds. Furthermore, a policy evaluation may wish to allow for welfare changes rather than simply income changes, since utilities are affected by labour supply variations. Hence the aim of the present chapter is to examine the implications for labour supply, inequality and social welfare, defined in terms of individuals' utilities, of the presence of an in-work transfer payment involving a discontinuity. The emphasis is on an attempt to understand the nature of potential labour supply incentive effects arising from the introduction of an hours threshold, along with the types of constraint imposed on the choice of policy parameters in such a tax and transfer system.

The following analysis therefore uses a highly simplified tax structure and allows only for variations in wage rates. For simplicity, the analysis is in terms of individuals, therefore ignoring any benefits affected by the number of children and the complexities of modelling household labour supply. The framework of analysis thus follows more closely the standard optimal income tax framework, in which individuals are assumed to maximise utility defined in terms of net income and leisure time. In making comparisons among alternative tax structures, attention is given to the government's bud-

[2] Sometimes a concern is expressed, in a standard means-tested system, over benefits being paid to high-wage but very low-hours individuals. However, it is not clear how large this group is in practice.

get constraint and all results are for budget-neutral structures.

It is necessary to stress that the analysis in the present chapter is exclusively of the supply side of the labour market, with wage rates assumed to remain fixed. The ultimate effects of any tax and transfer reform obviously depend also on labour demand considerations. There is a range of administration and other issues associated with this type of tax reform. These include the difficulty of monitoring hours worked and the problem of dealing with variability in hours over time. The latter can lead to horizontal equity problems. However, these issues are not examined here.

The basic specification of the tax structure is described in section 8.1. This is a flexible structure containing few parameters, but is nevertheless capable of displaying all the main features of complex budget constraints applying in practice. In particular, these characteristics concern the nature of labour supply behaviour generated by kinks and non-convexities in the budget set. The analysis of a simplified structure helps to clarify important design features and illustrates the effect of the government revenue constraint and other requirements on the ability to select parameters independently.

The modelling procedure is outlined in section 8.2. This describes the utility functions, the social evaluation function and the strategy used for obtaining budget-neutral comparisons. Analytical solutions are not available even in the simplest of models. The emphasis is on using numerical simulations to clarify the properties of alternative tax and benefit systems. Numerical simulations are reported in section 8.3. Results are reported for social welfare and inequality, for variations in the hours threshold and in the extent of the jump in net income produced by the in-work payment.

8.1 The Tax and Transfer System

This section describes the tax and transfer system examined. A simplified structure is required that nevertheless captures essential properties of realistic tax systems. The budget constraints facing individuals need to be specified in detail, in view of the later need to compute optimal hours of work for each individual. An in-work payment (IWP), which becomes available at a particular hours threshold, is used to augment a two-rate means-tested tax structure, often described as a modified minimum income guarantee. The various forms taken by budget constraints, depending on the wage rate faced by the individual, are discussed in subsection 8.1.1. The resulting way in which labour supply is expected to vary as the wage rate varies is analysed in subsection 8.1.2.

8.1.1 Budget Constraints

A convenient way to model an in-work payment with an hours threshold is to consider it as being added onto a basic tax and transfer system involving only two effective marginal rates. Suppose that all those with earnings, y, below an earnings threshold, a, receive a benefit equal to $s(a-y)$,where s is the taper or abatement rate at which the benefit is withdrawn as earnings increase. After this benefit is exhausted, earnings are taxed at a constant proportional rate, so that the tax paid is $t(y-a)$; this is effectively a proportional tax applied to earnings in excess of a tax-free threshold of a. For an individual with an hourly wage rate of w, and working h hours a week, the earnings threshold is reached where $a = wh$, that is, at the hours level a/w. This system is shown in Figure 8.1 as the line AKE. For a means-tested system, the taper or abatement rate exceeds the income tax rate, so that $s > t$. Each budget constraint in Figure 8.1 is drawn for a particular wage rate, and the lower part of the figure has a higher wage than the upper diagram. Hence the constraint for the higher wage reaches the tax-free threshold, a, at a lower hours level than for the lower wage rate.

The modified minimum income guarantee used here has several analytical advantages. It involves just two tax rates and one earnings threshold. The maximum benefit, which is available to those who do not work at all, is defined in terms of the benefit taper rate and the earnings threshold, since when $y = 0$, the benefit is equal to at. The use of a single threshold is convenient for the analysis of budget-neutral alternatives, as this one parameter can be allowed to adjust while others are varied. The specification also explicitly avoids any further discontinuities in budget constraints. This structure also provides a good approximation to many practical systems, though the latter can appear to produce very 'ragged' lines.[3] It is seen below that even an apparently simple system of this kind involves considerable complexities.[4]

Suppose that this basic system is augmented by an in-work payment whereby net income increases by an amount g_w at the hours level, h_1. Beyond this discontinuity in the budget constraint, the effective taper rate is r, where $s > r > t$. This means that the new section of the budget constraint, CD in Figure 8.1, must reach the old constraint somewhere along the range KE. This occurs at the hours level h_2, where $h_2 > a/w$. Here h_2 depends on the individual's wage rate, while h_1 is fixed and is the same for all individuals. Benefit receipt is thus extended further up the hours, and thus earnings, range compared with the basic transfer system. Although net incomes are higher than otherwise, it means that more people face a higher effective marginal tax rate.

In specifying this type of in-work payment, it seems desirable to make the extent of the discontinuous jump in the budget constraint, g_w, lower for those with higher wage rates. Without this property, the in-work payment would continue to be paid to very high-income individuals, for example those with high w and working at least h_1 hours. Hence, in addition to an hours of work condition, the benefit paid at, as well as beyond, the hours threshold is means tested. This property is illustrated in Figure 8.1, where there is

[3] However, many systems have a small tax-free range before the means testing applies.

[4] This type of means-tested system has been examined in detail in Lambert (1985, 1988) and Creedy (1996, 1998b).

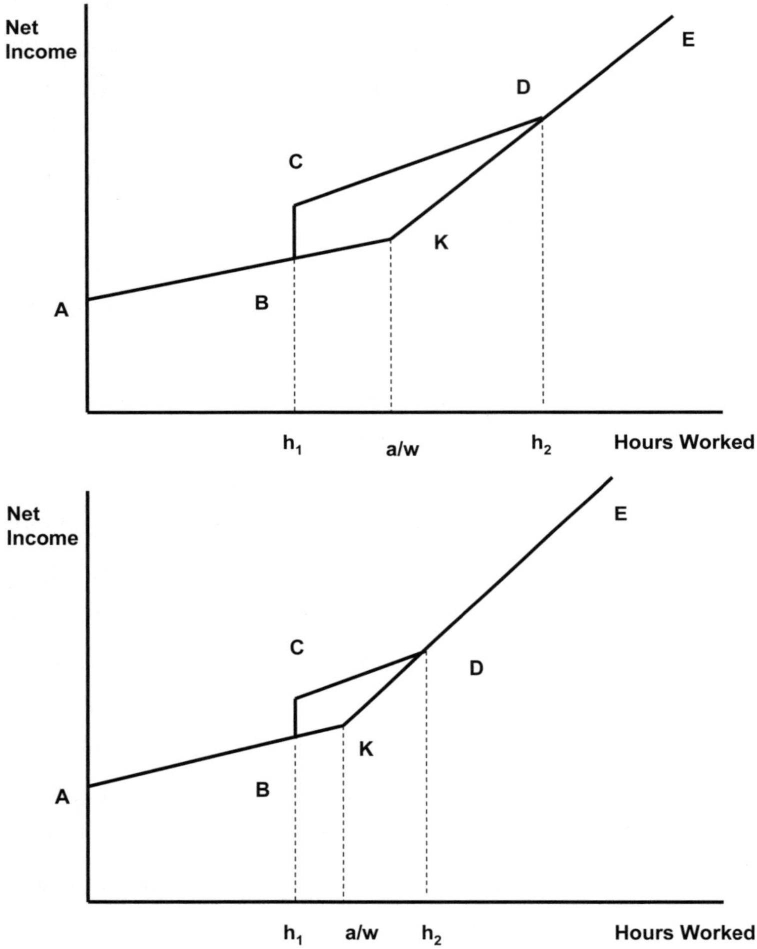

Figure 8.1: Budget Constraints For Two Wage Rates

a smaller jump in net income (a smaller distance BC) in the lower diagram where the wage rate is higher.

The question arises of how to specify this reduction. Suppose that the highest value, of $g_w = g$, occurs for the minimum wage, w_m. For higher wage rates, the vertical jump in the budget line at h_1 is assumed to decline at a linear rate. A convenient specification for this is:

$$\begin{aligned} g_w &= g - v\left(wh_1 - w_m h_1\right) \\ &= g - vh_1\left(w - w_m\right) \end{aligned} \tag{8.1}$$

The decline in g_w therefore depends on the extent to which gross earnings at the specified hours threshold exceed the earnings of someone with the minimum wage. Hence there is no in-work payment for w in the range:

$$w > w_m + \frac{g}{vh_1} \tag{8.2}$$

However, the value of v cannot be set arbitrarily. Net income at h_1 for wage $w > w_m$ must exceed that for w_m at the same hours level. That is, the higher-wage people must be better off than low-wage individuals at similar hours levels. Otherwise the system is 'incentive incompatible' and those with higher wages have an incentive to pretend to have lower wage rates. This means that:

$$as + wh_1\left(1 - s\right) + g - vh_1\left(w - w_m\right) > as + w_m h_1\left(1 - s\right) + g \tag{8.3}$$

or:

$$h_1\left(w - w_m\right)\left(1 - s - v\right) > 0 \tag{8.4}$$

which implies that $s + v < 1$.

Given these properties of the in-work payment it is possible to obtain the precise form of the equations of the various linear segments of budget constraints. Denoting net income as z, the equation of segment AB in Figure

8.1, which applies over the hours range $0 < h < h_1$, is therefore given by:

$$\begin{aligned} z &= wh + s(a - y) \\ &= as + wh(1 - s) \end{aligned} \tag{8.5}$$

The equation of the segment DE, where $h > h_2$, is:

$$z = at + wh(1 - t) \tag{8.6}$$

The equation of CD, for which $h_1 < h < h_2$, is:

$$\begin{aligned} z &= as + wh_1(1 - s) + g_w + w(1 - r)(h - h_1) \\ &= as + g - wh_1(s - r) - vh_1(w - w_m) + wh(1 - r) \end{aligned} \tag{8.7}$$

Hence the intersection of CD and DE, at D, occurs for hours equal to h_2, where:

$$h_2 = \frac{a(s - t) + g - h_1\{w(s - r) + v(w - w_m)\}}{w(r - t)} \tag{8.8}$$

As the wage rate increases, the hours level corresponding to the kink at K in Figure 8.1 moves to the left, and the height BC falls. This is demonstrated by comparing the two parts of the figure, where the lower section shows the budget constraint for a higher wage than in the upper section.

In Figure 8.1, the hours threshold is in each case below the kink point K, which occurs for hours a/w. However, it is possible that the wage is sufficiently high that $a/w < h_1$ while the in-work payment continues to be received. In this case, $a/h_1 < w < w_m + g/rh_1$. This situation is shown in Figure 8.2. The equation of the linear segment CD is:

$$\begin{aligned} z &= \{at + wh_1(1 - t) + g - vh_1(w - w_m)\} + w(1 - r)(h - h_1) \\ &= at + wh_1(r - t) + g - vh_1(w - w_m) + wh(1 - r) \end{aligned} \tag{8.9}$$

The corresponding expression for h_2 must differ from that given in equation (8.8). When $h_1 > a/w$, the in-work payment is exhausted at h_2 hours, where:

$$h_2 = h_1 + \frac{g - vh_1(w - w_m)}{w(r - t)} \tag{8.10}$$

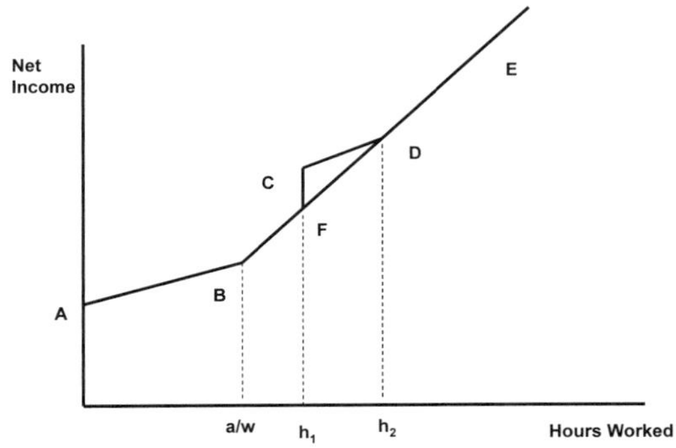

Figure 8.2: A Budget Constraint With $a/w < h_1$

Having assembled the various forms of budget constraint, the implications for labour supply behaviour are discussed in the following subsection.

8.1.2 Labour Supply

The budget sets generated by the above tax and transfer system have several non-convexities. These arise from the fact that $s > r > t$, combined with the non-convexity resulting from the discontinuity at the fixed hours threshold. These features can give rise to unusually shaped labour supply functions, explored in the present subsection. As usual, the approach proceeds by considering how the optimal position (enabling the highest indifference curve to be reached subject to the budget constraint) varies as the wage rate increases, causing the budget constraint to pass through the various phases shown in Figures 8.1 and 8.2.

Figure 8.3 shows a possible form of individual labour supply function. Some minimum wage level is necessary before the individual begins to work; this is shown as point A. As the wage rate increases above this minimum, labour supply expands along the segment AB of the supply curve in Figure 8.3, which also corresponds to the segment of the budget constraint marked AB in Figure 8.1. Then as the wage increases beyond some level (for which an indifference curve is simultaneously tangential to the segment AB and the corner at C of the budget constraint shown in Figure 8.1), there is a jump in labour supply to the corner at h_1 hours of work. This is shown by the vertical segment of the labour supply function illustrated in Figure 8.3. Labour supply remains fixed at this hours threshold for a range of wage rates, indicated by the vertical distance CD in Figure 8.3, before movement takes place along the range where the in-work payment is subject to abatement at the rate r.

The additional non-convexity means that an indifference curve can simultaneously be tangential to the two linear segments CD and DE of the budget constraint in Figure 8.1, for a particular wage rate. This means that as the wage passes that level, another jump is made from somewhere on CD to a point on the segment DE, where the marginal rate is t. This jump is shown in Figure 8.3 as the horizontal line EF. Beyond that point, further increases in the wage rate result in expansions of labour supply along the range FG in Figure 8.3. The labour supply curve therefore has two 'jumps' at certain wage levels, corresponding to the two non-convexities, and three ranges of steadily increasing hours as the wage increases, corresponding to movements of a tangency position along a linear segment of the budget constraint. These expansions are shown for convenience as straight lines in Figure 8.3, but of course their shape depends on the precise nature of the utility function.[5]

However, the labour supply curve need not take precisely this form. If the two taper rates r and s are relatively high, it is likely that there is simply a jump straight from zero hours of work to h_1, followed by another jump directly from h_1 to the segment where no benefits are received and the marginal income tax rate is t. The ranges AB and DE in Figure 8.3 are thereby eliminated. This possibility is shown in Figure 8.4. Other alternatives clearly exist, where just one of the ranges AB and DE is eliminated.

[5] In fact, for Cobb–Douglas utility functions, the segments are linear.

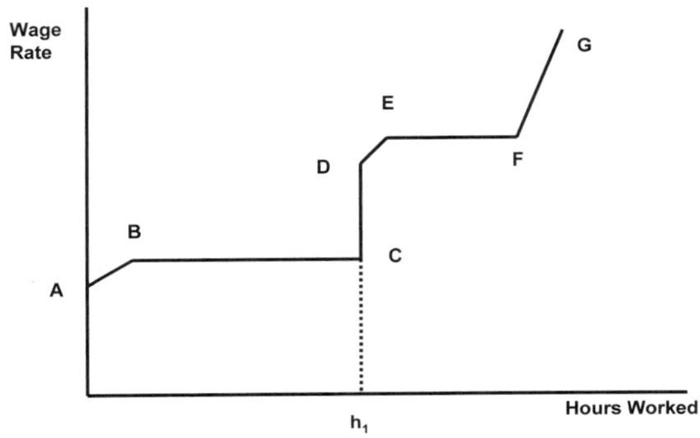

Figure 8.3: A Possible Labour Supply Function

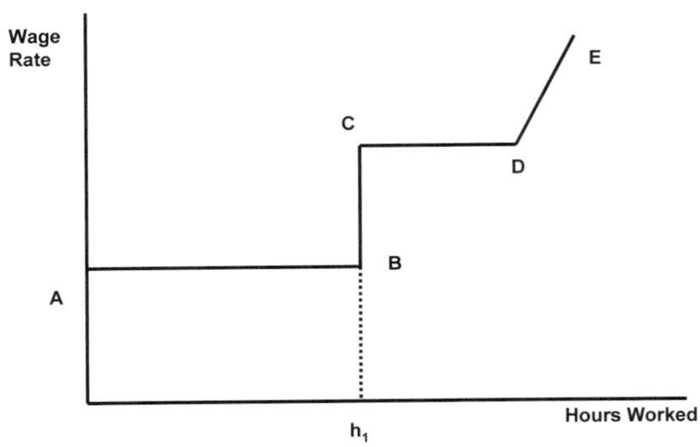

Figure 8.4: Labour Supply With High Abatement Rates

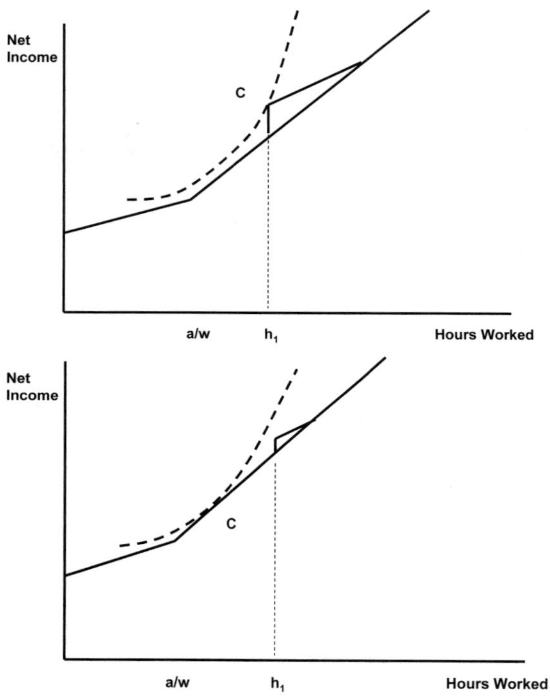

Figure 8.5: Labour Supply With High Hours Threshold

The budget constraints all have (other than at zero hours of work) only one convex kink at the point marked C in each of the Figures 8.1 and 8.2. In the standard case, such a kink usually arises at a fixed gross income level where a higher marginal tax rate starts to apply. As the wage rate increases, the kink in the budget constraint therefore moves horizontally. It gives rise to a range of wage rates where gross and net income are constant, but labour supply falls (along a rectangular hyperbola). But in the present context the convex kink arises from a fixed hours threshold, so the kink corresponding to C moves vertically rather than horizontally. It is therefore likely that there would be a substantial amount of 'bunching' of individuals at the hours threshold, with different associated income levels.

The vertical movement of C seems to suggest that labour supply would not have a 'backward bending' range. However, this property of the budget constraint, combined with the feature of the in-work payment, described above, whereby the benefit paid at the hours threshold h_1 falls as the wage rate increases, can give rise to a somewhat surprising result. In some cases, a reduction in labour supply can occur as the wage rate increases, particularly if the hours threshold h_1 is relatively large. Figure 8.5 shows the situation where labour supply is h_1 for a range of wage rates, but a point is reached where an increase in w leads to a reduction in labour supply. This arises because the discontinuity falls as w increases, even though, as discussed above, net income is higher at comparable hours. However, this case is unlikely to apply to most values of h_1 that are considered in practice.

8.2 The Modelling Procedure

Further analysis of the effects of the in-work payment with an hours threshold requires an explicit assumption to be made about preferences. This is discussed in subsection 8.2.1, where the assumption is made that individuals have Cobb–Douglas utility functions defined in terms of net income and leisure. More complex utility functions, such as the CES form, could be used, but are unlikely to affect the main comparisons below. The main characteristics of labour supply are driven, as seen above, by the nonlinear nature of the budget constraints rather than the properties of utility functions.[6] Multiple local optima can arise from the nonlinear budget constraint, and subsection 8.2.1 also describes a procedure for obtaining optimal hours worked for each individual.

An important feature of any tax and transfer system is that a degree of freedom in the choice of parameter values (the various thresholds and rates) is lost because of the government's budget constraint. The revenue from taxes must be sufficient to raise the amount required to finance both benefit and non-transfer government expenditure. That revenue, and the transfer expenditure requirements, depend crucially on the labour supply choices of individuals which are themselves determined in part by the tax parameters. It also depends on the precise form of the distribution of wage rates. As in standard optimal tax models, the government budget constraint cannot be solved analytically, so that iterative numerical methods must be used in conjunction with a simulated wage rate distribution. This is discussed in subsection 15.2, which also describes the form of social evaluation function used: this welfare function encapsulates the value judgements of an independent 'decision maker'.

8.2.1 Utility Functions

Suppose that utility functions follow the Cobb–Douglas form:

$$U = c^{\alpha} (T - h)^{1-\alpha} \tag{8.11}$$

where T is the maximum amount of time available per week, and c is an index of total consumption, whose price is normalised to unity. Hence, in

[6] On the use of the CES form, and comparisons of labour supply functions with the Cobb–Douglas case, see Creedy (1996, 1997).

this static framework, c is equivalent to net income, y. Consider tangency solutions along a linear budget constraint segment given by:

$$c = b + w_n h \tag{8.12}$$

where w_n is the net wage rate and b is the virtual income appropriate to the particular segment. Virtual income is the net income at the intercept of the segment, when it is extended, with the axis where hours of work are zero.

Labour supply analysis also requires the concept of full income. This is the total net income received if all available time is spent working, that is, if $h = T$. The individual is considered to convert the endowment of time, combined with virtual income, into full income, and to use this to purchase goods and leisure, at a price equal to the net wage. For the linear segment of equation (8.12), full income, M, is equal to $Tw_n + b$ and following the standard Cobb–Douglas results, $c = \alpha M$ and leisure, $T - h$, is equal to $(1 - \alpha) M/w_n$. Hence hours worked are given by:

$$h = \alpha T - \frac{b(1-\alpha)}{w_n} \tag{8.13}$$

The tax and transfer scheme described above combines a piecewise-linear budget constraint with non-convexities and a discontinuity. It can therefore give rise to multiple local optima. A procedure for solving the labour supply, given a wage rate, taste parameter and the parameters of the tax system, must involve examination of utility at all the possible corner solutions. In addition, equation (8.13) is used to search for tangency positions on each linear segment, by appropriate substitution of the net wage and virtual income, checking that such solutions fall within the relevant hours limits for that segment.

The algorithm must begin by determining whether w is such that the in-work payment is relevant and, if so, whether the budget constraint is like Figure 8.1 or Figure 8.2. In the latter case, the search for local optima includes four segments where tangency positions may be relevant. Finally, it is necessary to collect all interior and corner solutions and then find the one that gives rise to the global maximum utility.

8.2.2 Evaluation Procedure

This subsection describes the procedure used to evaluate alternative tax systems, that is, alternative parameter values for the flexible system described in section 8.1. Consider a population of individuals facing the same tax system. As in the standard optimal tax framework, it is assumed that tastes are identical, but each individual faces a different wage rate. Suppose the wage rate distribution, for wages above w_m, follows the lognormal form, so that w is distributed as $\Lambda(w|\,\mu, \sigma^2)$ where μ and σ^2 are respectively the mean and variance of log-wage rates. A simulated population can be generated by drawing observations at random from this lognormal distribution and setting any $w < w_m$ equal to w_m.

In the model considered here, there are seven tax parameters, s, t, r, a, g, h_1 and v. However, these cannot all be set independently because of the properties mentioned above and the need to satisfy the government's budget constraint. This constraint is highly complex in view of the nature of the constraints facing individuals. Hence it is not possible to write one of the tax parameters as a function of the other parameters. A numerical iterative method of solution is required, and it is appropriate to solve for the earnings threshold, a, for given values of the other parameters. This is because any value of a is consistent with both low and high values of tax rates, in view of labour supply behaviour. Hence, it is not sensible to try to solve for, say, t, given values of a and the other parameters. Starting from a trial value of a, and given values of the other parameters, all labour supplies and hence total net revenue are computed. If the resulting net revenue is greater than the desired amount specified, a is increased and the process is repeated.

Having solved the government's budget constraint, all the values of utility, hours worked and so on are available for a given set of tax parameters. Clearly, the 'outcome' can be evaluated in many different ways, depending on the basic value judgements applied. The approach followed here, as in standard optimal tax models, is to evaluate the tax and transfer system using a social welfare function expressed in terms of individuals' utilities. This is taken as summarising the values of an independent decision maker. The welfare function is the iso-elastic form commonly used in the literature, and is written as:

$$W = \sum_{i=1}^{n} \frac{U_i^{1-\varepsilon}}{1-\varepsilon} \tag{8.14}$$

where ε represents the constant relative inequality aversion. Tax reforms of the kind examined here inevitably involve losses for some individuals: Paretean improvements are seldom available. The welfare function encapsulates explicit interpersonal value judgements, based on (cardinal) utilities. In optimal tax calculations it is known that results depend on the particular cardinalisation of utility functions used, though of course the cardinalisation does not affect individuals' optimal labour supplies. However, this is not an issue in the present context, where comparisons are made among tax structures, rather than searching for an optimal rate in a given structure.

It is convenient to rewrite (8.14) in abbreviated form, where W is expressed in terms of the arithmetic mean utility, $\overline{U}$, and its inequality, as measured by the Atkinson index, $I_U = 1 - U_E/\overline{U}$. Here U_E is the equally distributed equivalent utility, equal to the value that, if obtained by everyone, would generate the same W as the actual distribution. On abbreviated social welfare functions, see Lambert (1993) and on the inequality measure, see Atkinson (1970). The abbreviated form is:

$$W = \overline{U}\,(1 - I_U) \tag{8.15}$$

which allows W to be expressed as average utility less the 'cost of inequality', $\overline{U} I_U$. For comparison, results are also reported below with net income replacing utility as the argument of the welfare function.

8.3 Simulation Analysis

This section provides simulation results using the framework described above. In view of the large number of parameters, no attempt is made here to search over all the dimensions to produce optimal tax rates. Instead, the emphasis is on policy changes and the effects of the size of the discontinuity in budget constraints and the value of the hours threshold at which the jump in net incomes occurs. Hence this section concentrates on the results of varying the parameters g and h_1. These are the main additional design features from a reform introducing an in-work payment with an hours threshold. Subsection 8.3.1 describes the other parameter values used, while the second subsection gives the main results of the comparisons. It is important to stress the need, in this type of exercise, to carry out extensive sensitivity analyses. It was found that the main features of the reported results are robust to variations in parameter values. All simulations reported in subsection 8.3.2 are for a population of 5,000 individuals.

8.3.1 Parameter Values

In view of the highly stylised nature of the model, it is possible only to calibrate it, that is impose parameter values, in such a way that sensible numerical results are produced; that is, the orders of magnitude of various characteristics can be made to bear some relation to selected observed magnitudes.[7]

The values assumed for s, r, t and v are respectively 0.8, 0.6, 0.4 and 0.1. Here 0.4 is similar to the top marginal income tax rate in New Zealand, and 0.8 is a reasonable value for the effective marginal rate arising from various abatement rates. The maximum time per week available for work, T, is set

[7]It may be tempting to think that comparisons could be made with empirical estimates of labour supply elasticities. However, single values are usually reported at arithmetic mean values of variables, whereas a major feature of the analysis here is that the elasticity varies substantially over the supply curve (given the various 'jumps' and stable points).

to 80. The taste parameter α is equal to 0.55. The arithmetic mean hourly wage $\bar{w}$ is 19, while the variance of logarithms of the wage rate distribution, σ^2, is 0.5; the implied value of the arithmetic mean log-wage is given, from the properties of the lognormal distribution, by $\mu = \log \bar{w} - \sigma^2/2$. These values are chosen to give a 'standard' working week of around 40 hours, and a resulting distribution of weekly income that roughly approximates the New Zealand distribution.

The social welfare function requires a value of relative inequality aversion, ε, to be specified. The following results are for $\varepsilon = 0.5$. In the context of incomes, x, for individuals i and j, with $x_j > x_i$, then $\left.\frac{dx_i}{dx_j}\right|_W = -\left(\frac{x_j}{x_i}\right)^{\varepsilon}$. Hence, if j has twice the income of i, a value of $\varepsilon = 1$ means that the judge is prepared to take \$1 from j and transfer only 50 cents to i, losing the remaining 50 cents from the 'leaky bucket'.[8]

8.3.2 Some Results

In view of the emphasis on the two parameters g and h_1 of the in-work payment, this section examines the implications of varying each one of these in turn, for the specified values of the other parameter. In all cases, a is endogenously adjusted to ensure budget neutrality, by solving the government's budget constraint iteratively as explained above. To give an idea of the order of magnitude, if g and h_1 are set at \$60 per week and 30 hours respectively (values that are associated with the New Zealand proposed system) and if non-transfer government revenue per person is \$25 per week, it is found that a value of $a =$ \$250 is required for a balanced budget.

Figure 8.6 shows the variation in W as the jump in net income, g, varies, for three values of the hours threshold, h_1. It can clearly be seen that social welfare falls systematically as g increases, although there is a very slight rise for further increases at high values of g. For the lower value of $h_1 = 25$, the

[8] For survey results on attitudes to inequality, producing values of ε substantially below 1, see Amiel *et al.* (1999).

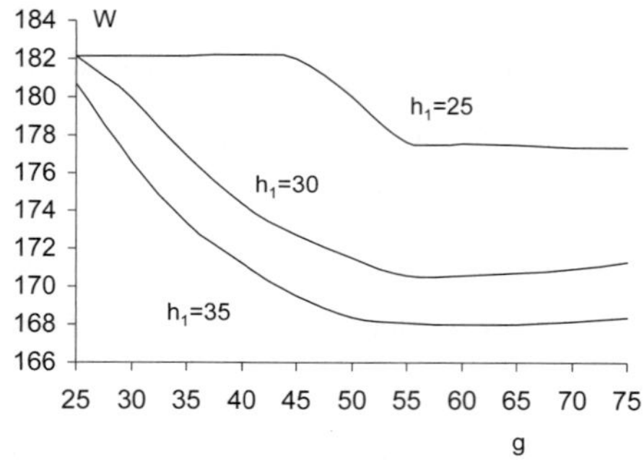

Figure 8.6: Social Welfare And The Discontinuity

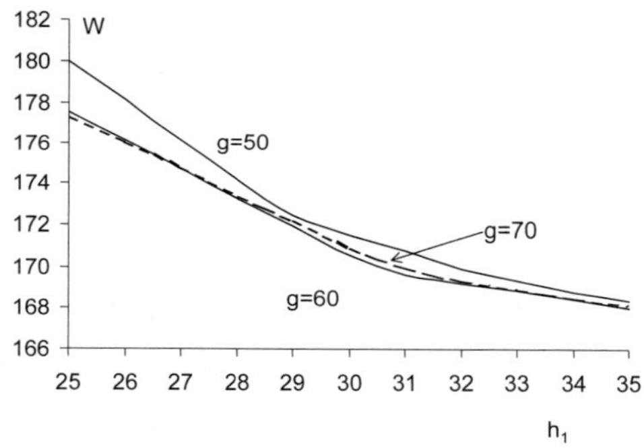

Figure 8.7: Social Welfare And The Hours Threshold

profile is flat for low values of g. This is because the discontinuity actually has no effect over this range of a low hours threshold: individuals either do not work or they jump across the discontinuity in the budget constraint and work and pay tax at the rate t. Beyond g of about \$60, the profile for $h_1 = 25$ is again flat. Here there are no non-workers, low-wage individuals (for w below about 14) are at the hours threshold of 25 hours, and those earning between about \$14 and \$18 per hour receive an abated in-work payment over this range of the schedule (subject to the taper rate of $r = 0.6$).

Figure 8.7 shows the variation in social welfare as the hours threshold,

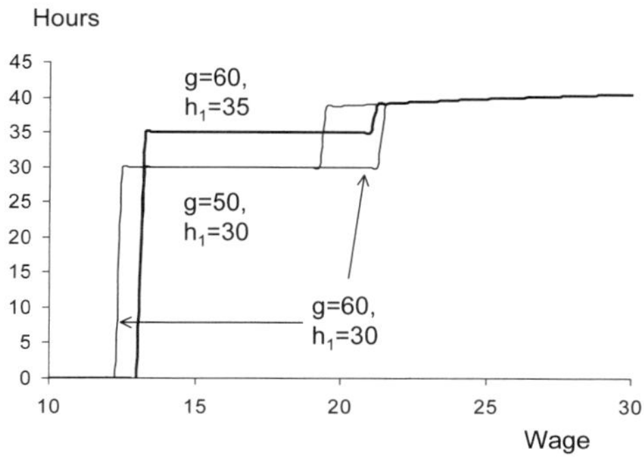

Figure 8.8: Labour Supply Curves

h_1, varies for three values of the discontinuous jump, g. Again it can be seen that for all values of g, social welfare unambiguously falls as the threshold is increased. The range excludes very low and high values of h_1. If h_1 is set very low, then even those on the lowest wages would work at h_1 and if it is set high, the labour supply response discussed above arises, whereby hours fall as the wage increases.

Figure 8.8 gives an idea of the typical labour supply functions obtained, with hours of work measured on the vertical axis. As suggested in section 8.1, the corner solutions at $h = 0$ and at $h = h_1$ dominate for lower wage levels. The different combinations of h_1 and g determine only the height and position of the steps in the diagram. The effect of the in-work payment is thus to lead to a bunching of individuals at hours of work of zero, h_1 hours and around full-time work of about 40 hours per week. The higher value of g leads to more people reducing their labour supply down to the hours threshold h_1.

An important role is played in generating these results by the imposition of the government's budget constraint and budget neutrality of the comparisons. As the discontinuity, or (maximum) in-work payment of g is increased with h_1 fixed, or as h_1 is increased with g fixed, the earnings threshold, a, has to fall to accommodate the higher payments. Hence, for example, as g increases, those who remain at zero hours of work suffer a decline in their benefit, and are therefore worse off. Those who receive no benefits in each situation, but pay income taxation at the rate t, are subject to a reduction in their tax-free income, since the tax they pay is equal to $t(y-a)$, and are therefore also worse off. These losses outweigh any gains experienced by those above h_1 who are induced to reduce their work hours slightly but benefit by the higher in-work payment. Also, those induced to jump from zero hours to the hours threshold may experience a discrete jump in net incomes, but the substantial loss of leisure may mean that there is very little increase in utility.

In view of these results it is of interest to compare the basic modified minimum income guarantee scheme, having just two rates s and t, with the structure having an additional in-work payment and hours threshold. For $g = 60$ and $h_1 = 30$, it was found (for values of other parameters as discussed above) that $W = 170$. Eliminating the in-work payment altogether is achieved by setting $g = 0$ and correspondingly increasing the earnings threshold, a, to maintain budget neutrality. This produces a value of social welfare of $W = 182$. Hence the introduction of the in-work payment reduces social welfare. An alternative reform would be to lower the effective marginal tax rate facing those in receipt of benefits. It is found, for example, that if s is reduced from 0.8 to 0.7 (with $g = 0$), social welfare increases yet again to $W = 184$. Hence flattening the tax rate structure is welfare enhancing.[9]

The above approach evaluates tax structures in terms of social welfare defined over individuals' utilities. This allows for the consumption of leisure time in addition to net income. However, it is also of interest to examine the effect of the in-work payment on the inequality of net income. Values of the Atkinson inequality measure, again for $\varepsilon = 0.5$, are shown in Figure 8.9,

[9]For extensive comparisons of means-tested structures in the context of the two-rate structure, see Creedy (1998b).

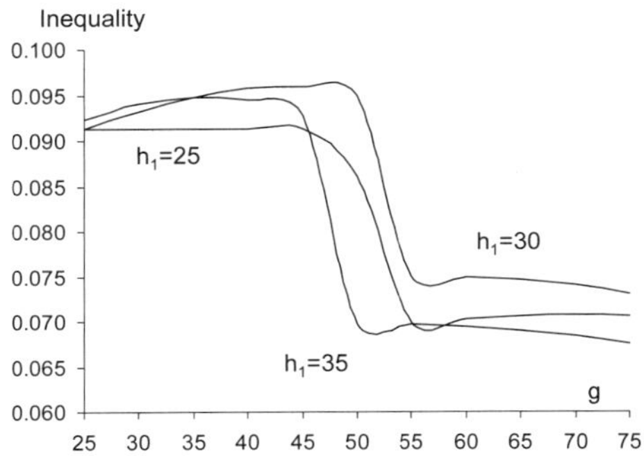

Figure 8.9: Inequality and The Discontinuity

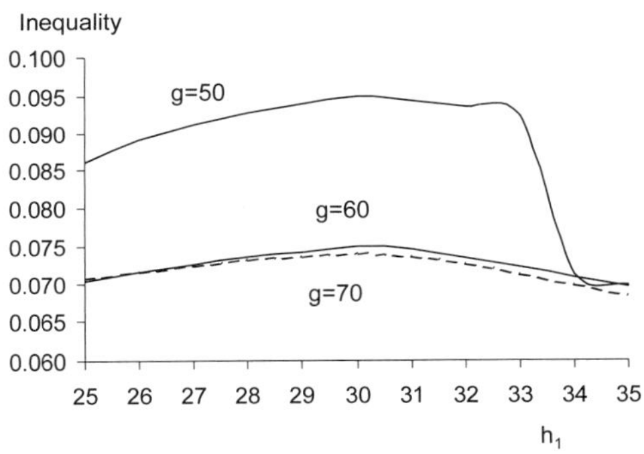

Figure 8.10: Inequality of Net Income and The Hours Threshold

for variations in g, and Figure 8.10, for variations in h_1. Figure 8.9 shows a reduction in inequality over a narrow range of h_1: here the inequality of net income falls as a result of a significant number of individuals moving to the hours threshold, as discussed above.

8.4 Conclusions

This chapter has examined the effect on a measure of social welfare of an in-work payment involving a discontinuity at an hours threshold. The in-work payment was modelled as augmenting a means-tested tax and transfer system having two tax rates (one relating to the abatement of benefits and the other being the income tax rate). This highly simplified tax structure was used in order to concentrate on the basic design problems involved, and to examine the potential labour supply effects of introducing a discontinuity in the budget constraint at a fixed hours level. The non-convexities introduced into individuals' budget sets were shown to lead to labour supply functions involving discrete jumps in hours worked for small variations in the wage rate. The in-work payment, while effective in inducing low-wage individuals to jump to the hours threshold, also raises marginal tax rates for a range of people above the threshold, who therefore reduce their labour supply. The choice of hours threshold in practice is difficult, and would clearly need to allow for demand-side considerations in view of the inevitable concentration at that hours level on the supply side of the labour market.

Alternative tax structures were examined using a social welfare function defined in terms of individuals' utilities, which depend on leisure and net income. Numerical simulations, which ensure that a fixed amount of net revenue per person is collected by the government, show that social welfare falls systematically as the extent of the discontinuity increases. It also decreases as the hours threshold, at which the jump in net income occurs, increases. Eliminating the discontinuity resulting from the in-work payment improves social welfare. Furthermore, it was found that a policy of improving labour supply incentives by flattening the rate structure in the means-tested system increases social welfare yet further.

The evaluation of alternative schemes here is positive rather than normative, in that it examines the implications of adopting a particular type of value judgement. Inevitably the value judgements modelled (involving the use of an additive, individualistic, Paretean function based on utilities and reflecting inequality aversion) are not likely to be held by all judges, and any policy recommendation cannot escape making value judgements (though these are seldom made explicit in practice, of course).

The welfare function used does not have an independent role for poverty, rather than inequality. The analysis is entirely static, and thus does not allow for any productivity-increasing effects of encouraging higher work hours of low-wage individuals. In addition, it does not model household labour supply in the presence of children and is therefore unable to examine any potential effects on secondary workers. All these important practical aspects are best examined using a behavioural tax microsimulation model which is able to produce a wide range of evaluation measures. Nevertheless, an analysis of this kind is useful in indicating the various awkward interdependencies involved, the nature of the constraints imposed on policy choices in designing tax and transfer systems, and the complexities of potential labour supply behaviour resulting from the additional non-convexities introduced into individuals' budget constraints.

Chapter 9

Welfare-Improving Tax Reforms

Analyses of optimal personal income taxation, from Mirrlees (1971), generally ask what tax structure maximises a specified social welfare function, subject to a government budget constraint. As discussed in earlier chapters, the partial equilibrium environment usually consists of individuals with identical preferences but different abilities (reflected in exogenous wage rates), and the welfare function is specified as a variant of the basic utilitarian form, allowing for inequality aversion.[1] The welfare metric is thus utility, which is necessarily considered to be cardinal and interpersonally comparable. Most analyses, instead of examining the nature of an optimal tax schedule, consider optimal parameters for simple tax functions. The emphasis is thus on the optimal linear tax rate, or two-rate or at most three-rate structures. A useful negative lesson is that extensive research has shown that few robust results are available: the optimal structure depends on the nature of the social welfare function examined as well as the wage rate distribution and the nature of individuals' preferences. For reviews of policy implications of optimal tax theory see, for example, Stern (1984), Heady (1993), Tuomala (1995) and Bradbury (1999). For a critique of the approach, see Slemrod

[1] However, as discussed below, non-welfarist forms of evaluation function have also been examined.

(1990).

It is suggested that practical policy advice about the effects of tax changes can be based on a behavioural microsimulation model in which the full extent of population heterogeneity is represented along with all the details of highly complex tax and transfer systems, rather than using simple stylised forms.[2] But this raises a number of challenges. First a reliable approach to modelling labour supply, at the intensive and extensive margins, is required. Modellers have settled on a discrete hours structural approach, allowing for heterogeneity as well as a stochastic utility component. This gives rise to a probability distribution of hours worked for each individual, with consequent difficulties raised for carrying out distributional analyses and computing measures of welfare change such as equivalent and compensating variations. The latter is further complicated by the considerable nonlinearity of tax functions.

A further fundamental difficulty arises in specifying a suitable welfare metric and social welfare function. In the basic optimal tax model, this is straightforward given the choice of cardinalisation of utility, where there are common preferences, particularly for leisure. Homothetic utility functions are usually used, such as Cobb–Douglas or constant elasticity of substitution forms. Theoretical work by public choice and welfare theorists on understanding interpersonal comparability problems and the aggregation problems involved in evaluating alternative structures, along with the conditions under which price-independent welfare comparisons can be made, has been well ahead of applied work.[3] The conditions required turn out to be highly restrictive: see, for example, Donaldson (1992) and Blackorby *et al.* (1993).[4]

[2]Nevertheless, when using such models it is important to be aware of their limitations. In particular, they deal only with the supply side of the labour market and, despite modelling labour supply, have no genuine dynamic element. Furthermore, they deal only with financial incentive effects rather than administrative behaviour and monitoring features designed to reduce moral hazard. On behavioural modelling, see Creedy and Kalb (2006).

[3]The same may be said of practical cost-benefit analyses, where consumer's surplus is still often used (without testing for the absence of income effects), or where policies are evaluated using simple aggregates of, say, equivalent variations.

[4]This has led to the adoption of non-welfarist approaches, such as that proposed by

Even a minimum requirement of homotheticity is not satisfied by the types of direct utility function used in practical labour supply analyses and, in particular, complications are raised by the existence of differences between individuals in their preference for leisure.[5]

In view of these problems, it is perhaps not surprising that few attempts have been made to examine optimal income taxation using a microsimulation model. One approach has recently been suggested by Aaberge and Colombino (2008) and Ericson and Flood (2009). Both studies use a discrete hours structural approach to modelling labour supply, allowing for a substantial amount of population heterogeneity. However, the welfare metric used in their social welfare function is a value of utility based on an independently estimated utility function which is considered to be the same for all individuals. This overcomes one problem at the cost of a type of schizophrenic behaviour by individuals, whereby their welfare metric may differ from the utility levels determining labour supply behaviour. Blundell and Shephard (2009) simply adopt a social welfare function based on a common (iso-elastic) utility transformation. They simplify the resulting expression for the aggregate, allowing for the stochastic utility component, which follows a Type-I extreme value distribution.

Any practical analysis must of course also restrict the number of options to consider, by applying a piecewise-linear tax function of some kind. Blundell and Shephard (2009), in looking at low-income groups, have seven marginal tax rates and an out-of-work income support level. Aaberge and Colombino (2008) use nine parameters including an exemption level, four marginal tax rates, three kink points (income thresholds) and a lump sum transfer. Ericson and Flood (2009) concentrate on looking at a series of struc-

Fleurbaey and Maniquet (1999), which abandons the requirement of independence of irrelevant alternatives.

[5]Boadway *et al.* (2002) examined optimal income taxation in a model with two wage rates, two preferences for leisure and quasi-linear utility. They deal in detail with the resulting incentive compatibility problems.

tures that were used historically. In the last two studies, a rank-dependent social welfare function is specified.

The present chapter has a more limited objective than the production of an optimal tax structure. The starting point is that practical policy debates usually concern changes to an existing structure rather than a complete redesign of an existing tax and transfer system. Hence the emphasis is on welfare-improving reform, that is, the determination of the optimal *direction* of changes in existing tax parameters in order to move towards an optimal structure. It may be said that the approach represents one iteration towards an optimal structure. It cannot be known – given the considerable complexity involved – whether the welfare function is concave over the whole range of structures, or whether more than one local optimum exists.

The welfare metric used is money metric utility per adult equivalent person, allowing fully for the fact that individuals have a probability distribution in the context of a discrete hours approach with a random utility component.[6] Comparisons are also made with the use of net income, rather than money metric utility. While the difficulties associated with metrics are recognised, it is also the case that, as Donaldson (1992, p. 89) stressed, 'no methodology in applied welfare economics is perfect. Practical work is always limited by the availability of data and the problem of estimating the economic consequences of projects. Different evaluation procedures are, therefore, bound to be differentially useful in different situations.'

The approach involves the computation of social welfare changes per dollar of revenue, for changes in each existing marginal income tax rate, using explicit forms of social welfare function. The approach is illustrated using the Melbourne Institute Tax and Transfer Simulator (MITTS).[7] Section 9.1 first

[6] An early exponent of the use of money metric utility in microsimulation was King (1983). However, this was not in the context of labour supply variations, but changes in commodity demands.

[7] MITTS is described briefly below and in detail in Creedy *et al.* (2002). Creedy and Kalb (2006) describe some further features of MITTS, and Kalb and Lee (2007, 2008)

briefly reviews the main results of optimal tax analyses and explains the approach used to examine income tax reforms. Implementation of the method in a microsimulation model is discussed in Section 9.2. This is complicated by the existence of highly nonlinear budget constraints facing individuals. This affects the computation of welfare changes and also leads to an asymmetry in the effects of tax rate increases and decreases. Furthermore, labour supply in the MITTS model is based on a discrete hours structural approach. Hence the method must also deal with the fact that simulations produce, for each individual, a probability distribution over the discrete hours levels rather than a single point. Section 9.3 presents numerical results relating to reforms to the Australian income tax structure. Actual tax structure changes in Australia are then examined in Section 9.4, where the degree of inequality aversion that is implicit in recent policy changes is considered.

9.1 Optimal Taxation and Tax Reform

This section briefly reviews the main lessons regarding tax design, from optimal tax theory. It then considers the problem of obtaining information about welfare-improving reforms, involving small changes to income tax rates leading to increases in a social welfare function.

9.1.1 Optimal Structures

Earlier optimal tax work suggested that, for a range of assumptions, the optimal structure is approximately linear. But in fact it is not difficult to produce models in which different tax structures are optimal.[8] A basic issue relates to the social welfare function itself. Much of the literature is

report updated wage and labour supply estimates underlying the labour supply responses. For a comparison of MITTS results with experimental evaluation results of the same policy change, see Cai *et al.* (2008).

[8]A small selection of examples includes those discussed by Diamond (1998), Chang (1994), Hashimzade and Myles (2004), Myles (1999), Saez (2001) and Tuomala (2006).

'welfarist' in that the welfare function is specified as some function of utilities; it is expressed in terms of variables which matter to individuals. But 'non-welfarist' forms are sometimes used. For example, social welfare may be based solely on an income-based measure of poverty, which can give quite different results: for further discussion see Kanbur, Keen and Tuomala (1994) and for a broader treatment of non-welfarist objectives, see Kanbur, Pirttilä and Tuomala (2004). Non-welfarist objectives may go further than simply attaching no value to leisure, in that they may prefer to encourage labour supply (whereas in a welfarist approach the existence of non-workers is acceptable in an optimal structure): see, for example, Besley and Coate (1992).

One approach has been to consider piecewise-linear tax functions with just two or three rates. This allows for consideration of the question of whether marginal tax rates should be higher for those with relatively low earnings, arising from the means testing of transfer payments. Means testing is preferred by those who advocate 'target efficiency' as the criterion by which schemes should be judged. Numerical analyses using welfarist social welfare functions show that in a very wide range of situations, social welfare is increased by a shift to lower taper rates and a flatter rate schedule.[9] Assumptions giving rise to means testing in an optimal structure are given in Diamond (1998). An emphasis on 'workfare', designed largely to encourage positive labour supply, rather than 'welfare', can also lead to high marginal rates imposed on low earners, as shown by Besley and Coate (1992). Results inevitably involve special cases in highly simplified models which were not designed to provide a strong basis for policy advice.

In practice, governments seldom have the 'luxury' of completely redesigning tax structures, so that from a practical point of view it is useful to consider welfare-improving reforms – involving small changes – rather than attempting the much more complex task of evaluating an optimal structure.

[9] See, for examples, simulation results reported in Creedy (1998b) and for wide-ranging discussions of means testing, see also Atkinson (1995) and Bradbury (1999).

9.1.2 Tax Reform

The problem of how to take one small step towards an optimal structure has previously been examined in the context of indirect taxation, involving fixed total expenditures but differential taxation on a range of goods.[10] The approach involves finding, for each commodity group, the welfare loss per dollar of extra revenue resulting from a small increase in the relevant tax rate. An optimal reform is such that those groups with the smallest cost per dollar have their tax rates increased, while those with the highest cost have their rates reduced. A revenue-neutral set of welfare-improving changes can thus be found. Let x_{ji} denote the consumption of the ith taxable good by the jth household, and t_i the unit tax on good i. The reduction in social welfare, W, resulting from an increase in the ith tax rate is:

$$\frac{\partial W}{\partial t_i} = -\sum_{j=1}^{n} v_j x_{ji} \tag{9.1}$$

where v_j is the social value of additional consumption by household j. Aggregate tax revenue, R, from indirect taxes on K goods is given by:

$$R = \sum_{j=1}^{n} \sum_{k=1}^{K} t_k x_{jk} \tag{9.2}$$

and $\partial R / \partial t_i$ can be expressed in terms of Marshallian demand elasticities, at observed consumption levels and expenditures. Multiplying $\partial R / \partial t_i$ by p_i allows the change to be expressed in terms of expenditures (rather than quantities) and cross-price elasticities. It can be shown that:

$$p_i \frac{\partial R}{\partial t_i} = \sum_{j=1}^{n} p_i x_{ji} + \sum_{j=1}^{n} \sum_{k=1}^{K} \tau_k \eta_{jki} p_k x_{jk} \tag{9.3}$$

where η_{jki} is household j's elasticity of demand for good k with respect to the price of good i, and τ_k is the ratio of the tax to the tax-inclusive price. Hence

[10] On marginal indirect tax reform see, for example, Ahmad and Stern (1984), Madden (1996) and Creedy (1999).

τ_i is the tax-inclusive *ad valorem* rate.[11] It is then possible to obtain for each commodity group the value of the required ratio, $\left|\frac{\partial W}{\partial t_i}\right| / \frac{\partial R}{\partial t_i}$, the welfare cost of raising tax rate i.

In considering income tax structures, a similar type of approach could be adopted to examine small adjustments to a piecewise-linear system. The social welfare function W is in this case a function of a set of marginal income tax rates and income thresholds, as well as summarising the value judgements involved. Similarly, total net revenue, R, is a function of the same set of tax parameters. It can be shown that if t_i now represents the ith marginal rate, and y_j is person j's earnings, a similar result to that given above holds, whereby $\frac{\partial W}{\partial t_i} = -\sum_{j=1}^{n} v_j y_j$. For any piecewise-linear tax function, the tax paid by household j, $T(y_j)$, can be expressed as:

$$T(y_j) = t_k (y_j - a'_k) \tag{9.4}$$

where y_j falls into the kth tax bracket and a'_k is a function of the kth and previous thresholds and marginal rates. The total tax revenue raised by those in the kth bracket, T_k, is thus:

$$T_k = t_k \sum_{j=1}^{n_k} (y_j - a'_k) \tag{9.5}$$

It would be possible to combine this kind of approach with a number of simplifying assumptions regarding elasticities of earnings with respect to tax rates and the proportions of earnings and people above a particular rate, to consider whether (for a given set of tax thresholds) that marginal rate should be reduced or increased. For an extensive discussion of the use of elasticities to derive optimal tax rates, see Saez (2001).

This appears to be an attractive route because, unlike the usual approach to optimal tax modelling, the conditions can be expressed in terms of what appears to be empirically observable counterparts such as elasticities. However, given the considerable complexities introduced by nonlinear budget

[11] Some studies simplify further by assuming that households have equal elasticities.

constraints – unlike the consumption tax case where linear pricing is a reasonable assumption – strong assumptions would be needed and results could only be regarded as illustrative rather than of practical relevance. Nonlinear budget sets make it difficult to generalise regarding labour supply responses and welfare changes even for workers with similar preferences and with relatively simple tax structures. In practice, populations display considerable heterogeneity in preferences and household circumstances, and tax and transfer structures are extremely complex.

However, given a behavioural tax microsimulation model, there is no need to make simplifying assumptions about elasticities of earnings with respect to tax rates. For small reforms, the required changes, from an initial actual tax structure, can be obtained numerically. Starting from the actual tax structure, and considering small changes in a range of tax parameters, it is possible to use a microsimulation model to obtain values of welfare and revenue changes, denoted ΔW and ΔR respectively, for each tax parameter in turn. The changes in welfare for small increases and decreases in revenue, $\Delta W/\Delta R$, should be similar for all tax parameters in an optimal system and so the direction of a welfare-improving reform is indicated by relative orders of magnitude of these ratios. However, there is a further complication arising from the nonlinearity of the budget constraints facing individuals. The effects of small tax rate changes are not symmetrical with respect to increases and decreases. Hence the investigation of welfare-improving reforms which are revenue neutral (whereby rate increases for one bracket must be matched by reductions for other brackets) must consider explicitly the resulting welfare and revenue changes for tax rate changes in each direction. In addition, the effects on welfare and revenue of further increasing (or reducing) the marginal tax rates are not expected to be linear.

9.2 Computation of the Welfare Metric

Computation of the welfare metric for each individual must allow for the complexity of budget constraints. The method used here of computing welfare changes for each individual in a discrete hours context follows that proposed in Creedy and Kalb (2005), and implemented and extended to the calculation of money metric utility in a microsimulation context in Creedy, Hérault and Kalb (2008). The MITTS model uses a discrete hours labour supply model. Hence the behavioural simulations produce a frequency distribution of post-reform hours for each individual, conditional on the individual's optimal pre-reform hours being equal to observed discretised hours.[12] Similarly a frequency distribution of welfare and net income changes is obtained for each individual. A method of dealing with the distributions of net income and welfare metrics, when each person faces a probability distribution, was proposed by Creedy, Kalb and Scutella (2006), involving the production of a 'pseudo' distribution. This provides more accurate results than taking, say, the arithmetic mean values for each person.

Value judgements concern three aspects: the welfare metric, the form of the social welfare function to be used and the definition of the unit of analysis. As mentioned above, money metric utility is used here as the welfare metric, but is also compared with the use of a 'non-welfarist' metric based on net income. The choice of welfare function is closely related to value judgements regarding inequality, and different values of inequality aversion are used in the analyses in this chapter. Any evaluation for a broad group of income units involves comparisons of units of different size and composition. The reported results are based on the use of money metric utility per adult equivalent, using parametric equivalence scales described below.

The steps in the social evaluation are as follows. For each income unit,

[12] The conditional distribution is obtained using the method of generating conditional draws described in Bourguignon, Fournier and Gurgand (1998). The error terms are drawn from the set of error terms which all result in observed labour supply.

the initial money metric utility, M_0, is obtained, using pre-reform taxes as 'reference prices'. This is equal to 'full income' under the pre-reform system, defined as the net income which could be obtained if all the endowment of time were devoted to work at the going wage rate. For each income unit, the net income at 80 hours of work (the assumed maximum number per week) by all adult members of the income unit under pre-reform taxes is calculated, giving full income for the income unit. Following the approach introduced by Creedy, Hérault and Kalb (2008), the equivalent variation from a tax policy change, EV, is obtained by searching all discrete labour supply points for the minimum value for each conditional draw, while taking into account the nonlinearity and non-convexity of the budget constraint.[13] Then, given the equivalent variation, EV, resulting from the reform for each of the discrete hours levels, money metric utility is computed as $M_1 = M_0 - EV$. A probability distribution of EVs and thus money metric utilities is obtained for each unit.

For each income unit, the adult equivalent size, s, is obtained, following Banks and Johnson (1994) and Jenkins and Cowell (1994), using the following parametric scales:

$$s = (n_a + \theta n_c)^\alpha \tag{9.6}$$

where n_a and n_c are respectively the number of adults and children in the unit, θ is the weight attached to children and α represents the extent of economies of scale. The size, s_i, is used to compute money metric utility per adult equivalent, m_{ji}, where j refers to the tax structure and i refers to the income unit. The distributions of pre-reform and post-reform money metric utility can be used to calculate social welfare measures.

In computing inequality and welfare measures with the individual as the unit of analysis, each value of m_{ji} is weighted by the actual number of persons in the income unit, n_i. This chapter uses Atkinson's inequality measure, $A(\varepsilon)$,

[13] Hence welfare measures crucially depend on the specific characteristics of each income unit as reflected in the utility function's parameters.

where ε is the degree of relative inequality aversion. The inequality measure is the proportional difference between the arithmetic mean and the equally distributed equivalent value, where the latter is the value which, if obtained by everyone, gives the same social welfare as the actual distribution. Using an additive welfare function based on constant relative inequality aversion, ε, of the form:

$$W = \frac{1}{1-\varepsilon} \sum_{i=1}^{n} y_i^{1-\varepsilon} \tag{9.7}$$

the equally distributed equivalent value, y_{ede}, is in general, for a set of values y_i, for $i = 1, \ldots, N$, equal to:

$$y_{ede} = \left(\frac{1}{N} \sum_i y_i^{1-\varepsilon} \right)^{1/(1-\varepsilon)} \tag{9.8}$$

Results can be obtained for a range of inequality aversion parameters, ε. Finally, social welfare in each system is most conveniently obtained using the abbreviated form of the welfare function in (9.7), given by:

$$W_j = \bar{m}_j \left(1 - A_j(\varepsilon)\right) \tag{9.9}$$

where $\bar{m}_j$ is the arithmetic mean value of the money metric utility per adult equivalent. The use of the abbreviated form, showing the trade-off between equity and efficiency, is convenient because it ensures that W is positive for all values of ε.

The orders of magnitude of ε can be interpreted by considering the 'leaky bucket' experiment of making a transfer from a richer to a poorer person. A transfer from person 2 to person 1, in the context of incomes, $y_2 > y_1$, which leaves social welfare unchanged is given by:

$$\left.\frac{dy_1}{dy_2}\right|_W = -\left(\frac{y_2}{y_1}\right)^{-\varepsilon} \tag{9.10}$$

Hence if, for discrete changes and a transfer of 1 from the richest person, $\Delta y_2 = -1$, and if incomes are such that $y_2 = 2y_1$, then the amount which must be given to the poorest person is $\Delta y_1 = 2^{-\varepsilon}$. For example, if $\varepsilon = 0.5$, $\Delta y_1 = 0.71$ and a 'leaky bucket' involving a loss of 29 cents from the dollar is tolerated. If ε is 1.4, it can be seen that $\Delta y_1 = 0.39$ and the judge is prepared to lose 61 cents from the dollar.

As mentioned above, the approach involves obtaining reductions in social welfare per dollar of extra revenue, for increases in marginal tax rates, and increases in social welfare for tax rate reductions. Unlike the indirect tax context, these welfare changes are not symmetric with respect to rate reductions and increases. A tax reform, consisting of a set of small increases and decreases in tax rates, is then investigated which is revenue neutral. Thus total net revenue, allowing for changes in social transfers as income tax rates are varied, is unchanged. The imposition of revenue neutrality is important, as otherwise an adjustment to some other kind of expenditure, tax or debt policy is involved.

9.3 Simulation Results

The following simulation results are based on the Australian tax and transfer system for the financial year of 2003/2004, using the Melbourne Institute Tax and Transfer Simulator (MITTS) model with the 2003/2004 Survey of Income and Housing Costs (SIHC).[14] Population values were obtained by using the sample weights provided. The behavioural simulation model allows for endogenous responses of labour supply to income tax changes. However, other sources of non-wage and non-transfer income (such as rental and interest income) are held constant. For details of this behavioural microsimulation model of direct tax and transfers, see Creedy *et al.* (2002). All results are aggregated to the population level using the household weights provided with the SIHC. Pre-reform net incomes at alternative hours levels are based on

[14]It is desirable to use the actual tax structure in operation at the time of the survey, so that calibration places individuals at their labour supplies corresponding to actual incentives faced.

the MITTS calculation of entitlements, not the actual receipt. Furthermore, MITTS applies only income tests, as there is at present no asset imputation in the model. All major social security payments, family payments, rebates and income taxes are included, ensuring a reasonable approximation to net income.

MITTS consists of two components. MITTS-A is the arithmetic tax and benefit modelling component and provides, using the wage rate of each individual, the budget constraints that are crucial for the analysis of behavioural responses to tax changes. For those individuals in the data set who are not working, an imputed wage is obtained. MITTS-B examines the effects of any specified tax reform, allowing individuals to adjust their labour supply. Behaviour is based on quadratic preference functions where the parameters are allowed to vary with individuals' characteristics. Individuals are considered as being constrained to select from a discrete set of hours levels. For singles, 11 discrete points are distinguished. For couples, two sets of discrete labour supply points are used. The female hours distribution covers a wider range of part-time and full-time hours than the male distribution, which is mostly divided between non-participation and full-time work. Therefore, women's labour supply is divided into 11 discrete points, whereas men's labour supply is represented by just 6 points. The joint labour supply of couples is estimated simultaneously, unlike a popular approach in which female labour supply is estimated with the spouse's labour supply taken as exogenous. Thus for couples there are 66 possible joint labour supply combinations.

Simulations are probabilistic, as utility at each hours level is the sum of a deterministic component (depending on hours worked and net income) and a random component. Hence MITTS generates a probability distribution over the discrete hours levels. The self-employed, disabled, students and those over 65 have their labour supply fixed at observed hours. Simulations begin by recording the discrete hours level for each individual that is closest to the observed hours level. The deterministic component of utility is obtained using the parameter estimates of the quadratic preference function. To generate the random component, a draw is taken from the distribution of the error term for each hours level (an Extreme Value Type I distribution). The utility-maximising hours level is found by adding the two components of utility for each hours level and choosing the hours with the highest utility. Draws from the error terms are taken conditionally on the observed labour supply; that is, they are taken in such a way that the optimal pre-reform labour supply is equal to the actually observed labour supply. As a result, post-reform labour supply is simulated conditional on the observed pre-reform labour supply. A user-specified number of draws is produced.

For the post-reform analysis, the new net incomes cause the deterministic component of utility at each hours level to change, so using the same set of draws from the calibration stage, a new set of optimal hours of work is produced. This gives rise to a probability distribution over the set of discrete hours for each individual under the new tax and transfer structure.

The income tax structure is given in Table 9.1, where t_i is the marginal rate applied above an annual income of a_i, for $i = 1, ..., 5$. The simulations reported here are for small tax changes, such that each of these marginal rates was in turn decreased by one percentage point, and then increased by one percentage point, and the resulting changes in total revenue and social welfare were obtained. The use of small changes means that the labour supply adjustments are expected to be quite small, given the use of a discrete hours approach (since a characteristic of corner solutions is a certain amount of 'stickiness' in response to price changes, here reflected in the price of leisure). The use of a common percentage point change in tax rates implies that the net-of-tax rates, $1 - t_i$, change by different percentage amounts.

Table 9.1: The Australian Income Tax 2003/2004

No.	Income threshold (in AU$)	Marginal tax rate
1	$a_1 = 0$	$t_1 = 0$
2	$a_2 = 6,000$	$t_2 = 0.17$
3	$a_3 = 21,600$	$t_3 = 0.30$
4	$a_4 = 52,000$	$t_4 = 0.42$
5	$a_5 = 62,500$	$t_5 = 0.47$

9.3.1 Aggregate Effects

Before presenting the main results of the reforms, Table 13.2 presents summary information about simple aggregate effects, for increases and decreases in each marginal tax rate by one percentage point, obtained by adding all expected EV and net incomes across all income units without equivalising the amounts. Changes in net government revenue account both for changes in income tax revenue and for consequent changes in expenditures on social security.[15] Indeed, government spending on pensions, allowances and rebates is affected by changes in income taxes and labour supply. Table 13.2 also presents labour supply responses by demographic group. For couples, the first amount relates to the male partner while the second amount is for the female partner.

Changes in t_2 and t_3 have the largest effects. Changes in other tax rates have smaller effects either because they apply over a smaller income range (as in the case of t_1) or because they concern fewer households (as for rates t_4 and t_5). Increases in tax rates typically lead to a net decrease in labour supply. The latter implies a further reduction in household income and thus a smaller increase in government revenue than would be expected under fixed labour supply. Therefore, the reduction in household net income is larger than the increase in government revenue. By contrast, reductions in taxes typically increase labour supply, leading to reductions in government revenue

[15] To give a point of comparison, total government revenue (from households) is 103 billion dollars. On 1 January 2004, the Australian dollar was valued at USD 0.75.

Table 9.2: Aggregate Effects of Increases and Decreases in Income Tax Rates

	Change in:		EV	Average hours change in hours per week				
	Net rev ($m)	Net inc ($m)	($m)	Couples	Single males	Single females	Single parents	ALL
Increase in marginal tax rate t_i								
t_1	542	-654	600	-0.01, -0.02	-0.01	0.00	-0.05	-0.01
t_2	1,181	-1,548	1,367	-0.03, -0.05	-0.03	-0.01	-0.10	-0.04
t_3	1,256	-1,834	1,522	-0.04, -0.04	-0.04	-0.02	-0.11	-0.04
t_4	182	-255	216	0.00, 0.00	-0.01	0.00	0.00	0.00
t_5	429	-626	532	-0.02, 0.00	-0.01	0.00	0.00	-0.01
Reduction in marginal tax rate t_i								
t_2	-1,258	1,501	-1,369	0.03, 0.03	0.03	0.02	0.10	0.03
t_3	-1,349	1,781	-1,524	0.03, 0.03	0.04	0.03	0.10	0.04
t_4	-177	263	-216	0.01, 0.00	0.00	0.00	0.00	0.00
t_5	-306	764	-534	0.02, 0.01	0.01	0.00	0.00	0.01

that are smaller than the increases in household income.

For tax increases, reductions in welfare, as measured by changes in aggregate EV, are smaller than reductions in household income because welfare measures account for the increase in leisure and home production time, following the decrease in labour supply. Similarly, changes in welfare are smaller than changes in net income for tax reductions because welfare measures value the decrease in leisure and home production time. Overall, increases and decreases in tax rates have fairly symmetric effects on aggregate welfare and average hours worked.

9.3.2 Income Tax Reforms

Table 9.3 shows the resulting absolute values, $\left|\frac{\Delta W}{\Delta R}\right|$, of the changes in welfare per dollar of revenue for increases and decreases in each marginal tax rate by one percentage point. The social welfare function is based on money metric utilities as described above. Results are shown for two values of the economies of scale parameter, α, in the parametric adult equivalence scales, and three values of inequality aversion, ε. The weight attached to children,

θ, was set at 0.6.

Table 9.3: Values of $|\frac{\Delta W}{\Delta R}|$ Using Money Metric Utility

	Increase in t			Reduction in t		
		ε			ε	
	0.2	0.8	1.4	0.2	0.8	1.4
Scale parameter: $\alpha = 0.8$						
t_1	1.35	1.30	1.25			
t_2	1.40	1.33	1.24	1.32	1.25	1.17
t_3	1.46	1.31	1.15	1.36	1.22	1.07
t_4	1.42	1.16	0.94	1.46	1.19	0.97
t_5	1.43	0.99	0.69	2.01	1.38	0.96
Scale parameter: $\alpha = 0.4$						
t_1	1.85	1.77	1.69			
t_2	1.93	1.81	1.68	1.81	1.70	1.58
t_3	2.03	1.79	1.54	1.89	1.67	1.43
t_4	2.01	1.60	1.24	2.07	1.65	1.28
t_5	2.08	1.37	0.90	2.92	1.91	1.25

The table indicates that welfare gains and losses are not symmetric. Given ε and α, the welfare gain associated with a decrease in t_2 or t_3 is always smaller than the corresponding welfare loss associated with a tax increase. The opposite result is found for t_4 and t_5, with welfare gains from tax rate reductions always larger than the welfare losses from tax rate increases. Since changes in aggregate EV are largely symmetric, this can only be explained by an asymmetric behaviour of inequality changes or net government revenue, ΔR. Table 9.4 reports changes in inequality measures of money metric utility for increases and decreases in the marginal income tax rates. This shows that inequality changes are symmetric, so that the asymmetric behaviour of the welfare gains and losses is determined by differences in ΔR. For increases in t_1 to t_5 by one percentage point, the increases in net revenue are respectively \$542m, \$1,181m, \$1,256m, \$182m and \$429m. For decreases in t_2 to t_5, the reductions in net revenue are respectively \$1,258m, \$1,349m, \$177m and \$306m.

Welfare gains for reductions in t_2 and t_3 are smaller than the corresponding welfare losses associated with increases in these tax rates because ΔR is larger for reductions than for increases in t_2 and t_3. The opposite is true for t_4 and t_5, with ΔR larger for tax increases than for tax reductions.

Table 9.4: Atkinson's Index Based on Money Metric Utility and Net Income: Changes in Per Cent

	Increase in t			Reduction in t		
		ε			ε	
Tax rate	0.2	0.8	1.4	0.2	0.8	1.4
Based on money metric utility						
Scale parameter: $\alpha = 0.8$						
t_1	0.03	0.01	0.01			
t_2	0.01	-0.04	-0.06	0.00	0.04	0.06
t_3	-0.20	-0.27	-0.30	0.21	0.27	0.30
t_4	-0.08	-0.08	-0.09	0.08	0.09	0.09
t_5	-0.45	-0.42	-0.37	0.46	0.42	0.37
Scale parameter: $\alpha = 0.4$						
t_1	0.03	0.02	0.01			
t_2	0.02	-0.02	-0.05	-0.02	0.02	0.05
t_3	-0.17	-0.23	-0.27	0.17	0.23	0.27
t_4	-0.07	-0.08	-0.08	0.07	0.08	0.08
t_5	-0.45	-0.40	-0.34	0.45	0.40	0.35
Based on net income						
Scale parameter: $\alpha = 0.8$						
t_1	0.11	0.08	0.05			
t_2	0.15	0.05	-0.03	-0.10	-0.01	0.06
t_3	-0.32	-0.41	-0.48	0.39	0.48	0.54
t_4	-0.15	-0.15	-0.14	0.15	0.15	0.15
t_5	-0.79	-0.65	-0.54	0.93	0.77	0.65

Under a fixed labour supply assumption, ΔR would be symmetric. But after allowing for labour supply changes, the reduction in the extra government revenue generated by increases in t_2 or t_3 is larger than the reduction in the extra government expenditure generated by a tax rate reduction. The explanation is that although aggregate labour supply responses are quite symmetric, those reducing their labour supply in the face of an increase in t_2 or t_3 on average have higher incomes than those increasing their labour supply when the same tax rate is reduced, so that the impact of labour supply responses on government revenue is larger for a tax increase. By contrast, those experiencing the largest increases in labour supply following a reduction in t_4 or t_5 have higher incomes than those with the largest reductions in labour supply after an increase in t_4 or t_5, which means that changes in government revenue are more limited for reductions than for increases in t_4 or t_5.

The last segment of Table 9.4 gives changes in inequality measures when net income is used as the welfare metric. These are still approximately symmetric, but to a lesser extent than inequality changes based on money metric utility. In addition, they are substantially larger in magnitude compared with the corresponding results obtained using money metric utility (with two exceptions for a reduction in t_2 with $\varepsilon = 0.4$ or $\varepsilon = 1.4$). This arises because of the failure to value leisure time in measures based on net income only. By contrast, measures based on money metric utility account for the fact that increases in income are due to some extent to an increase in labour supply. In some cases, for changes in lower tax rates, the inequality measures move in different directions.

Welfare changes per dollar of revenue for reductions and increases in tax rates indicate the direction of welfare-increasing changes to the tax system. In the simple case where it is required to obtain a small increase in revenue by adjusting one rate, the appropriate strategy is to increase that marginal rate resulting in the smallest welfare cost. Conversely, for a small reduction in revenue, a reduction is made in the tax rate associated with the largest welfare gain. However, the importance of examining adjustments to the tax system that keep total tax revenue unchanged, by combining an increase in a tax rate to fund a decrease in another tax rate, has been stressed above. Such adjustments are of particular interest because they contribute to a movement towards an optimal tax system, at no cost for the government. The change that maximises welfare improvements while keeping total tax revenue unchanged is the one involving an increase in the tax rate with the lowest welfare cost combined with a decrease in the tax rate with the highest welfare gain.

Consider the welfare gains and losses for an inequality aversion of $\varepsilon = 0.2$, along with the use of $\alpha = 0.8$ for the scale economy parameter in the adult equivalence scales. The largest welfare gain per dollar is of 2.01 for a reduction in the top marginal income tax rate. Then moving to the column relating to tax increases, the smallest welfare loss per dollar of extra revenue is for the imposition of a 1 per cent tax rate in the tax-free income range. Thus the revenue-neutral change maximising welfare gains involves a flattening of the rate structure from a combination of reducing the top rate and increasing (from zero) the lowest rate. The specific changes in rates for a revenue-neutral change involving a reduction in t_5 and an increase in t_1 can be obtained using:

$$\left.\frac{dt_1}{dt_5}\right|_R = -\frac{\partial R/\partial t_5}{\partial R/\partial t_1} \tag{9.11}$$

and the resulting welfare increase from such a revenue-neutral change is:

$$\frac{dW}{dt_1} = \frac{\partial W}{\partial t_1} + \left(\frac{\partial W}{\partial t_5}\right)\left.\frac{dt_5}{dt_1}\right|_R \tag{9.12}$$

For this value of $\varepsilon = 0.2$, the next biggest welfare gain from reducing a marginal tax rate is for a reduction in t_4, and the next smallest welfare loss is for an increase in t_2. This means that a further flattening of the rate structure can also improve social welfare.

This welfare-improving flattening of the rate structure contrasts with the implications of adopting the very high degree of inequality aversion of $\varepsilon = 1.4$. In this case the highest welfare gain arises from a reduction in t_2, and the smallest welfare loss is for an increase in t_5. Hence the tax reform that keeps total tax revenue unchanged and maximises social welfare gains involves a small increase in the degree of rate progression. Further welfare-improving adjustments to other rates involve a reduction in t_3 along with an increase in t_4.

In the case of $\varepsilon = 0.8$, determining the revenue-neutral change that maximises social welfare gains is slightly more difficult since t_5 is associated with both the largest welfare gain for tax reductions and the smallest welfare loss for tax increases. In this particular case, the rule used above is insufficient. It is appropriate to use a more general rule that the revenue-neutral change improving social welfare the most is the one involving the largest difference between the welfare cost of the tax increase and the welfare gain of the tax decrease. Accordingly, the use of $\varepsilon = 0.8$ implies a reduction in t_2 along with an increase in t_5 because it is the combination leading to the largest welfare gain per dollar of revenue shifted from one tax bracket to another. Hence this involves an increase in the degree of rate progression, as with $\varepsilon = 1.4$. This is despite the fact that, with this degree of inequality aversion, the single rate change leading to the largest welfare gain per dollar results from a reduction in the top tax rate t_5. Examination of the lower half of Table 9.3 confirms that the policy reform for each value of inequality aversion is not affected by a reduction in α, involving a greater degree of scale economies within households.

9.3.3 The Use of Net Income

Table 9.5 presents tax reform results when using net income per adult equivalent person in the social welfare function. This shows that the results, in terms of the single marginal tax rate adjustments maximising social welfare gains, are the same when the welfare metric is net income instead of money metric utility. That is, the largest welfare gains are obtained by reducing the top tax rate for $\varepsilon = 0.2$ or $\varepsilon = 0.8$ and by reducing the second tax rate for $\varepsilon = 1.4$. The smallest welfare costs are obtained by increasing the first tax rate for $\varepsilon = 0.2$, and by increasing the top tax rate for $\varepsilon = 0.8$ or $\varepsilon = 1.4$.

Table 9.5 also shows that, for $\varepsilon = 0.2$ and $\varepsilon = 1.4$, the results, in terms of the direction of revenue-neutral adjustments maximising welfare gains, are not affected when the welfare metric is net income instead of money metric utility.

Table 9.5: Values of $\left|\frac{\Delta W}{\Delta R}\right|$ Using Net Income

	Increase in t			Reduction in t		
		ε			ε	
	0.2	0.8	1.4	0.2	0.8	1.4
Scale parameter: $\alpha = 0.8$						
t_1	1.48	1.42	1.32			
t_2	1.60	1.49	1.34	1.45	1.34	1.20
t_3	1.75	1.49	1.24	1.56	1.31	1.07
t_4	1.62	1.23	0.90	1.73	1.31	0.95
t_5	1.62	1.01	0.63	2.78	1.75	1.09
Scale parameter: $\alpha = 0.4$						
t_1	2.05	1.94	1.77			
t_2	2.21	2.03	1.79	2.00	1.83	1.61
t_3	2.43	2.05	1.64	2.17	1.80	1.41
t_4	2.30	1.70	1.17	2.46	1.81	1.24
t_5	2.35	1.40	0.81	4.02	2.43	1.41

However, in the case of $\varepsilon = 0.8$, the direction of the revenue-neutral change maximising welfare gains is modified by the use of net income instead of money metric utility in the welfare metric. Based on net income measures, the most welfare-improving change now involves a reduction in t_5 along with an increase in t_4. This is not, as before, a flattening of the rate structure from the bottom to the top of the income scale, but a flattening at the top end only. This result is essentially due to the substantially higher value of the welfare gains for a reduction in the top tax rate when net income is used instead of money metric utility in the welfare metric.

9.3.4 Changes to Income Thresholds

The previous discussion has concentrated on adjustments to income tax rates. However, it is of interest to consider the effects of changes in income thresholds. Clearly, any change in tax thresholds which does not move an individual into a different tax bracket does not affect the marginal rate faced, but there is a change in net income if the threshold is below gross income (since a portion of lower income is taxed at a different rate). Individuals who are moved across thresholds experience changes in both marginal and average rates (at the pre-change gross income level).

Table 9.6: Values of $|\frac{\Delta W}{\Delta R}|$ Using Money Metric Utility: Income Threshold Changes (Equivalence Scale Parameter $\alpha = 0.8$)

	Increase			Decrease		
Threshold	$\varepsilon = 0.2$	$\varepsilon = 0.8$	$\varepsilon = 1.4$	$\varepsilon = 0.2$	$\varepsilon = 0.8$	$\varepsilon = 1.4$
a_2	1.31	1.24	1.17	1.39	1.32	1.24
a_3	1.36	1.26	1.16	1.46	1.36	1.25
a_4	1.42	1.18	0.98	1.41	1.18	0.98
a_5	1.58	1.25	1.00	1.45	1.17	0.93

Table 9.6 shows absolute values of welfare changes per dollar of revenue arising from increases and decreases of $1,000 in annual income thresholds, using a value of $\alpha = 0.8$ for the adult equivalence scale parameter (along with $\theta = 0.6$). Increases in thresholds a_2 to a_5 involve reductions in aggregate revenue of $1,449m, $897m, $256m and $59m respectively, and give rise to welfare increases. Reductions in the thresholds involve increases in revenue of $1,374m, $853m, $271m and $67m respectively, and are associated with welfare reductions. As for changes in tax rates, given ε and α, welfare gains are smaller than the corresponding welfare losses for the lowest thresholds a_2 and a_3, but larger for the top threshold a_5. However, the welfare changes per dollar of revenue are generally smaller than when the tax rates are modified, and display smaller ranges. In addition, differences between welfare gains

and losses are more limited, which implies a lower potential for social welfare improvements following revenue-neutral adjustments.

For inequality aversion of $\varepsilon = 0.2$, the revenue-neutral change that maximises welfare gains implies an increase in a_5 along with a reduction in a_2. The effect is a yet longer income range between thresholds two and five. The use of a high degree of inequality aversion of $\varepsilon = 1.4$ leads to changes which are the reverse of those arising from $\varepsilon = 0.2$. The value of $\varepsilon = 0.8$ implies similar changes to the use of $\varepsilon = 1.4$, except that the increase in a_3 takes first priority over a_2.

9.4 Actual Tax Policy Changes

The Australian income tax structure has been changed in several ways since 2003/4. In particular there have been annual changes in the thresholds, except for a_2 which has remained constant in nominal terms (and a_1 which remains at zero). Furthermore, all the marginal tax rates have been reduced slightly, except for t_3 which has remained unchanged. The 2008/9 thresholds and marginal rates are shown in Table 9.7. This table also shows the thresholds adjusted to 2003/4 prices using the consumer price index. Hence in real terms a_2 has been reduced, while the biggest changes have been the increase in a_5, which more than doubled, followed by the increases in a_3 and a_4. These changes effectively reflect two types of policy change, since they combine changes in the income tax structure with a change in the total tax revenue collected.

From results reported above, the adoption of inequality aversion of $\varepsilon = 0.2$ would lead, given a policy of revenue reduction, to reductions in t_5, t_4 and t_3 along with increases in income thresholds a_5, a_4 and a_3: these rates and thresholds are listed in order, with the first mentioned giving the highest welfare increase per dollar of reduced revenue. This pattern of changes is not precisely reflected in the actual policy changes, since the latter include a

Table 9.7: The Australian Income Tax 2009/2010

No.	Income Threshold (AU$ per year)	Inflation Adjusted (to 2003/4)	Marginal tax rate
1	$a_1 = 0$	0	$t_1 = 0$
2	$a_2 = 6,000$	5,155	$t_2 = 0.15$
3	$a_3 = 35,000$	30,072	$t_3 = 0.30$
4	$a_4 = 80,000$	68,736	$t_4 = 0.38$
5	$a_5 = 180,000$	154,657	$t_5 = 0.45$

reduction in a_2 along with a reduction in t_2, with t_3 unchanged. Nevertheless, they are much closer to the tax reforms implied by the high values of $\varepsilon = 0.8$ and $\varepsilon = 1.4$.

This suggests that the actual policy changes would imply a larger increase in the social welfare function with the adoption of a value of 0.2 for ε, with either net income or money metric utility per adult equivalent person as the welfare metric, compared with the value judgements of higher aversion. Indeed, using the inflation adjusted thresholds and the new rates, compared with the actual 2003/4 structure, and using money metric utility (with $\alpha = 0.8$ and $\theta = 0.6$), the value of social welfare, as defined by (9.9), increases by 2.27 per cent for $\varepsilon = 0.2$, compared with 2.03 and 1.81 per cent for inequality aversion of, respectively, 0.8 and 1.4. When net income is used as the welfare metric, the percentage increases in (abbreviated) social welfare are 5.58, 4.83 and 4.08 for inequality aversion parameters of 0.2, 0.8 and 1.4 respectively. In each case social welfare increases despite the increase in inequality arising from the threshold increases and lower tax rates.

Of course it would be extremely foolish to suggest that actual policy could be described as being decided by a single judge with sufficient information to plan policy reforms based on a social welfare function of the kind considered here. However, it is not unreasonable, as an exercise in ex-post rationalisation, to ask what value judgements might be found to be implicit in actual policy changes. In this case a relative inequality aversion of 0.2

implies changes which are closer to actual reforms than the higher values examined here.[16]

9.5 Conclusions

This chapter began with the observation that the extensive optimal tax literature does not provide clear guidance about tax structures. Instead, the literature has clarified the precise way in which the optimal tax system depends on a wide range of factors, some of which relate to value judgements while others concern behavioural responses or basic conditions, such as abilities, which display considerable heterogeneity in practice. In looking for practical advice, it was suggested that a behavioural microsimulation model can provide the kind of detail needed, and can deal with the considerable complexity of actual tax systems and the large degree of population heterogeneity found in practice. An approach to the analysis of welfare-improving reforms was proposed and implemented using the Australian microsimulation model MITTS. Welfare changes per dollar of revenue were obtained using additive Paretian welfare functions displaying constant relative inequality aversion. Two alternative welfare metrics were used in the social welfare function. One, for 'welfarist' functions, involves the use of money metric utility per adult equivalent person. A 'non-welfarist' alternative, that of net income, was also investigated.

It was found that the welfare changes for the Australian income tax structure were not symmetric with respect to increases and decreases in tax rates, largely because of the asymmetry in tax revenue changes arising from differential labour supply effects in different ranges of the income distribution. It was also found that the degree of relative inequality aversion plays a substantial role in the determination of the direction of welfare-improving rate

[16] Using questionnaires based on the 'leaky bucket' experiment, Amiel *et al.* (1999) reported an average value of around 0.2 for economics students in three countries.

changes. For moderate levels of aversion, a flattening of the rate structure is recommended. However, for high degrees of aversion, a further increase in rate progression arises as the preferred direction of change. The extent of inequality aversion was found to play a much larger role than the form of the welfare metric or the specification of adult equivalence scales. However, although the specification of adult equivalence scales did not affect the direction of welfare-improving tax reforms, the form of the welfare metric was found to modify, for one particular value of inequality aversion, the direction of the revenue-neutral tax reform that maximises welfare gains.

Changes to income tax thresholds were also investigated. Overall, they lead to smaller differentials between welfare gains and losses than when the tax rates are modified. Finally, results were compared with the actual income tax structure changes made to the Australian tax structure since 2003/4 regarding income tax rates and thresholds. It was found that, as anticipated from the results for welfare changes, the actual changes lead to the highest increases in social welfare in the case of the low, rather than high, relative inequality aversion parameter investigated.

Chapter 10

The Elasticity of Marginal Valuation

This chapter examines a number of frameworks in which the concept of the 'elasticity of marginal valuation', in the context of evaluating a social welfare function, is central. This arises in assigning welfare weights in inequality comparisons and in cost–benefit analyses involving discounting. Stress is placed on the need to distinguish these contexts and models clearly. This elasticity concept cannot be measured objectively but necessarily involves value judgements. Hence the role of economists is not to propose the use of particular values, which is equivalent to imposing judgements, but to examine the implications of adopting alternative value judgements.

Social welfare functions are used both in static contexts, involving a distribution over appropriately defined units, and in dynamic contexts, involving a distribution over time periods. Decisions must be made regarding the welfare metric (for example, income, consumption or utility) and the unit of analysis (for example, households, individuals or equivalent adults). Both of these decisions also involve value judgements, but they are not the concern of the present chapter. The emphasis here is on the fact that, in attaching welfare weights to each unit or time period, the concept of the elasticity of marginal valuation plays an important role.[1]

[1] For example, it is prominent in the debate on climate change: see, for example, Stern

Many contributions to the literature appear to regard this elasticity as something that can be objectively measured. For examples, see Pearce and Ulph (1998), Cowell and Gardiner (1999) and Evans (2005). The UK Treasury recommends a value for the elasticity of around unity, based on empirical estimates. Evans (2005) argued that the Treasury recommendation, when forming distributional welfare weights or computing a social time preference rate in cost–benefit studies, is too low. Pearce and Ulph (1998, p. 282) argued that the earlier UK Treasury recommended discount rate was too high, saying that 'we find it impossible to support the continued use of rates in the region of 6% for the UK. Such rates are far too high.' In each of these examples, the view was presented as an objective finding, rather than a value judgement.

Section 10.1 introduces the form of social welfare function and welfare weights widely adopted in the literature on policy evaluation in the single-period context. The concept of the elasticity of marginal valuation is defined and the use of 'estimates' based on empirical information about a sample of individuals' consumption behaviour is criticised. Section 10.2 turns to the multi-period context and its additional complications. Much emphasis has been placed on the estimation of a value of the elasticity that is thought to be implicit in an income tax structure. Attempts to impute such a value include Mera (1969), Stern (1977), Christiansen and Jansen (1978), Moreh (1981), Brent (1984), Cowell and Gardiner (1999) and Evans (2005). This approach, based on an assumption of equal absolute sacrifice as a policy objective, necessarily produces for a progressive tax a value of the elasticity of marginal valuation in excess of unity. Section 10.3 considers, first, whether this approach can actually provide reliable evidence of implicit judgements and, second, whether it could legitimately be used as the foundation of an argument in favour of using those values.

(2006) and criticisms of the discount rate used by Stern which include Nordhaus (2006), Dasgupta (2006) and Carter *et al.* (2006).

The fundamental difference between what 'is' and what 'should be' is stressed. Given the need to make value judgements, economists have no special qualifications or authority to impose their own judgements, and cannot use 'estimates' as support for their views. Economists have an obligation to make value judgements explicit, and their role is to examine the implications of adopting a range of such judgements. Having been presented with alternative results, readers can then form their own opinions.

10.1 Social Evaluations: A Single Period

Any attempt to answer the question, 'when is a change an improvement?', faces the fundamental difficulty that it cannot avoid the use of value judgements. Hence complete agreement in any particular context – say the effect of a proposed change to a tax and transfer system – is most unlikely, even if there are no losers.[2] The approach adopted in economics is to specify explicit value judgements in a formal manner, using a social evaluation function or, following Samuelson (1947), a social welfare function. Crucially, this function formally expresses the value judgements of a fictional judge or policy maker. It is not, despite the use of the term 'social', intended to represent any kind of aggregate or representative views of society.[3] Indeed the judge is considered to be an independent person who is not affected by the outcomes. This section discusses the form of social welfare function commonly used and the associated elasticity of marginal valuation.

[2]The Pareto criterion has little practical use as it refuses to pass judgement where losers exist, and is certainly not a value-free criterion. There are also well-known problems with the use of potential Pareto improvements.

[3]The extreme case of a representative agent, mentioned below, is the exception where the welfare function corresponds to the utility function of the fictional representative.

10.1.1 The Welfare Function

Some simple properties of welfare functions are typically specified, with the hope that while they cannot be expected to represent any kind of consensus, they are at least likely to appeal to a large number of people. It is in this spirit that the form of evaluation function widely adopted reflects adherence to value judgements such as the 'principle of transfers' (whereby a transfer from a richer to a poorer person is judged to produce an 'improvement'[4]) as well as being individualistic, additive and Paretian.[5]

The first choice is to select a welfare metric, say x_h for unit h, and to define the unit of analysis itself, with both choices involving value judgements. The definition of x, the welfare metric, is problematic and usually depends on the context. It is variously defined as income, consumption, utility or money metric utility, where each concept may, in addition, be expressed in adult equivalent terms, and such equivalence scales themselves involve difficult value judgements. The choice of unit of analysis, between for example individuals and adult equivalents, also involves incompatible value judgements. This important issue is not discussed here, and for simplicity the unit is referred to below simply as the individual.[6]

An additive social welfare function is typically formed as an appropriate weighted sum. Thus the problem is to specify precisely how those welfare weights are formed.[7] Define the contribution to social welfare of individual

[4]This is conditional on the transfer being such that the transferee does not become richer than the transferor.

[5]However, other approaches are widely used. For example, the welfare function implicit in the use of the Gini inequality measure involves quite different value judgements.

[6]On these aspects see, for example, Shorrocks (2002). The choice of different units can have quite different implications for policy evaluations; for examples in the single-period evaluation of tax reforms see Creedy and Scutella (2004) and in the multi-period case, see Creedy and Guest (2008).

[7]For 'classical utilitarians', the evaluation criterion was simply the sum, over all individuals, of utilities. The welfare weights were thus all unity.

h as $W(x_h)$. Social welfare, W_S, is thus defined as:

$$W_S = \sum_{h=1}^{H} W(x_h) \tag{10.1}$$

Importantly, $W(x_h)$ is *not* individual h's utility function. Indeed, the welfare metric may itself be utility (or some money metric measure of utility), as in the optimal tax literature. In the marginal indirect tax reform literature it represents indirect utility.[8]

10.1.2 The Elasticity of Marginal Valuation

Any change – which may be induced by a policy reform to an income or indirect tax structure – gives rise to a total change in social welfare of:

$$dW_S = \sum_{h=1}^{H} \frac{\partial W(x_h)}{\partial x_h} dx_h \tag{10.2}$$

Letting $v_h = \frac{\partial W(x_h)}{\partial x_h}$ denote the 'marginal valuation', the contribution to the change in W_S of a change in x_h, (10.2) becomes:

$$dW_S = \sum_{h=1}^{H} v_h dx_h \tag{10.3}$$

The term v_h represents the welfare weight attached to the hth individual. An aversion to inequality on the part of the hypothetical judge is specified

[8] In the literature on marginal tax reform, W is defined in terms of (indirect) utilities, V_h, so that $W = \sum_{h=1}^{H} W(V_h)$ and the effect of a change in the price of good i, p_i, say arising from a tax change, is:

$$\frac{\partial W}{\partial p_i} = \sum_{h=1}^{H} \frac{\partial W(V_h)}{\partial V_h} \frac{\partial V_h}{\partial p_i}$$

From Roy's Identity, $x_{hi} = -(\partial V_h / \partial p_i) / (\partial V_h / \partial m_h)$, where m is total expenditure, and:

$$\frac{\partial W}{\partial p_i} = \sum_{h=1}^{H} \left(\frac{\partial W}{\partial V_h} \frac{\partial V_h}{\partial m_h} \right) x_{hi}$$

In specifying the term in brackets, W is usually re-interpreted in terms of total expenditures, with $W(m_h) = m_h^{1-\varepsilon} / (1 - \varepsilon)$ and so the term in brackets becomes $m_h^{-\varepsilon}$.

by an assumption that $W(.)$ is concave, so that it satisfies the principle of transfers. A measure of relative inequality aversion, R, is therefore based on the concavity measure:

$$R = -\frac{x d^2 W(x) / dx^2}{dW(x) / dx} \tag{10.4}$$

This is equivalent to the elasticity of marginal valuation, $\left(\frac{dv}{dx}\right)\left(\frac{x}{v}\right)$. This elasticity plays an important role in what follows. Importantly, the term 'marginal valuation' is used here rather than using 'marginal utility' since, as stated above, $W(x)$ is not a utility function. The function $W(x)$ represents the contribution to social welfare (the social evaluation function) of the hth person, however x is defined.

10.1.3 Choice of Values

The function $W(x)$ is specified in the vast majority of studies as:

$$W(x) = \frac{x^{1-\varepsilon_s}}{1-\varepsilon_s} \tag{10.5}$$

for $\varepsilon_s \neq 1$, and $W(x) = \log x$, where $\varepsilon_s = 1$. In this case, substitution in (10.4) gives $R = \varepsilon_s$ and ε_s thus reflects a constant degree of relative inequality aversion of the judge or policy maker.

Importantly, ε_s is not an objective measure relating to individuals in society, but reflects the subjective value judgements of a fictional judge who is evaluating the effects of alternative policies or outcomes. However, a superficially similar-looking, but very different, concept of the 'elasticity of marginal utility' plays a central role in some consumer demand systems, particularly where directly additive utility functions are involved; this was first clarified by Frisch (1959). Define the elasticity of the marginal utility of total expenditure with respect to total expenditure as ξ. If $\delta_{\ell j}$ denotes the Kroneker delta, such that $\delta_{\ell j} = 0$ when $\ell \neq j$, and $\delta_{\ell j} = 1$ when $\ell = j$, and e_ℓ is the total expenditure elasticity for good ℓ, and w_j is the budget share of good j,

Frisch showed that the price elasticities, $e_{\ell j}$, can be written as:

$$e_{\ell j} = -e_\ell w_j \left(1 + \frac{e_j}{\xi}\right) + \frac{e_\ell \delta_{\ell j}}{\xi} \tag{10.6}$$

This can be used to obtain ξ, given independent values of the elasticities. In the special case of the Linear Expenditure System, the elasticity of marginal utility has a convenient interpretation: it is the ratio of total expenditure to supernumerary expenditure, that is, expenditure above a committed amount. The use of the LES in empirical demand studies therefore necessarily involves an elasticity value of, say, ε_{LES}, which is well above unity, and studies typically obtain a value of around 2.

In view of the entirely different contexts, of welfare comparisons involving social evaluation functions and empirical studies of household consumption behaviour, there is no relationship whatsoever between ε_s and ε_{LES}. In other words, there is absolutely no reason why a value of ε_s, to be imposed by economists in making comparisons, could be 'estimated' using information from studies of household budgets. Nevertheless, this suggestion is sometimes made; for example, elasticities obtained on the basis of the Linear Expenditure System are discussed by Evans (2005, pp. 204–206).

In using ε_s values to compute values of social welfare functions, or carry out cost–benefit evaluations, there is no alternative but to consider a range of alternative values, implying different degrees of aversion to inequality. In some cases, 'dominance' results may be obtained. In other words one policy may be judged to give rise to a higher value of social welfare than another policy for all values of ε_s. In other situations, readers can make up their own minds given the reported computations.

In considering alternative values of ε_s, it is clearly useful to ensure that they are within a range that is considered appropriate by a reasonable number of users of the results. Hence questionnaire studies have been designed to elicit information about individuals' value judgements. It was in this spirit that the questionnaire study of Amiel *et al.* (1999) was carried out. Nevertheless, there was no suggestion that questionnaires can produce any single value that should be used in policy evaluations.[9] A substantial number of respondents did not adhere to the constant relative inequality aversion form. In addition, Amiel and Cowell (1992, 1994) have found that a large number of questionnaire respondents do not actually share the value judgements that are explicit in the most common forms of social welfare function used in evaluation work, such as the one discussed above. This presents a challenge to produce alternative flexible specifications.[10]

10.2 Multi-period Contexts

Evaluations are also made in a multi-period context. Some models use a representative individual, and hence subsection 10.2.1 begins by looking at a single individual optimisation in a multi-period framework. Subsection 10.2.2 then considers social evaluation functions.

10.2.1 A Single Individual

Consider a single individual where C_t represents consumption in period t. An additive utility function defined over T periods, where ρ is the 'pure time preference' rate of the individual is thus:

$$U_T = \sum_{t=1}^{T} \left(\frac{1}{1+\rho} \right)^{t-1} U(C_t) \tag{10.7}$$

Consider periods 1 and 2. The pure time preference, or impatience, rate measures the extent to which the slope of an indifference curve, at a point where $C_1 = C_2$, deviates from a downward-sloping (from left to right) 45 degree line.[11] It reflects impatience, or an aversion to waiting, on the part of

[9] There is sometimes confusion about this, as in Evans (2005).

[10] Early questionnaire studies were carried out by Glesjer *et al.* (1977) and Gevers *et al.* (1979), although no attempt was made to estimate precise specifications of distributional preferences.

[11] The terminology is not universally accepted. For example, Pearce and Ulph (1998) refer to this simply as the 'rate of time preference (the rate at which *utility* is discounted',

the individual. Faced with a constant consumption stream the individual is prepared to give up more than one unit of C_2 in order to obtain one more unit of C_1. For any combination of C_1 and C_2, the marginal rate of substitution between consumption in the two periods, MRS_{c_1,c_2}, is the absolute value of the slope of the individual's indifference curve, and is thus $\frac{\partial U_T/\partial C_1}{\partial U_T/\partial C_2}$.

The discount rate, r, at any combination of C_1 and C_2, is defined as:

$$1 + r = MRS_{c1,c2} \tag{10.8}$$

Suppose that $U(C_t)$ is the iso-elastic form:

$$U(C_t) = \frac{C_t^{1-\varepsilon_p}}{1-\varepsilon_p} \tag{10.9}$$

where ε_p is the absolute value of the individual's elasticity of the marginal utility of consumption.[12] Then:

$$MRS_{c_1,c_2} = \left(\frac{C_2}{C_1}\right)^{\varepsilon_p}(1+\rho) \tag{10.10}$$

An example is shown in Figure 10.1. At the point of intersection with the 45 degree line from the origin, along which consumption is equal in both periods, the solid indifference curve shown is steeper than the downward sloping 45 degree line, indicating a degree of pure time preference. The convexity of the indifference curve is affected by the value of ε_p, so that the solid curve reflects a lower value than the broken curve. If $\varepsilon_p = 0$, the indifference curves are straight lines and the individual's optimal position would be a corner solution, consuming everything either in period 1 or 2, depending on whether the market rate of interest (assuming equal borrowing and lending rates) is less than or greater than the pure time preference rate.

---

and decompose it into a 'pure rate' and a term reflecting the rate of growth of life chances. They refer to what is below called the 'social time preference rate' as the 'consumption rate of interest'.

[12] It is also the absolute value of the elasticity of the marginal rate of substitution with respect to the ratio of consumption levels.

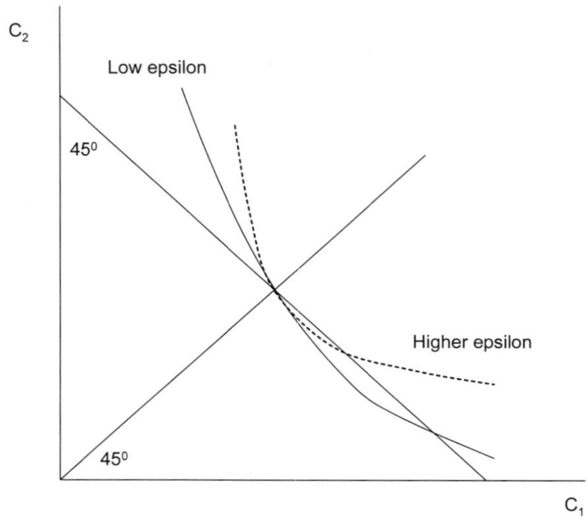

Figure 10.1: Time Preference

In general the individual's optimal position is a tangency where the market rate of interest equals the discount rate.

A convenient expression for the discount rate can be obtained using an approximation which holds when the various rates are small. Let g denote the (constant) growth rate of consumption, so that $\frac{C_2}{C_1} = 1 + g$ and:

$$r = (1+g)^{\varepsilon_p}(1+\rho) - 1 \tag{10.11}$$

Expanding $(1+g)^{\varepsilon_p}$ and neglecting squared and higher-order powers gives $(1+g)^{\varepsilon_p} \approx 1 + \varepsilon_p g$. Hence $r = (1+\varepsilon_p g)(1+\rho) - 1$, and making the further assumption that $\varepsilon_p g \rho \approx 0$, the individual's discount rate is:

$$r = \rho + \varepsilon_p g \tag{10.12}$$

Hence the discount rate is equal to the pure time preference rate plus the product of the growth rate of consumption and the individual's (absolute) elasticity of the marginal utility of consumption. The growth rate affects the difference between consumption in the present and future, and ε_p reflects an aversion to inequality between periods (not impatience to consume in the present), and the combination of these involves an addition to pure time preference.

The above applies to an individual person; hence the p subscript is used. However, a substantial literature is based on the concept of a representative individual. In this case, optimal plans are unambiguously based on the preferences of this representative individual and there are no difficulties over the aggregation of preferences.[13] In fact, macroeconomic models using a so-called representative individual are, strictly speaking, constructed in terms of just one individual: there is no consideration of aggregation requirements.[14]

10.2.2 Social Evaluations

In practical social evaluations or cost–benefit evaluations involving multi-period contexts, it is often inappropriate to think of a single individual. Evaluations may be based on a social welfare function, as in the single-period case. A choice of welfare metric for each period must be made. In the following discussion this is taken to be aggregate consumption, which in the case of a fixed population size translates simply to consumption per person.[15]

Hence, where the Cs now represent aggregates, the welfare function can be written as:

$$W_T = \sum_{t=1}^{T} \left(\frac{1}{1+\rho_m} \right)^{t-1} W(C_t) \tag{10.13}$$

[13]In some growth models, the representative individual is assumed to be infinitely lived. In order to prevent the individual simply accumulating huge debts, a condition is imposed such that the rate of interest and the individual's discount rate are equal. In turn, this means that ε_p and ρ cannot be set independently, given g.

[14]From the demand analysis literature, it is known that quasi-homothetic (Gorman) preferences are required for aggregates to be interpreted as arising from the preferences of a representative individual. In this case demands are linear, with a common slope, although intercepts may differ to allow for, say, demographic factors.

[15]The questions of the welfare metric and the unit of analysis in the multi-period case are examined in detail by Creedy and Guest (2008).

In this case, $W(C_t)$ represents the contribution of period t's aggregate consumption to the evaluation function, and ρ_m represents the pure time preference rate of the hypothetical judge. The corresponding ubiquitous iso-elastic function is thus:

$$W(C_t) = \frac{C_t^{1-\varepsilon_m}}{1-\varepsilon_m} \tag{10.14}$$

In this context the discount rate is commonly referred to as the 'social time preference rate', r_m, and is given, where g_m is the aggregate growth rate of consumption, by:

$$r_m = \rho_m + \varepsilon_m g_m \tag{10.15}$$

Although equations (10.12) and (10.15) have the same basic form, there are no grounds for taking values appropriate to one and substituting in the other. Again, it must be stressed that the term ε_m represents the value judgements of a judge or policy maker. It may be possible to obtain empirical estimates of ε_p using data on saving behaviour over time for a sample of individuals; on the approach used, with a review of alternative estimates, see Pearce and Ulph (1998). However, there are no grounds for imposing $\varepsilon_m = \varepsilon_p$; the former involves a value judgement and there is no logical connection between the two rates.

In thinking about the appropriate values for ε_m in this context, quite different considerations apply compared with the case of single-period distributional judgements involving inequality aversion, ε_s, discussed earlier. The term ε_m is, in the multi-period framework, more accurately interpreted in terms of an aversion on the part of the judge towards variability – inequality between periods rather than inequality between persons. Yet unfortunately these terms are often conflated in the literature, where discussion proceeds as if ε_m, ε_p, ε_{LES} and ε_s were measuring the same thing.

10.3 Taxation and Equal Absolute Sacrifice

This section turns to a different approach involving attempts to estimate the implicit value judgements revealed by tax and transfer policies. Some authors, such as Stern (1977), Cowell and Gardiner (1999) and Evans (2005), have suggested that estimates provide a guide to ε values which should be applied in policy evaluations.

There are two steps to such an approach. The first step attempts to infer, from tax policy decisions, value judgements which are not otherwise made explicit. Such an attempt can be defended – provided of course that the model used to make inferences is plausible. For example, such estimates may be useful in checking whether there is in fact any correspondence between policies and basic value judgements of policy makers. Given the complexities involved in tax policy design, it may be useful to know if a particular structure is associated with implicit judgements that may actually be very different from those held (though seldom made explicit). This is the view taken by van de Ven and Creedy (2005) when examining adult equivalence scales implicit in tax and transfer systems.

The second step is the illegitimate one of suggesting that estimates of implicit value judgements 'should' be used in making social evaluations. This criticism applies even in the most unlikely case where implicit views can be identified precisely.

This section considers the first step taken by the authors mentioned above, and suggests that the model used is inadequate. The approach is based on the assumption that income tax policy makers aim to achieve equal absolute sacrifice. It assumes that incomes are exogenously given, rather than arising from endogenous labour supply behaviour (subject to endowments and education which give rise to individual productivities). Suppose x represents income and the tax function is $T(x)$. Equal absolute sacrifice requires, for all x, that the absolute difference between pre-tax and post-tax utility is the same for all individuals. Hence:

$$U(x) - U(x - T(x)) = k \tag{10.16}$$

where $U(.)$ represents a utility function which is considered to be the same for all individuals. The parameter k depends on the amount of revenue per person.[16] The combination of equal absolute sacrifice with the iso-elastic function, $U(x) = x^{1-\varepsilon_T}/(1-\varepsilon_T)$ for $\varepsilon_T \neq 1$, gives, from (10.16) above:[17]

$$\frac{x^{1-\varepsilon_T}}{1-\varepsilon_T} - \frac{(x - T(x))^{1-\varepsilon_T}}{1-\varepsilon_T} = k \tag{10.17}$$

Differentiation and simplification give, as in Evans (2005, p. 207), the result that:

$$\log(1 - T'(x)) = \varepsilon_T \log\left(1 - \frac{T(x)}{x}\right) \tag{10.18}$$

where $T'(x)$ and $T(x)/x$ are marginal and average tax rates. This expression has been used to carry out ordinary least squares regressions using income tax schedules, so that ε_T and its standard error are obtained as a regression coefficient. There is some difference of opinion over whether to include a constant in the regression: compare Cowell and Gardiner (1999) and Evans (2005), who also use different income measures. Alternatively, (10.18) can be rearranged to get $\varepsilon_T = \log(1 - MTR)/\log(1 - ATR)$, and estimates of ε_T are obtained and compared using simply the marginal and average tax rates at different income levels.

The first point to stress regarding this approach is that it automatically produces a value of ε_T in excess of unity for a progressive tax system, for which the marginal tax rate exceeds the average tax rate. This feature was

[16] This differs from an alternative view that would replace $U(x)$ with $W(x)$. Thus, as with inequality measurement, a judgement is made regarding the welfare metric, and then a view is taken about variations in x. This judgement is quite separate from the way individuals may themselves view such variations.

[17] Young (1987) actually showed that the iso-elastic form is required if an indexation requirement is imposed on the tax structure in addition to equal sacrifice. But of course fiscal drag is a common, indeed almost universal, feature of income tax structures.

first discussed by Edgeworth (1897) and formally shown by Samuelson (1947). The values of ε_τ obtained in this way are thus severely constrained by the specification of the objective of equal absolute sacrifice. Furthermore, those using the approach to estimate ε ignore the objections raised by Edgeworth and others concerning the various interpretations of sacrifice theories.[18]

For $\varepsilon_\tau > 1$, equation (10.17) can be rearranged as:[19]

$$T(x) = x - \left\{x^{1-\varepsilon_\tau} - k(1-\varepsilon_\tau)\right\}^{1/(1-\varepsilon_\tau)} \tag{10.19}$$

Examples of marginal and average rate schedules based on this function are shown in Figure 10.2.[20] Of course, in practice tax functions are multi-step functions with ranges where the marginal rate is constant. In structures like that in the UK, there is a standard rate over a wide range of taxable income, so the above function obviously has difficulty capturing this range.[21] The imposition of $\varepsilon > 1$ is also highly restrictive (as with the use of the linear expenditure system mentioned above). Furthermore, the model applies only to positive taxes. It can thus relate at best to a small component of a much broader set of taxes and transfers.

---

[18]This does not apply to those, such as Richter (1982) and Young (1987), who were interested only in deriving the implications of various axioms.

[19]In stating this result, Young (1987, p. 212) rewrote $-k(1-\varepsilon)$ as $\lambda^{1-\varepsilon}$, so that the tax function compares with a constant elasticity of substitution form.

[20]The coefficient k is determined by the amount of revenue raised by the tax. Suppose that x follows a lognormal distribution with mean and variance of logarithms of $\mu = 10$ and $\sigma^2 = 0.5$ respectively. These values imply an arithmetic mean income of \$28,282. Suppose it is required to raise revenue per person of \$10,000 and that $\varepsilon_\tau = 1.5$. Using a numerical iterative search procedure, it is found that this requires $k = 0.0025$. This is based on a simulated population obtained from 5,000 random draws from the assumed income distribution.

[21]If equal absolute sacrifice is combined with a welfare function displaying constant absolute inequality aversion, α, such that $W = 1 - \exp(-\alpha x)$, a tax function of the form $T(x) = x + \frac{1}{\alpha}\log\{k + e^{-\alpha x}\}$ arises. This can be made to display rate schedules similar to those illustrated above. Dalton (1954, pp. 68–70) discussed several examples using alternative utility functions and sacrifice principles, and showed that if equal absolute sacrifice produces progression, equal proportional sacrifice produces a more progressive tax structure. In an early study, Preinreich (1948) considered the form of the utility schedule consistent with the US tax legislation, without imposing a specific functional form over the whole income range. He assumed equal proportional sacrifice.

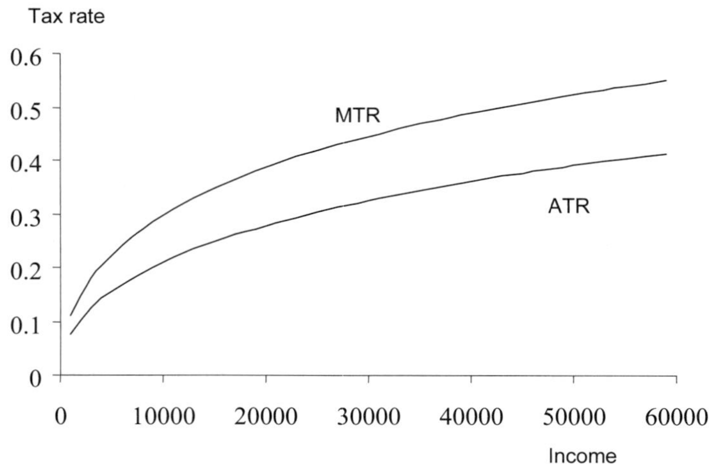

Figure 10.2: Marginal and Average Tax Rates: Equal Absolute Sacrifice

Hence some scepticism must be attached to interpretations of estimates obtained using this model as implicit value judgements. It seems most likely that the approach has been chosen largely – or indeed only – for its simplicity. On the other hand, the optimal tax framework has demonstrated the considerable complexity involved in the link between value judgements and the tax structure and, importantly, progression can arise with values of $\varepsilon < 1$. But even if the estimation of implicit preferences were plausible, they cannot qualify as value judgements which should be imposed. There is no alternative to accepting that value judgements are required and the best attitude of professional economists is to report a range of results based on alternative value judgements.

10.4 Conclusions

This chapter was concerned with the use of social welfare functions in evaluating actual or potential changes resulting from policies or other factors affecting a well-defined group of individuals. In particular, it has considered suggestions regarding the welfare weights to be used in comparing the gains and losses of different individuals, and a social time preference rate for use in cost–benefit evaluation. While these variables essentially reflect value judgements, some authors have argued that they can be estimated either from consumers' behaviour or from the judgements implicit in tax policy. It was instead suggested here that results are highly sensitive to the context and model specification assumed.

More importantly, the argument that an estimated elasticity of marginal utility or social time preference rate *should* be used in policy evaluations fails to recognise that fundamental value judgements are involved. The various estimates and models may be of interest, but they cannot be used by economists to *impose* value judgements. The main contribution economists can make is to examine the implications of adopting a range of alternative value judgements. This argument is of course not new. Indeed it was stated most forcefully and eloquently by Robbins (1935) in his important book on the *Nature and Significance of Economic Science*. He argued, 'propositions involving the verb "ought" are different in kind from propositions involving the verb "is". And it is difficult to see what possible good can be served by not keeping them separate, or failing to recognise their essential difference' (1935, p. 149). It seems worthwhile to repeat these warnings of Robbins, along with his view that:

> All this is not to say that economists may not assume as postulates different judgments of value, and then on the assumption that these are valid enquire what judgment is to be passed upon particular proposals for action. On the contrary, as we shall see, it is just in the light that it casts upon the significance and consistency of different ultimate valuations that the utility of economics consists. (1935, p. 149)

Part IV

Tax Revenue

Chapter 11

Fiscal Drag and Revenue Elasticities

This chapter provides an introduction to tax revenue elasticities – the extent to which revenues increase in response to an increase in income, with an unchanged tax structure – in the context of personal income and consumption taxes. It provides a framework within which analytical expressions for the revenue elasticities of various taxes may be compared and combined.[1] The approaches are illustrated using a range of empirical estimates for the UK. The issue of revenue responsiveness is popularly thought of as 'fiscal drag', whereby growth in nominal incomes, with a fixed tax structure, raises the average tax rate facing individuals, causing income tax revenues to grow faster than incomes.[2]

Measuring the long-run growth of tax revenues reliably is important for the design of tax policy. For example, when fiscal authorities set a revenue

[1] Early studies based on analytical expressions for income tax revenue elasticities include Hutton and Lambert (1980, 1982a) and Creedy and Gemmell (2002) for the UK; and Friedlaender *et al.* (1973) and Fries *et al.* (1982) for the US. Dorrington (1974), Spahn (1975) and Hutton and Lambert (1982b) used simulation methods to examine the elasticity of income taxation. Attempts have been made to measure tax elasticities using regression methods applied to data on tax revenue, tax base and income aggregates. These include Dye and McGuire (1991), Ram (1991) and Sobel and Holcombe (1995).

[2] Tax elasticity is also closely related to tax progressivity – the redistributional properties of a tax. Hence tax changes designed to affect progressivity may have unintended consequences for elasticity, and *vice versa.*

target, the need for discretionary changes in tax parameters (such as tax rates, income thresholds and allowances) is conditional on the expected automatic revenue growth generated by the tax system in the absence of any discretionary change. The automatic revenue changes are described in terms of the 'built-in flexibility', or revenue responsiveness, of the tax. A unit-free measure of this responsiveness is the revenue elasticity of the tax: this is the percentage change in tax revenue in response to a given percentage change in income, for a constant tax structure. Estimates of tax revenue elasticities can assist in long-run revenue forecasting.[3] Furthermore, the built-in flexibility of taxation is known to affect the stability properties of macroeconomic models.[4] An elastic tax acts as an automatic stabiliser: when the economy is in recession and incomes are falling (or rising slowly), tax revenues fall proportionately more (or rise more slowly), so helping to maintain the growth of disposable incomes or spending.

11.1 Income Tax Revenue Elasticities

This section introduces general expressions for individual and aggregate income tax revenue elasticities which apply to any tax structure.

11.1.1 Individual Revenue Elasticities

Consider revenue elasticities at the individual level. Suppose $T(y_i)$ denotes the income tax paid by individual i with a nominal income of y_i. All references to income variables relate to nominal values. The individual revenue

[3] For discussion of H.M. Treasury and Institute for Fiscal Studies revenue-forecasting methods, see Pike and Savage (1998) and Giles and Hall (1998) respectively. For a number of OECD countries, van den Noord (2000) and Heinemann (2001) use regression methods to estimate various tax revenue elasticities for personal income and indirect taxes, with respect to changes in GDP or other income measures. Also Giorno *et al.* (1995) provide some comparisons of aggregate income tax revenue elasticities based both on regressions and on tax-share weighted individual values for OECD countries.

[4] The large literature on this issue includes Delorme and Hayakawa (1977), Özmucur (1979), Smyth (1978), Peel (1979) and Pohjola (1985).

elasticity of income tax with respect to a change in income, η_{T_y,y_i}, is defined as the proportional change in tax divided by the proportional change in the individual's income. Hence:

$$\eta_{T_y,y_i} = \frac{dT(y_i)/T(y_i)}{dy_i/y_i} \tag{11.1}$$

so that a simple rearrangement gives:

$$\eta_{T_y,y_i} = \frac{dT(y_i)/dy_i}{T(y_i)/y_i} = \frac{mtr_i}{atr_i} \tag{11.2}$$

where mtr_i is the marginal tax rate and atr_i is the average tax rate faced by i. The general scheme adopted here for notation is that the first subscript of the revenue elasticity, η, refers to the type of tax revenue considered and the second subscript refers to the income that is considered to change. However, in the present case of the individual elasticity, the first subscript T_y is used as a shorthand for $T(y_i)$. In a progressive tax structure, $mtr_i > atr_i$ for all i, so that $\eta_{T_y,y_i} > 1$. This elasticity is also the local measure of liability progression defined by Musgrave and Thin (1948).

Further insight into the revenue elasticity can be obtained by considering the variation in the average tax rate as income increases. This is Musgrave and Thin's measure of average rate progression. It can be shown that:

$$\eta_{T_y,y_i} = 1 + \eta_{atr,y_i} \tag{11.3}$$

Hence an increase in η_{atr,y_i}, that is a higher rate of increase in the average tax rate at y_i, results in a higher revenue elasticity at y_i. The elasticity η_{atr,y_i} can change even though mtr_i is fixed if, for example, allowances change. Furthermore, a progressive tax, for which $\eta_{atr,y_i} > 0$, is necessarily an elastic tax. Measuring this elasticity requires only information about average tax rates at different income levels, which is often readily available.

11.1.2 The Aggregate Revenue Elasticity

Suppose there are N individuals, with incomes $y_1, ..., y_N$, so that total income is $Y = \sum_{i=1}^{N} y_i$, and total income tax revenue is $T_Y = \sum_{i=1}^{N} T(y_i)$. Totally differentiating aggregate revenue gives:

$$dT_Y = \sum_{i=1}^{N} \frac{\partial T(y_i)}{\partial y_i} dy_i \tag{11.4}$$

so that the aggregate elasticity, $\eta_{T_Y,Y}$, is:

$$\eta_{T_Y,Y} = \sum_{i=1}^{N} \left(\eta_{T_y,y_i}\right)\left(\eta_{y_i,Y}\right)\left(\frac{T(y_i)}{T_Y}\right) \tag{11.5}$$

Therefore $\eta_{T_Y,Y}$ is a tax-share weighted average of the product of individual revenue elasticities, η_{T_y,y_i}, and the elasticity of individual income with respect to total income, $\eta_{y_i,Y}$, with $\sum_{i=1}^{N} \eta_{y_i,Y} = 1$. This means that the aggregate elasticity cannot be obtained without specifying the distribution of proportionate income changes, dy_i/y_i, associated with any proportional increase in total income, dY/Y. For non-equiproportional changes, the aggregate revenue elasticity can be less than 1; for example it is zero if the only incomes which increase are below a tax-free threshold and none crosses the threshold.

The simplest form of (11.5) is for the special case where all individuals experience an equal proportionate increase in income. Any relative measure of inequality is unchanged and $dy_i/y_i = dY/Y$, so that $\eta_{y_i,Y} = 1$ for all i. Substituting into (11.5) gives:

$$\eta_{T_Y,Y} = \sum_{i=1}^{N} \eta_{T_y,y_i} \frac{T(y_i)}{T_Y} \tag{11.6}$$

Hence the aggregate elasticity is in this case simply a weighted average of the individual elasticities, with weights equal to the proportion of total revenue paid by each individual. The majority of empirical analyses have used this simplifying assumption.[5]

[5]However, the assumption was relaxed by Creedy and Gemmell (2003, 2004) when examining UK and NZ taxes.

11.2 The Multi-step Income Tax Function

The most common form of income tax function used in practice is the multi-step function.[6] Hence it is useful to examine this case closely. The multi-step tax function is described by a series of marginal tax rates and income thresholds over which the rates apply. Between two adjacent thresholds, the marginal tax rate is constant, giving the appearance of a step. Formally, the multi-step income tax function can be written as:

$$\begin{aligned} T(y_i) &= 0 && 0 < y_i \leq a_1 \\ &= t_1(y_i - a_1) && a_1 < y_i \leq a_2 \\ &= t_1(a_2 - a_1) + t_2(y_i - a_2) && a_2 < y_i \leq a_3 \end{aligned} \tag{11.7}$$

and so on. If y_i falls into the kth tax bracket, so that $a_k < y_i \leq a_{k+1}$, and $a_0 = t_0 = 0$, $T(y_i)$ can be written for $k \geq 1$ as:

$$T(y_i) = t_k(y_i - a_k) + \sum_{j=0}^{k-1} t_j(a_{j+1} - a_j) \tag{11.8}$$

which can be rearranged as:

$$T(y_i) = t_k(y_i - a_k') \tag{11.9}$$

where:

$$a_k' = \sum_{j=1}^{k} a_j \left(\frac{t_j - t_{j-1}}{t_k} \right) \tag{11.10}$$

The implication of (11.9) and (11.10) is that the tax function facing any individual taxpayer is equivalent to a tax function with a single marginal tax rate, t_k, applied to income measured in excess of a single threshold, a_k'. The term, a_k', is the effective threshold for individuals in the kth class, and is a weighted sum of the a_js, with weights, $(t_j - t_{j-1})/t_k$, determined by the structure of marginal rate progression. Therefore, a_k' differs across

[6] Not surprisingly, it has received most attention in the conceptual literature; see Hutton and Lambert (1980), Fries *et al.* (1982), Caminada and Goudswaard (1996) and Creedy and Gemmell (2002, 2003).

individuals, unlike a_j, depending on the marginal income tax bracket into which they fall.

From (11.9), for $k \geq 1$, differentiation gives, for income changes which do not involve a movement between tax brackets:

$$\eta_{T_y,y_i} = \frac{y_i - a_k' \eta_{a_k',y_i}}{y_i - a_k'} \tag{11.11}$$

The term η_{a_k',y_i} captures the impact on the revenue elasticity of changes in effective deductions as y_i increases. Hence for the simpler case where $da_k'/dy_i = 0$, the elasticity becomes:[7]

$$\eta_{T_y,y_i} = 1 + \frac{a_k'}{y_i - a_k'} \tag{11.12}$$

Table 11.1: A Multi-step Tax Function

a_k	t_k	a_k'
5,000	0.20	5,000.00
15,000	0.25	7,000.00
25,000	0.30	10,000.00
40,000	0.35	14,285.71

To illustrate the properties of a multi-step function, suppose the rates and fixed thresholds are as shown in the first two columns of Table 11.1, for a structure with four rates above zero. The associated values of a_k' are shown in the final column. For $y_i < a_1$ the elasticity is zero, since tax revenue remains constant at zero. As income crosses the a_1 threshold, the revenue elasticity becomes infinitely large, after which, for $a_1 < y_i < a_2$, it declines because, from (11.12), $\eta_{T_y,y_i} = 1 + a_1/(y_i - a_1)$. The average and marginal rates for the tax structure in Table 11.1 are shown in Figure 11.1, and the variation in the revenue elasticity as y_i increases is illustrated in Figure 11.2.[8]

[7] The result in (11.12) can be compared with that in Hutton and Lambert (1983, p. 224), who use a different terminology. They point out that the elasticity of any tax, j, can be expressed as $\eta_j = 1 + K_j/T_j$, where T_j is the tax paid and K_j depends on the tax structure. The result in (11.12) can easily be rewritten in this general form, where K_j becomes $t_k a_k'$ and is an effective transfer payment, since net income is $t_k a_k' + y_i(1 - t_k)$.

[8] Fries *et al.* (1982) and Hutton and Lambert (1983) note that it is possible to decom-

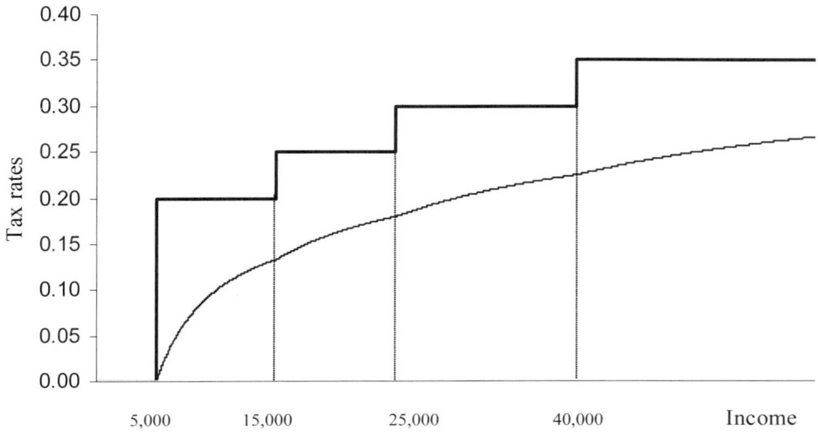

Figure 11.1: Marginal and Average Tax Rates

11.3 Estimates for Income Taxes in the UK

It has been seen that individual elasticities can be computed using information about the tax structure, along with details of the way in which allowances change with income. The computation of the aggregate elasticity requires information about the distribution of income at any time, along with details of the dynamics of income change from one period to the next. The simplest case is of course where the income changes are assumed to be equiproportional, that is, where all values of $\eta_{y_i,Y}$ are unity. Here, the preferred approach depends on the available form of information about the income distribution.

First, suppose that a cross-sectional survey of a large number of individuals is available. The aggregate elasticity can be obtained as the tax-share weighted average of these individual elasticities. If it is required to project

pose the revenue elasticity, η_{T_y,y_i}, into components reflecting the effect on the tax base of a change in income, η_{B,y_i}, and the effect on tax payments of a change in the tax base, $\eta_{T_y,B}$, such that $\eta_{T_y,y_i} = (\eta_{T_y,B})(\eta_{B,y_i})$.

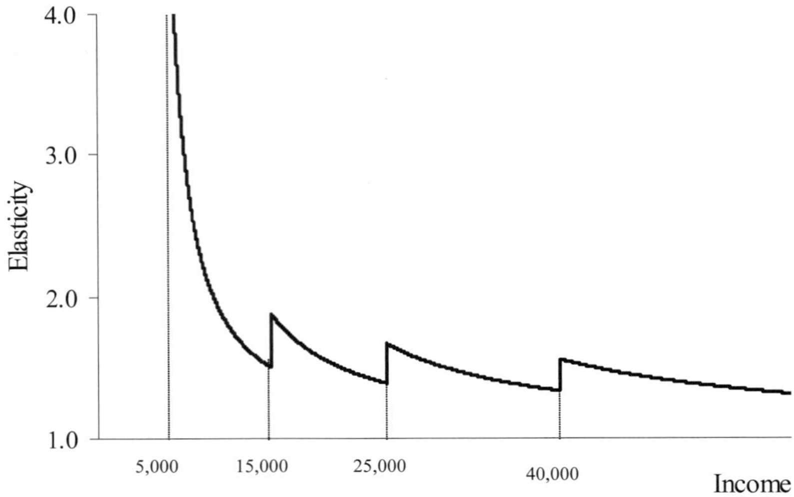

Figure 11.2: Tax Revenue Elasticity

the aggregate elasticity, after a period of income growth, then for the equi-proportional case it is simply a matter of increasing each individual's income by the same amount and re-calculating the values of η_{T_y,y_i}, and so on.

Alternatively, data are often available only in the form of a grouped income distribution, or other summary information, such as several percentiles of the distribution. Such data may be used to estimate the parameters of a specified functional form to describe the distribution. Given the estimates, a pseudo cross-sectional sample may be generated by taking a large number of random draws from the specified distribution, and then proceeding as described in the previous paragraph.[9] This approach was used by Creedy and Gemmell (2003) to examine the UK income tax system. Annual estimates of $\eta_{a',y}$ were obtained from data on allowances and deductions using regressions

[9]This kind of simulation method has been used to investigate income tax revenue elasticities by, for example, Dorrington (1974), Spahn (1975), Hutton and Lambert (1982b) and Creedy and Gemmell (2003, 2004).

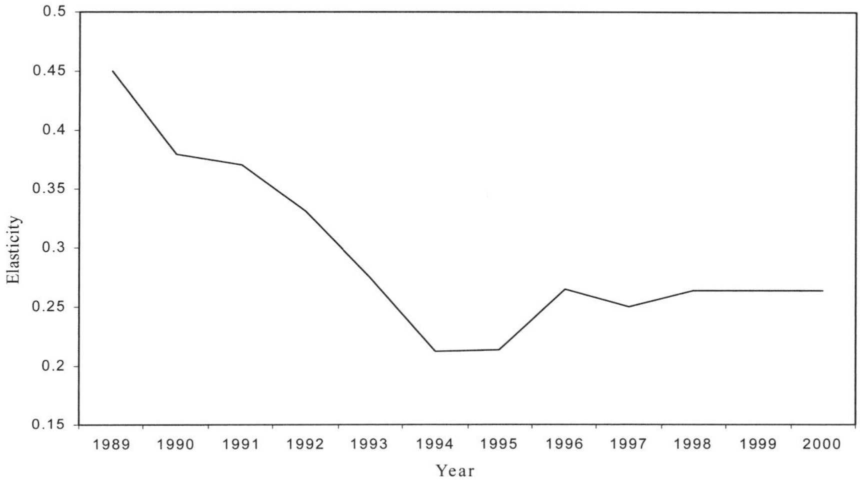

Figure 11.3: Elasticity of Allowances: UK

of the form:

$$\log a_j^{'} = \alpha + \beta \log y_j \tag{11.13}$$

where there are $j = 1, ..., n$ income groups. Estimates of the coefficient β provide estimates of the required $\eta_{a',y}$ values. Elasticities are illustrated in Figure 11.3.[10] The elasticity of allowances with respect to income declined from 0.45 in 1989 to around 0.2 in 1994, thereafter stabilising and rising slightly to around 0.26 in 1998. The decline largely reflects the falling real value of mortgage interest tax relief, while occupational and personal pension deductions, which disproportionately benefit those on higher incomes, dominate the total deductions data from 1994.

Aggregate income tax revenue elasticities for each year were obtained using a simulated population of 20,000 individuals drawn at random from a lognormal income distribution, where the mean and variance of logarithms

[10]Regressions for each year were based on cross-sections of up to 16 income groups. The double logarithmic form gives a very good fit; see Creedy and Gemmell (2003).

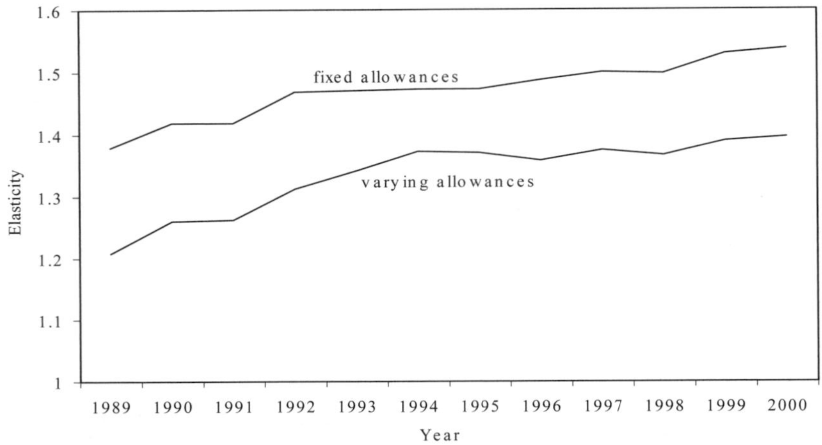

Figure 11.4: Income Tax Revenue Elasticities: UK

for each year were estimated using grouped data. Figure 11.4 shows the two sets of income tax revenue elasticities over the 1989–2000 period; that is, using the assumption that $\eta_{a'_k,y} = 0$ for all individuals, as well as using the estimates of $\eta_{a'_k,y}$ presented above. Ignoring this, by setting $\eta_{a'_k,y_i} = 0$ for all individuals, increases the revenue elasticity substantially. While elasticities rose during the 1990s, they were nevertheless lower than values found for the mid-1980s, because of the decline in the marginal tax rate faced by most taxpayers, and the rise in real incomes relative to tax thresholds.

11.4 Consumption Tax Revenue Elasticities

This section extends the analysis to include consumption tax revenue. Elasticity expressions for combined income and consumption tax revenues are also obtained. In many cases these revenue elasticities can be calculated using limited information on expenditure patterns in addition to data on the tax parameters. For consumption taxes, the direct tax base is expenditure, or tax-liable expenditure. Estimating the impact of changes in gross income on revenues is therefore less straightforward for consumption taxes. There are several responses to changes in gross incomes: changes in disposable income (affected by income tax changes), changes in total expenditures (if saving behaviour changes) and changes to tax-liable expenditure (for example, if consumption patterns change towards or away from taxed goods). Only after these responses have been modelled or estimated can information on consumption tax structures be applied to generate the automatic change in consumption tax revenues arising from a change in income.

11.4.1 Individual Revenue Elasticities

Consider an individual with income of y_i and facing a multi-step income tax function. This determines the individual's disposable income, $z_i = y_i - T(y_i)$. For many individuals, savings represent a non-negligible fraction of their disposable income. Consider first the case where there are no savings, so that consumption expenditure by individual i, m_i, is simply z_i. Hence:

$$m_i = a_k' t_k + y_i \left(1 - t_k\right) \tag{11.14}$$

Suppose that the tax-exclusive *ad valorem* indirect tax rate imposed on the ℓth good (for $\ell = 1, ..., n$) is v_ℓ, giving rise to the equivalent tax–inclusive rate of $v_\ell' = v_\ell / \left(1 + v_\ell\right)$.[11] Defining w_ℓ as the budget share of the ℓth good, $m_{i\ell}/m_i$, the consumption tax paid by i on all $\ell = 1, ..., n$ goods, $T_v(y_i)$, is given by:

$$T_v(y_i) = m_i \sum_{\ell=1}^{n} v_\ell' w_{i\ell} \tag{11.15}$$

The total consumption and income tax paid by the individual, $R\left(y_i\right) =$

[11] Any indirect taxes that are not imposed as *ad valorem* rates can be expressed as equivalent to *ad valorem* rates. For example, a unit tax of $t_{u\ell}$ imposed on the tax-exclusive price, $p_{E\ell}$, of the ℓth good, yields the tax-inclusive price of $p_\ell = p_{E\ell} + t_{u\ell}$, which is equivalent to an *ad valorem* rate of $\left(t_{u\ell}/p_\ell\right) / \left(1 - t_{u\ell}/p_\ell\right)$.

$T_y(y_i) + T_v(y_i)$, is therefore given by:

$$R(y_i) = t_k(y_i - a'_k) + \{a'_k t_k + y_i(1 - t_k)\} \sum_{\ell=1}^{n} v'_\ell w_{i\ell} \tag{11.16}$$

For simplicity, consider the case where the income tax thresholds are fixed, so that $\eta_{a'_k, y_i} = 0$ in equation (11.11). Then the change in total revenue resulting from an increase in the individual's income, assuming that the individual does not move into a higher tax bracket, is given by:

$$\frac{dR(y_i)}{dy_i} = t_k + (1 - t_k) \sum_{\ell=1}^{n} v'_\ell w_{i\ell} + m_i \sum_{\ell=1}^{n} v'_\ell \frac{dw_{i\ell}}{dy_i} \tag{11.17}$$

The last term in (11.17) involves changes in budget shares as income increases. Define e_ℓ as the total expenditure elasticity of demand for good ℓ, so that:

$$e_\ell = \frac{dm_{i\ell}/m_{i\ell}}{dm_i/m_i} \tag{11.18}$$

It can be shown that:

$$\eta_{R,y_i} = \frac{mtr_y + (1 - mtr_y) \sum_{\ell=1}^{n} v'_\ell w_{i\ell} e_{i\ell}}{atr_y + (1 - atr_y) \sum_{\ell=1}^{n} v'_\ell w_{i\ell}} \tag{11.19}$$

In (11.19) the marginal and average rates of income tax have three effects. First, higher rates affect the total revenue elasticity directly since the income tax revenue elasticity is simply mtr_y/atr_y. Secondly higher income tax rates simultaneously reduce the total revenue elasticity by reducing expenditure available to be taxed via indirect taxes, as captured by the terms in $(1 - mtr_y)$ and $(1 - atr_y)$. Thirdly, there is a compositional effect via changes in the share of income tax in total tax revenue.

Further insight into the roles played by the various components in the η_{R,y_i} expression in (11.19) can be gained by decomposing η_{R,y_i} into its income and consumption tax components. Thus, η_{R,y_i} is the weighted average of the elasticities for income and consumption taxes, η_{T_y,y_i} and η_{T_v,y_i} respectively; that is:

$$\eta_{R,y_i} = \left(\frac{T_v}{R}\right) \eta_{T_v,y_i} + \left(\frac{T_y}{R}\right) \eta_{T_y,y_i} \tag{11.20}$$

where the weights are the shares of each tax in total tax revenue. As the income tax elasticity is $\eta_{T_y,y_i} = mtr_y/atr_y$, inspection of (11.19) gives the contribution of the consumption tax elasticity as:

$$\eta_{T_v,y_i} = \left(\frac{1-mtr_y}{1-atr_y}\right)\sum_{\ell=1}^{n}\left(\frac{T_{i\ell}}{T_{v_i}}\right)e_{i\ell} \tag{11.21}$$

where $\sum_{\ell=1}^{n}(T_{i\ell}/T_{v_i})\,e_{i\ell}$ is simply the tax-share weighted sum of the expenditure elasticities for taxed goods. These results show, in addition to the tax parameters, it is necessary to have information about individuals' budget shares (or indirect tax shares) and the total expenditure elasticity of demand for each good. This information can generally be obtained from cross-sectional household budget surveys.

In the case where there are savings, consider the linear function:

$$m_i = a\,(z_i + b) \tag{11.22}$$

It can be shown that equation (11.21) becomes:

$$\eta_{T_v,y_i} = \left(1-\frac{ab}{m_i}\right)\left(\frac{1-mtr_y}{1-atr_y}\right)\sum_{\ell=1}^{n}\left(\frac{T_{i\ell}}{T_{v_i}}\right)e_{i\ell} \tag{11.23}$$

The consumption tax revenue elasticity therefore has three components. These are: the extent to which the relationship between disposable income and consumption is non-proportional; the residual progression of the income tax system; and the tax-share weighted average total expenditure elasticity of demand for each taxed good.

11.4.2 The Aggregate Consumption Tax Revenue Elasticity

As in the case of income taxes, the aggregate rather than the individual consumption tax elasticity is often more important for tax policy. Let $T_V = \sum_{i=1}^{N} T_v(y_i)$ where, as earlier, $T_v(y_i) = m_i\sum_{\ell=1}^{n} v'_\ell w_\ell$. Total differentiation gives:

$$dT_V = \sum_{i=1}^{N} \frac{\partial T_v(y_i)}{\partial y_i} dy_i = \sum_{i=1}^{N} \eta_{T_v,y_i} T_v(y_i) \frac{dy_i}{y_i} \tag{11.24}$$

For the equiproportional income growth case, substitute dY/Y for dy_i/y_i and divide by T_V to get:

$$\eta_{T_V,Y} = \sum_{i=1}^{N} \eta_{T_v,y_i} \frac{T_v(y_i)}{T_V} \tag{11.25}$$

Thus, as in the case of the income tax, the aggregate consumption tax elasticity is a consumption-tax-share weighted average of the individual revenue elasticities.

The aggregate revenue elasticity, $\eta_{T_R,Y}$, including both income and consumption taxes, again in the equiproportional growth case, is given by:

$$\eta_{T_R,Y} = \sum_{i=1}^{N} \eta_{T_R,y_i} \left\{ \frac{T_y(y_i) + T_v(y_i)}{T_Y + T_V} \right\} \tag{11.26}$$

and using (11.25) it can be found that (11.26) becomes:

$$\eta_{T_R,Y} = \left(\frac{T_Y}{T_Y + T_V} \right) \eta_{T_Y,Y} + \left(\frac{T_V}{T_Y + T_V} \right) \eta_{T_V,Y} \tag{11.27}$$

Hence the aggregate revenue elasticity is simply a revenue-share weighted average of the aggregate income tax and consumption tax elasticities.

11.4.3 Empirical Estimates for the UK

Consider again the UK tax structure. This section reports estimates for UK consumption tax revenue elasticities during 1989–2000, obtained by Creedy and Gemmell (2003). With the exception of savings proportions, the required information is readily available annually by income group, or can be calculated, from family expenditure surveys, Inland Revenue, UK Treasury and other official sources. To compute the values reported below, annual Family Expenditure Survey data were used to calculate budget shares and expenditure elasticities for each of a range of total expenditure groups, distinguishing between 10 groups of consumer goods currently subject to different levels of indirect tax. The categories are: goods subject to Value Added Tax (VAT) at the standard rate of 17.5 per cent; domestic fuel and power which are currently subject to VAT of 5 per cent; those for which VAT is zero-rated or exempt (non-VAT); beer; wines; spirits; other alcohol; tobacco; motor fuel; and insurance. Though domestic fuel and power, and insurance were not subject to these tax rates throughout the period, they are examined separately for the entire 1989–2000 period so that each category is composed of the same goods throughout.

Calculation of the required total expenditure elasticities requires modelling of the budget shares. Define w_{ki} $(i = 1, ..., n)$ as the average expenditure weight, or budget share, for the ith commodity group and kth total expenditure group. Expenditure elasticities were obtained by first fitting a separate regression for each commodity group and year, of the form:

$$w_{ki} = \alpha_{0,ik} + \alpha_{1,ik} \log(m_k) + \alpha_{2,ik} \left(\frac{1}{m_k}\right) \tag{11.28}$$

where m_k $(k = 1, ..., K)$ is the arithmetic mean expenditure of the kth total expenditure group.

Since over 80 per cent of expenditure is accounted for by non-VAT and 17.5 per cent VAT items, expenditure on those two categories is the most influential for revenue elasticity estimates. Aggregate budget shares over the period for standard rate (17.5 per cent) and non-VAT items are shown in Figure 11.5. There is a general tendency towards greater spending on VAT-liable items over time as real incomes grow. However, there is also a pronounced but temporary fall in the share of standard VAT items in 1991, and a similar rise in 1995. While the former change most likely represents a response to the increase in the standard rate of VAT in 1991, the reason for the large rise in the VAT-liable share in 1995, and its subsequent fall, is less clear.

Consumption tax revenue elasticities require values for the parameters a

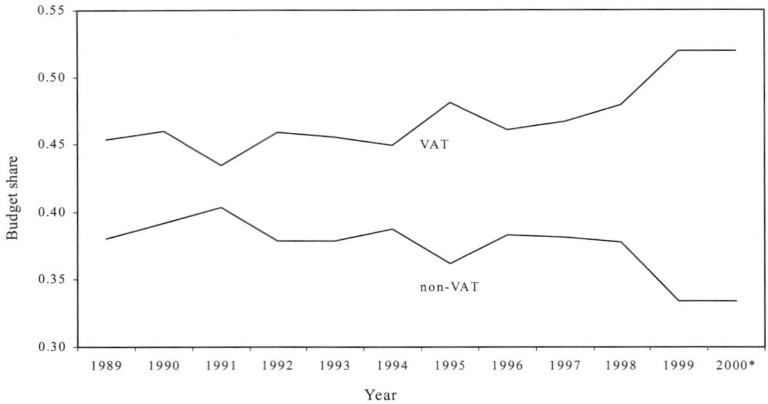

Figure 11.5: Aggregate Budget Shares for Standard and Zero-rate VAT

and b in equation (11.22). Benchmark values were chosen such that $a = 0.95$, with b calculated such that (for each year) a person with $z_i = 0$ has consumption, $m_i = ab$ equal to the value of the single person's income tax allowance. Using the simulated distribution of 20,000 taxpayers used for examining the income tax revenue elasticities described above, consumption tax revenue elasticity estimates for each year were obtained, and are illustrated in Figure 11.6, which compares the combined consumption tax revenue elasticities with those for income taxes. The consumption tax revenue elasticity generally fell during the period, from around 0.8–0.9 in the early 1990s to about 0.7 by 2000. As expected, Figure 11.6 also reveals a tendency for the consumption tax elasticity to move inversely with the elasticity of income taxes. The more elastic are income tax revenues (mtr_i exceeds atr_i), the lower is the residual progression component of the consumption tax revenue elasticity and hence, *ceterus paribus*, the lower is the revenue elasticity of consumption taxes.

Setting $b = 0$ and $a = 1$ has a substantial effect on consumption tax revenue elasticity estimates. The allowance for transfers and savings reduces the revenue elasticity to well below unity in each year, whereas failure to include

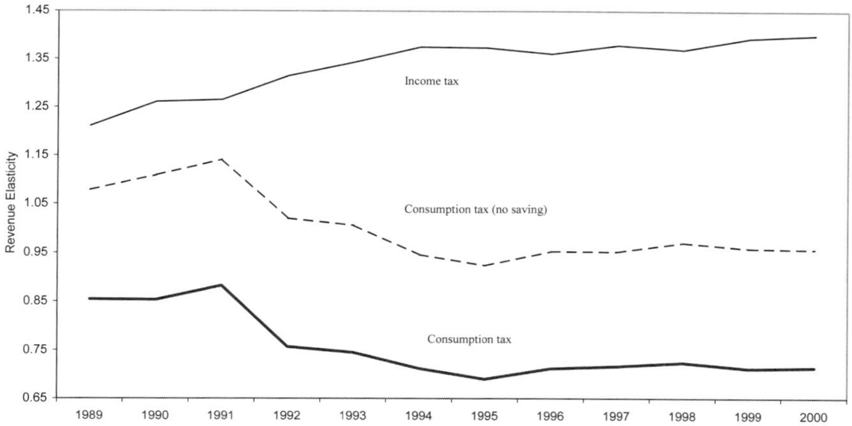

Figure 11.6: Consumption Tax Revenue Elasticities

a savings effect makes consumption tax revenues appear to be elastic in the early 1990s, and approximately proportional thereafter. Experiments showed that allowing for alternative values of the consumption function parameters, a and b, around the benchmark case, suggests that revenue elasticity results are not especially sensitive to particular values.

The changes in the revenue elasticity of consumption taxes arise both from changes to fiscal parameters (income and consumption taxes) and from changes in consumers' budget shares. Some changes in consumers' spending patterns may arise from income growth while others may be partly in response to the fiscal changes. For example, the temporary reduction in expenditures on VAT-liable items in 1991 may have been partly in response to the tax rate increase to 17.5 per cent. There is also a longer-term trend towards a lower domestic fuel expenditure share following the introduction of VAT in 1994 (not shown in Figure 11.5).

11.5 Conclusions

This chapter has examined convenient analytical expressions for the tax revenue elasticities of income and consumption taxes. The results help to provide both an understanding of the determinants of the revenue responsiveness properties of different taxes and convenient expressions for the calculation of elasticities in practice. It has been seen that the magnitude of revenue elasticities can be expected to differ substantially for alternative forms of income and consumption tax, and for the same tax over time as, for example, incomes change relative to tax thresholds. The properties were illustrated using estimates obtained for the UK tax structure.

The various parameters in the tax elasticity expressions highlight a number of potential impacts of tax reform on revenue elasticities. For example, tax reforms are often undertaken to achieve particular revenue and/or redistributive objectives in the short-to-medium run, or to be revenue-neutral or distribution-neutral. However, it is less well appreciated that changes in tax progressivity often imply changes in elasticities, while (short-run) revenue-neutral changes are not necessarily elasticity-neutral. Many industrialised countries have undertaken significant tax reform in the last 20 years, often involving shifts towards less progressive income taxes and greater use of indirect taxes, as well as experiencing rising mean incomes relative to tax thresholds. Results here suggest that each of these changes can be expected to affect tax revenue elasticities, while commonly observed increases in the inequality of pre-tax incomes also affect these elasticities.

This chapter has shown that tractable analytical expressions can be produced for the built-in flexibility, or revenue elasticities, of various indirect taxes and for combined direct-plus-indirect taxes, where the indirect tax system is combined with a general multi-step income tax structure. These results clarify the determinants of the revenue responsiveness properties of different taxes, and demonstrate that indirect tax elasticities can be estimated from information that is generally available for most tax systems: summary tax parameters and total expenditure elasticities for commodity groups.

For the common two-rate or multi-rate cases, whether or not consumption tax revenue is elastic is ambiguous but depends on two simple conditions: whether the income tax is regressive or progressive, and the average expenditure elasticity of zero-rated (lower-rated) goods. Consumption taxes are more likely to be elastic if income taxes are regressive and if zero-rated goods are mainly necessities. In practice, while the latter condition often holds, the former does not, so that consumption taxes are expected typically to display inelastic revenue properties.

The various tax parameters in the elasticity expressions obtained here also highlight the potential impact of tax reform on built-in flexibility. When governments make discretionary changes to tax parameters, such as tax rates and allowances, the direct effect on tax revenue is of immediate concern both to the Treasury and to the taxpayers. However, the effects of such changes on the built-in flexibility of individual taxes or the tax system as a whole are often less well appreciated.

Chapter 12

The Elasticity of Taxable Income

This chapter provides an introduction to the concept of the elasticity of taxable income with respect to the net-of-tax rate, concentrating on the basic analytics involved. This elasticity aims to capture all potential responses to income taxation in a single elasticity measure, without the need to specify the nature of the various adjustment processes involved or consider the details of tax regulations.[1] These adjustments include, as well as labour supply changes (both in terms of hours worked and intensity of effort), income shifting between sources which are taxed at different rates, and tax evasion through non-declaration of income. Under certain assumptions, the elasticity is sufficient in order to obtain a measure of the excess burden of income taxation.

It is therefore not surprising that many applications have been made in numerous countries since its introduction by Feldstein (1995).[2] The aim of the present chapter is to provide an introductory treatment of the basic concepts and analytical results. Stress is placed on the assumptions involved in specifying a reduced-form relationship and in obtaining welfare results. Many

[1] Some details may of course be needed at the estimation stage, as discussed below.

[2] A survey of the empirical literature, by Saez, Slemrod and Giertz (2009), includes 111 references, and the list could easily be extended.

of the results are well known, but are typically stated without proof. Here, careful attention is given to the derivation of results. These are reinforced by numerical examples which help to give some idea of the orders of magnitude involved, and their sensitivity to changes in parameters. Furthermore, motivation for the use of the elasticity of taxable income concept is provided by clarifying the difficulties involved in attempting to extend the standard structural approach to the analysis of labour supply to cover a wider range of tax responses. However, some new analytical results are presented below. Welfare effects are usually discussed only in terms of the top marginal income tax rate: the approach is extended to cover all income tax brackets. Also, a potential source of bias in estimating the elasticity is examined.

First, the standard basic approach to labour supply modelling is briefly discussed in section 12.1. The reduced form approach is then introduced in section 12.2. A top marginal income tax rate and its revenue effects are examined in section 12.3. In section 12.4, attention turns to the use of the elasticity of taxable income in welfare measurement, particularly concerning the excess burden of taxation, and the sensitivity of results to parameter changes. In considering excess burdens and marginal welfare costs, emphasis in the literature has been on the effects of changes in a top tax rate. The appropriate measures for any income tax bracket are also discussed in this section. Section 12.5 turns to a brief consideration of estimation methods, making use of actual tax reforms which affect a (relatively) small group of individuals, and changes in marginal rates faced by individuals as a result of fiscal drag.

12.1 A Structural Approach

This section briefly describes, in subsection 12.1.1, the standard approach to modelling labour supply. Subsection 12.1.2 discusses the problems of extending this model to allow for tax shifting.

12.1.1 The Standard Labour Supply Model

Suppose hours of work can be varied continuously, and an individual maximises a direct utility function $U(c, h)$, where c is net income (or consumption, with the price index normalised to unity) and h is the proportion of time spent in leisure (so that the endowment of time is effectively normalised to 1 unit). The fixed wage rate is w and, faced with a piecewise-linear budget constraint, a tangency solution along any section is equivalent to a tangency along the linear constraint:

$$c = w(1-h)(1-\tau) + \mu \tag{12.1}$$

where τ is the relevant tax rate and μ is 'virtual income', defined as disposable income at the intercept of the linear section extended to the c axis, where $h = 1$. For corner solutions, w is replaced by the 'virtual wage', given by the slope of the appropriate indifference curve at the corner. Equation (12.1) can be rewritten as:

$$c + wh(1-\tau) = w(1-\tau) + \mu \equiv M \tag{12.2}$$

where M is 'full income'. Gross earnings are $y = w(1-h)$.

Solving for c and h, and substituting into the direct utility function, gives the indirect utility function, V, and inverting this gives the expenditure function, $M(w(1-\tau), U)$, the minimum full income needed to attain utility, U, with net wage, $w(1-\tau)$. Alternatively, the expenditure function can be expressed in terms of virtual income. Welfare changes are expressed in terms of the expenditure function. For example, the equivalent variation resulting from a non-marginal increase in the tax rate from τ_0 to τ_1, involving a new utility level of U_1, is given by:

$$EV = \{M_1 - M(w(1-\tau_0), U_1)\} - \{M_0 - M_1\} \tag{12.3}$$

where M_i is full income under tax rate i. The first term in curly brackets is the standard equivalent variation for the reduction in the 'price' of leisure, and the second term in curly brackets is the 'full income' effect of the tax change. For small changes in τ, the equivalent variation can be written as:

$$EV = \frac{dW}{d\tau} = \frac{\partial M\left(w\left(1-\tau\right), U_1\right)}{\partial\tau} - \frac{dM}{d\tau} \tag{12.4}$$

A well-known problem arises from the fact that each individual's net wage and hours of work supplied are jointly determined, and depend on the particular range (or corner) of the budget constraint producing maximum utility. Hence any attempt to measure labour supply behaviour using a reduced-form specification in which hours of work are regressed on the net wage and some measure of the tax rate is subject to serious endogeneity problems. Furthermore, given kinks and non-convexities in budget constraints, labour supply functions do not correspond to the simple smooth specifications used in such regressions.

12.1.2 Under-reporting of Income

The labour supply adjustment to a tax change may not be the only adjustment. For example, there is an incentive not to declare some of the income. To illustrate using a simple specification, suppose that $z < y$ is declared for tax purposes, but there is a cost of concealing income, given by $A\left(y-z\right)$. A more extensive model would consider factors such as the probability of being audited and the size of a fine if evasion is detected. The budget constraint then becomes:

$$c = y - \tau z + \mu - A\left(y-z\right) \tag{12.5}$$

Maximising $U\left(c,h\right)$ subject to this constraint, income is concealed up to the point where the cost per unit concealed, $A\left(y-z\right)/\left(y-z\right)$, is equal to τ. Indeed, unless $A\left(y-z\right)$ is increasing in $y-z$, all income will be concealed unless, in addition, there is a non-pecuniary cost or the individual suffers some feeling of guilt, in which case $y-z$ can be regarded as entering the direct utility function with a negative effect. The utility function is thus written as $U\left(c,h,y-z\right)$.

The case where $A(y-z) = \delta(y-z)$, so that the cost per unit concealed is constant, is equivalent to an assumption that instead of not declaring the income component, $y-z$, it is declared under a different income schedule, attracting a tax rate of $\delta < \tau$. Again, an interior solution exists only if $y-z$ is included in the utility function, so that $U = U(c, h, y-z)$.

The possibilities of modelling taxable income responses to tax rate changes following this kind of structural approach are clearly severely limited. Even a fairly narrow range of income-shifting options would give rise to a complex nonlinear programming problem, where corner solutions and inequality constraints would be expected to play an important role. Instead of trying to construct a structural model which includes labour supply adjustments and income concealment (or some form of shifting) as part of a number of possible responses to tax changes, the approach underlying the elasticity of taxable income is to use a reduced-form equation, as shown in the following section.

12.2 A Reduced-Form Approach

The aim of a reduced-form relationship between total income and declared income is to capture all possible responses to tax rate changes in a single elasticity measure, without attempting to model each form of response. The elasticity concept is that of the elasticity, η, of declared income with respect to the net-of-tax rate, $1-\tau$, defined as:

$$\eta = \left(\frac{1-\tau}{z}\right)\frac{dz}{d(1-\tau)} \tag{12.6}$$

Typically a reduced form-equation, including this elasticity as a parameter, is written down as a starting point. However, the present section discusses utility specifications giving rise to a functional relationship between declared and total income, involving the marginal tax rate. In this context, a different approach to specifying utility is needed, in comparison with that used in the previous section when considering labour supply behaviour. The special and popular case of a constant elasticity form is then derived.

Instead of specifying utility in terms of consumption and leisure, consider a specification involving total income, net income and declared income. Consumption, or disposable income, c, clearly has a positive effect on utility. However, total income, y, enters the utility function with a negative effect, reflecting the fact that some effort is required to obtain it. In addition, where as before z denotes declared income, the amount $y - z$ is assumed to enter utility in view of the effort or psychic costs involved in non-declaration. Hence a general utility function may be written as:

$$U = U\left(c, y, y - z\right) \tag{12.7}$$

Ignoring also the considerable complexity of actual budget constraints, the linear form given in equation (12.5) may be adopted. Maximisation of utility subject to this linear constraint would give rise to a solution for z in terms of the tax rate, the cost of income shifting and virtual income. The solution would be obtained by substituting for c in U using the budget constraint and solving the two equations $\partial U/\partial y = 0$ and $\partial U/\partial z = 0$. However, even for simple utility functions these equations become nonlinear.

With the emphasis only on the effect on declared income (from all sources) of a tax change, a common approach is to consider a yet more abbreviated form of this kind of model, in which utility is written simply as $U\left(c, z\right)$, with z entering negatively. Suppose that the tax rate, τ, applies to income measured above a threshold, z_T. For those with $z > z_T$, and ignoring any cost of shifting, the budget constraint is:

$$\begin{aligned} c_i &= \mu_{Vi} + z_i - \tau\left(z_i - z_T\right) \\ &= \left(\mu_{Vi} + \tau z_T\right) + z_i\left(1 - \tau\right) \end{aligned} \tag{12.8}$$

where μ_{Vi} depends on the nature of the tax and transfer structure and the total income, y, of the individual: these components do not need to be considered explicitly. Hence, writing virtual income as $\mu_i = \mu_{Vi} + \tau z_T$, the budget constraint is written simply as:

$$c_i = \mu_i + z_i (1 - \tau) \tag{12.9}$$

To illustrate this approach, consider the Cobb–Douglas case where $U = c^{\beta} (\xi - z)^{1-\beta}$, and ξ is a parameter. This formulation allows for z to enter the utility function (separately from its contribution to c) with negative marginal utility, again reflecting the effort required to aquire it. Substituting for c using (12.9), z can be found by solving $\partial U/\partial z = 0$, where:

$$\frac{\partial U}{\partial z} = \frac{\beta U}{c} (1 - \tau) - \frac{(1-\beta) U}{\xi - z} \tag{12.10}$$

giving:

$$z = \beta \xi - (1 - \beta) \left(\frac{\mu}{1 - \tau} \right) \tag{12.11}$$

In the absence of a tax, that is when $\tau = 0$, then $z = z_0 = \beta \xi - (1 - \beta) \mu$. Declared income can thus be written as:

$$z = z_0 + (1 - \beta) \left(1 - \frac{1}{1 - \tau} \right) \tag{12.12}$$

and it is found that:

$$\eta = \frac{\frac{1}{1-\tau} + \tau \left(\frac{z_T}{\mu} \right)}{\frac{1}{1-\beta} \left(\frac{z_0}{\mu} \right) - \frac{\tau}{1-\tau}} \tag{12.13}$$

The elasticity is therefore a function of $1-\tau$, z_0, z_T and virtual income, μ; the latter is of course expected to vary among individuals. Clearly, η increases as τ increases. These results apply to tangency solutions and in general, with a tax structure containing a number of marginal rates, it would be necessary to consider corner solutions.

Considerable further simplification arises if income effects are not present. A specification which has received much attention is the quasi-linear form:

$$U = c - \left(\frac{1}{1 + \frac{1}{\varepsilon}} \right) \left(\frac{z}{z_0} \right)^{1+\frac{1}{\varepsilon}} \tag{12.14}$$

The linear term in c and the absence of μ from the term involving z ensure that income effects are zero.[3] Then z is obtained by solving $\partial U/\partial z = 0$, so that:

$$\frac{\partial U}{\partial z} = 1 - \tau - \left(\frac{z}{z_0}\right)^{\frac{1}{\varepsilon}} \tag{12.15}$$

and:

$$z = z_0 \left(1 - \tau\right)^{\varepsilon} \tag{12.16}$$

Thus the elasticity is constant at $\eta = \varepsilon$. If ε is assumed to be the same for all individuals, then they necessarily all have the same elasticity, η, despite having different incomes. It is seen below that the assumption of zero income effects is central in obtaining results regarding welfare changes. However, it should be recognised that the widespread and often implicit assumption of zero income effects is largely untested in this context.[4]

12.3 A Top Marginal Income Tax Rate

Most attention in the literature has been given to the top marginal income tax rate in a multi-rate system. This is partly because the initial policy changes which were used to estimate the elasticity of taxable income involved changes to only the top rate. The revenue effects of such a top rate are considered in this section. Suppose that in a multi-rate structure with K brackets, the kth tax bracket has a marginal tax rate of τ_k above the income threshold a_k, for $k = 1, ..., K$. Furthermore, $a_{k+1} = \infty$. For $a_k < z < a_{k+1}$ the tax paid at the rate τ_k is simply $\tau_k (z - a_k)$, and for $z > a_{k+1}$ the tax paid at that rate is $\tau_k (a_{k+1} - a_k)$.

Hence income above the top threshold, a_K, is taxed at a fixed rate, τ_K. As this is the top marginal rate, the tax paid at that rate by an individual

[3] Marshall (1890) first used the assumption of additive utility with one good having constant marginal utility, when wishing to avoid income effects in disequilibrium trading.

[4] In the context of labour supply, some evidence for Australia is presented in Kalb and Ghantous (2006). Their results show that income effects are nontrivial for various demographic groups.

with $z_i > a_K$ is equal to $\tau(z_i - a_K)$. Total revenue collected by the top marginal rate, R_K, is thus:

$$R_K = \tau_K \sum_{z_i > a_K} (z_i - a_K) = N_K \tau_K (\bar{z}_K - a_K) \tag{12.17}$$

where $\bar{z}_K$ is the arithmetic mean of those above the threshold and N_K is the number of people above the threshold. It is important to recognise that $\tau_K(z_i - a_K)$ is not the total tax paid by person i, since the latter has to include tax paid at lower rates. However, changes in the top rate have no effect on revenue from the lower rates. As it is clear that concentration is on the top marginal rate only, for convenience the K subscript is omitted from R, τ and N in this section and in the first part of the following section.

The effect on R, and thus on total revenue, of a change in τ is thus:

$$\frac{dR}{d\tau} = \frac{\partial R}{\partial \tau} + \frac{\partial R}{\partial \bar{z}_K}\frac{\partial \bar{z}_K}{\partial \tau} \tag{12.18}$$

The first term is a pure 'tax rate' effect while the second term is a 'tax base' effect of the tax rate change. Using $\partial R/\partial\tau = N(\bar{z}_K - a_K)$, $\partial R/\partial \bar{z}_K = N\tau$, and from the definition of η, $\partial \bar{z}_K/\partial\tau = -\eta\bar{z}_K/(1-\tau)$, the revenue change becomes:[5]

$$\frac{dR}{d\tau} = N(\bar{z}_K - a_K)\left\{1 - \eta\left(\frac{\bar{z}_K}{\bar{z}_K - a_K}\right)\left(\frac{\tau}{1-\tau}\right)\right\} \tag{12.19}$$

Define the term γ as:

$$\gamma = \frac{\bar{z}_K}{\bar{z}_K - a_K} \tag{12.20}$$

so that (12.19) is more succinctly written as:

$$\frac{dR}{d\tau} = N(\bar{z}_K - a_K)\left\{1 - \eta\gamma\left(\frac{\tau}{1-\tau}\right)\right\} \tag{12.21}$$

The tax rate, τ^*, which maximises revenue from the top marginal rate, is obtained by setting $dR/d\tau = 0$, and is thus a simple function of γ and the elasticity, η, whereby:

$$\tau^* = (1 + \gamma\eta)^{-1} \tag{12.22}$$

[5] This is equivalent to the result stated by Saez *et al.* (2009, p. 5).

The term, γ, is simply the arithmetic mean income above the income threshold, a_K, divided by the difference between that arithmetic mean and the threshold itself. The characteristics of γ are clearly determined by the nature of the distribution of declared income. This is examined as follows.

Let $f(z)$ and $F(z) = \int_0^z f(u)\,du$ denote respectively the density function and the distribution function (the proportion of people with income less than or equal to z) of declared income, where $\int_0^\infty f(u)\,du = 1$. The arithmetic mean of the complete distribution of z is given by $\bar{z} = \int_0^\infty u dF(u)$. Hence the proportion of total declared income obtained by those with income less than or equal to z is given by $\int_0^z u dF(u) / \int_0^\infty u dF(u)$, which may be denoted $F_1(z)$. The well-known Lorenz curve is, for example, the relationship between $F(z)$ and $F_1(z)$, and the term $F_1(z)$ is called the first moment distribution function of z.

In general it can be shown that:

$$\gamma = \frac{\bar{z}_K}{\bar{z}_K - a_K} = \left[1 - \left(\frac{a_K}{\bar{z}}\right)\frac{1 - F(a_K)}{1 - F_1(a_K)}\right]^{-1} \tag{12.23}$$

In general, the value of γ is expected to increase at a decreasing rate as the income threshold, a_K, increases. However, there is one special case where it remains fixed. If it is assumed that declared incomes above a_K are distributed as a Pareto Type I distribution, the density function (for $z > a_K$) is $f(z) = \delta/z^{1+\rho}$, where δ and ρ are parameters. In this special case it can be shown that $\gamma = \bar{z}_T/(\bar{z}_T - a_K)$ is constant and equal to ρ. Therefore, unlike the general case, γ does not depend on the threshold income level itself. However, the lower is a_K in relation to $\bar{z}$, the less likely it is that declared incomes above a_K can be approximated by the Pareto distribution. In practice, there is nothing to be gained by assuming that γ has this property since it is easy enough to compute values from observed distributions. The various components of (12.23) can be obtained directly from information about the actual distribution of declared incomes.

12.4 Welfare Changes

This section derives welfare changes, expressed in terms of the excess burden and the marginal welfare cost of taxation. As mentioned in section 12.1, welfare changes are defined in terms of the 'expenditure function', which in this case gives the minimum amount needed to attain a specified utility level at a given tax rate. In the more familiar case of consumer demands for commodities, it measures the minimum expenditure needed to attain a specified utility level at a given set of prices, and welfare changes are measured as the change in expenditure required to remain on a fixed indifference curve as prices change.

The first subsection examines welfare costs relating to the top marginal tax rate in a multi-rate structure, on which attention is concentrated in the literature. The second subsection extends the analysis to any tax bracket.

12.4.1 A Top Marginal Rate

Consider a change in the top marginal tax rate, for which $z > a_K$. As in the previous section, the K subscript is omitted for convenience where it is clear that reference is to the top marginal rate. Let $E_i = E(\tau, U_i)$ denote the expenditure function for individual i, expressed in terms of virtual income. The welfare change for a small tax change, following the expression for welfare changes in equation (12.4) above, is:

$$\frac{dW_i}{d\tau} = \frac{\partial E(\tau, U_i)}{\partial \tau} - \frac{d\mu_i}{d\tau} \tag{12.24}$$

Strictly speaking it would be necessary to consider whether equivalent or compensating variations are used (that is, depending on whether the utility level held constant is the post- or pre-change level). But the assumption that there are no income effects means that this can be ignored here. Using Shephard's Lemma (the Envelope theorem), it is known that $\partial E(\tau, U_i)/\partial \tau = z_i^H$, where the superscript indicates that it is the Hicksian, or compensated, value. However, if income effects are zero, Marshallian and Hicksian demands are equal for each individual.

Furthermore, from the budget constraint defined above and for the top tax rate, $\mu_i = \mu_{Vi} + \tau a_K$, and so $d\mu_i/d\tau = a_K$ for all individuals above the threshold. Hence the welfare change is simply:[6]

$$\frac{dW_i}{d\tau} = z_i - a_K \tag{12.25}$$

Comparing this result with (12.18), this welfare change is equivalent to $\partial R/\partial \tau$ for each individual; this is the 'tax rate' effect on revenue of a change in τ. Adding these changes over all those individuals above a_K gives the aggregate welfare change as:

$$\frac{dW}{d\tau} = N\left(\bar{z}_K - a_K\right) \tag{12.26}$$

The aggregate marginal excess burden, MEB, arising from the tax change is:

$$MEB = N\left(\bar{z}_K - a_K\right)\eta\gamma\left(\frac{\tau}{1-\tau}\right) \tag{12.27}$$

The MEB is thus equal to the absolute value of the 'tax base' effect on tax revenue of a rate change.[7] The term $\tau/\left(1-\tau\right)$ is in fact the tax-inclusive marginal tax rate. That is, applying this rate to net income generates the same revenue as applying τ, the tax-exclusive rate, to the corresponding gross income.

The marginal welfare cost, MWC, is defined as the marginal excess bur-

[6] Alternatively, consider changes in indirect utility resulting from a change in τ, again omitting the K subscript for convenience. The indirect utility function, omitting the individual subscript, V, is defined as $Max_z U\left(\mu + (1-\tau)z, z\right)$. The total differential is $dV = \frac{\partial V}{\partial c}\frac{\partial c}{\partial \tau}d\tau + \frac{\partial V}{\partial c}\frac{\partial c}{\partial \mu}d\mu$. From the budget constraint, $\frac{\partial c}{\partial \tau} = -z$ and $\frac{\partial c}{\partial \mu} = 1$, and writing $\frac{\partial V}{\partial c} = u_c$, gives $dV = -u_c\left(zd\tau - d\mu\right) = -u_c\left(z - d\mu/d\tau\right)d\tau$. Using, as shown above, $d\mu/d\tau = a_K$, gives $dV = -u_c\left(z - a_K\right)d\tau$. With no income effects, and the quasi-linear utility function above, the term u_c is the same for everyone.

[7] This is equivalent to the result given by Saez *et al.* (2009, p. 6).

den divided by the change in tax revenue. Hence:[8]

$$MWC = \frac{\eta\tau\gamma}{1-\tau-\eta\tau\gamma} \tag{12.28}$$

This expression is relevant only when the marginal tax rate is below the revenue-maximising rate in (12.22), so that $dR/d\tau > 0$.

The above discussion has ignored the possibility of shifting some income to another schedule where it is taxed at a lower rate. Suppose a proportion, s, of the reduction in declared income attracts a tax rate of $t < \tau$. It can then be shown that:[9]

$$\frac{dR}{d\tau} = N\left(\bar{z} - a_K\right)\left\{1 - \eta\gamma\left(\frac{\tau - st}{1-\tau}\right)\right\} \tag{12.29}$$

and:

$$MWC = \frac{\eta\gamma\left(\tau - st\right)}{1-\tau-\eta\gamma\left(\tau - st\right)} \tag{12.30}$$

Again this expression is relevant only for parameter values for which $dR/d\tau > 0$, that is for values of τ which are less than τ^*, given by:

$$\tau^* = \frac{1+st\gamma\eta}{1+\gamma\eta} \tag{12.31}$$

and which is higher than in (12.22).

Consider the effect of variations in the parameters in (12.30). Differentiating with respect to γ, τ and s gives the respective elasticities, $\varepsilon_{MWC,\gamma}$, $\varepsilon_{MWC,\tau}$ and $\varepsilon_{MWC,s}$, of the marginal welfare cost with respect to the parameter of interest as:

$$\varepsilon_{MWC,\gamma} = 1 + \gamma MWC \tag{12.32}$$

$$\varepsilon_{MWC,\tau} = \left(1 + \frac{1+\eta\gamma}{\eta\gamma}MWC\right)\left(\frac{\tau}{\tau - st}\right) \tag{12.33}$$

and:

$$\varepsilon_{MWC,s} = -\left(1 + MWC\right)\left(\frac{st}{\tau - st}\right) \tag{12.34}$$

[8]Saez *et al.* (2009, p. 6) call the MWC the 'marginal efficiency cost of funds (MECF)'. However, the 'marginal cost of funds', or MCF, is usually defined as $1+MWC$. On these concepts, see Creedy (1998a, pp. 54-59).

[9]See Saez *et al.* (2009, p. 9).

Table 12.1: Marginal Welfare Cost of Top Marginal Tax Rate

γ	s	t	τ	Elasticity of taxable income, η				
				0.2	0.4	0.6	0.8	1.0
1.6	0	0	0.3	0.159	0.378	0.699	1.215	2.182
1.6	0	0	0.4	0.271	0.744	1.778	5.818	
1.6	0	0	0.5	0.471	1.778	24.000		
1.6	0	0	0.6	0.923	24.000			
1.6	0.2	0.2	0.3	0.135	0.312	0.554	0.906	1.465
1.6	0.2	0.2	0.4	0.238	0.623	1.358	3.310	24.000
1.6	0.2	0.2	0.5	0.417	1.432	7.562		
1.6	0.2	0.2	0.6	0.812	8.615			
1.6	0.2	0.4	0.5	0.368	1.163	4.165		
1.6	0.2	0.4	0.6	0.712	4.952			
1.6	0.6	0.2	0.3	0.090	0.197	0.328	0.491	0.699
1.6	0.6	0.2	0.4	0.176	0.426	0.812	1.483	2.947
1.6	0.6	0.2	0.5	0.321	0.947	2.698	35.765	
1.6	0.6	0.2	0.6	0.623	3.310			
1.6	0.6	0.4	0.5	0.200	0.499	0.997	1.990	4.952
1.6	0.6	0.4	0.6	0.404	1.358	6.353		
1.6	0.8	0.2	0.3	0.068	0.147	0.238	0.344	0.471
1.6	0.8	0.2	0.4	0.147	0.344	0.623	1.049	1.778
1.6	0.8	0.2	0.5	0.278	0.771	1.880	6.716	
1.6	0.8	0.2	0.6	0.543	2.378			
1.6	0.8	0.4	0.5	0.130	0.299	0.528	0.855	1.358
1.6	0.8	0.4	0.6	0.289	0.812	2.049	8.615	
1.8	0.2	0.2	0.4	0.276	0.761	1.841	6.353	
1.8	0.2	0.2	0.5	0.495	1.962	155.255		
1.8	0.2	0.2	0.6	1.016				
1.8	0.2	0.4	0.5	0.433	1.530	9.776		
1.8	0.2	0.4	0.6	0.880	14.625			
1.8	0.6	0.3	0.4	0.152	0.359	0.656	1.119	1.941
1.8	0.6	0.3	0.5	0.299	0.855	2.238	11.755	
1.8	0.6	0.3	0.6	0.608	3.098			
1.8	0.6	0.4	0.5	0.230	0.598	1.281	2.981	14.625
1.8	0.6	0.4	0.6	0.479	1.841	34.715		
1.8	0.8	0.2	0.3	0.078	0.168	0.276	0.404	0.563
1.8	0.8	0.2	0.4	0.168	0.404	0.761	1.358	2.571
1.8	0.8	0.2	0.5	0.324	0.959	2.765	47.077	
1.8	0.8	0.2	0.6	0.656	3.808			

Furthermore, given the symmetry involved, the elasticity, $\varepsilon_{MWC,t}$, takes the same form as (12.34) but with s replaced by t. Hence the marginal welfare cost unambiguously rises when τ and γ increase, and falls when s and t fall. However, it is not immediately clear just how sensitive the MWC is to variations in these parameters. To give an indication of the sensitivity, illustrative examples are provided, using (12.30), in Table 12.1. Where there is no entry in a cell, this means that an increase in the marginal tax rate produces a reduction in revenue. This arises for many cases, and is more likely where the elasticity of taxable income is relatively high and the marginal tax rate is high.

The values of γ of 1.6 and 1.8 are around the typical values of γ found for industrialised countries. Many of the values of MWC are greater than unity – some substantially higher. It can also be seen from the table that the marginal welfare cost arising from the top marginal income tax rate can be highly sensitive to the value of that rate. For example, if the elasticity of taxable income is $\eta = 0.4$ and $\gamma = 1.6$, a change in the tax rate from 0.5 to 0.6, when $s = t = 0$, raises the marginal welfare cost from 1.778 to 24. When $s = t = 0.2$ the same tax rate change involves an increase in the marginal welfare cost from 1.432 to 8.615, showing not only the sensitivity to the tax rate but the effect of shifting some of the income to a taxed source, though at a lower rate. This sensitivity is increased for the higher elasticity of taxable income of 0.6, where an increase in the tax rate is from 0.4 to 0.5: consider the cases where $\gamma = 1.6$ and $s = t = 0$ and $s = t = 0.2$, and in particular where $\gamma = 1.8$ and $s = t = 0.2$. The latter combination gives rise to welfare costs of 1.841 and 155.255 for tax rates of 0.4 and 0.5 respectively. This sensitivity must be borne in mind when considering empirical estimates of η, which are obviously subject to error.

12.4.2 All Tax Brackets

The same approach can be applied to any tax bracket in a multi-rate system. As mentioned above, in the kth tax bracket the marginal tax rate is τ_k, above the income threshold a_k, for $k = 1, ..., K$. For $a_k < z < a_{k+1}$ the tax paid at the rate τ_k is simply $\tau_k (z - a_k)$, and for $z > a_{k+1}$ the tax paid at that rate is $\tau_k (a_{k+1} - a_k)$. It is now necessary to define a set of terms, $\bar{z}_k$, which denotes the arithmetic mean declared income in the kth tax bracket. Furthermore, let γ_k be defined, following the previous discussion, as:

$$\gamma_k = \frac{\bar{z}_k}{\bar{z}_k - a_k} \tag{12.35}$$

Hence if $F(z)$ denotes the distribution function of taxable income, the total tax paid at the rate τ_k, denoted R_k, is given by:

$$R_k = \tau_k \int_{a_k}^{a_{k+1}} (z - a_k)\, dF(z) + \tau_k (a_{k+1} - a_k) \int_{a_{k+1}}^{\infty} dF(z) \tag{12.36}$$

Expanding terms, and letting $F_1(z)$ denote the first moment distribution function of z, and N the total population size:

$$\begin{aligned} \frac{R_k}{N} &= \tau_k \left[\bar{z} \left\{ F_1(a_{k+1}) - F_1(a_k) \right\} - a_k \left\{ F(a_{k+1}) - F(a_k) \right\} \right] \\ &\quad + \tau_k \left[(a_{k+1} - a_k) \left\{ 1 - F(a_{k+1}) \right\} \right] \end{aligned} \tag{12.37}$$

where $\bar{z}$ is the arithmetic mean of the complete distribution of z. The number of individuals with income in the kth tax bracket, N_k, is:

$$N_k = N \left\{ F(a_{k+1}) - F(a_k) \right\} \tag{12.38}$$

The number of people with income above the threshold a_{k+1}, that is the number above the kth tax bracket, N_{k+1}^{+}, is:

$$N_{k+1}^{+} = N \left\{ 1 - F(a_{k+1}) \right\} \tag{12.39}$$

Furthermore, if $\bar{z}_k$ denotes the arithmetic mean of z within the kth tax bracket, then:

$$\bar{z}_k = \frac{\bar{z} \left\{ F_1(a_{k+1}) - F_1(a_k) \right\}}{\left\{ F(a_{k+1}) - F(a_k) \right\}} \tag{12.40}$$

Thus revenue raised by the kth rate is:

$$R_k = \tau_k N_k \left(\bar{z}_k - a_k\right) + \tau_k N_{k+1}^{+} \left(a_{k+1} - a_k\right) \tag{12.41}$$

The change in tax revenue from a small change in τ_k is:

$$\frac{dR_k}{d\tau_k} = \frac{\partial R_k}{\partial \tau_k} + \frac{\partial R_k}{\partial \bar{z}_k}\frac{\partial \bar{z}_k}{\partial \tau_k} \tag{12.42}$$

The first term is the pure 'tax rate' effect while the second term is the 'tax base' effect of the tax rate change. Here:

$$\frac{\partial R_k}{\partial \tau_k} = N_k \left(\bar{z}_k - a_k\right) + N_{k+1}^{+} \left(a_{k+1} - a_k\right) \tag{12.43}$$

Furthermore, $\partial R_k / \partial \bar{z}_k = \tau_k N_k$, and if the elasticity of taxable income in the kth bracket is η_k:

$$\frac{\partial \bar{z}_k}{\partial \tau_k} = -\frac{\eta_k \bar{z}_k}{1 - \tau_k} \tag{12.44}$$

The revenue change thus becomes:

$$\frac{dR_k}{d\tau_k} = N_k \left(\bar{z}_k - a_k\right) \left\{1 - \eta_k \left(\frac{\bar{z}_k}{\bar{z}_k - a_k}\right) \left(\frac{\tau_k}{1 - \tau_k}\right)\right\} + N_{k+1}^{+} \left(a_{k+1} - a_k\right) \tag{12.45}$$

In considering the welfare change, allowance must be made for the income change of those above the threshold, a_{k+1}, though they do not experience a change in their effective marginal tax rate and there is no excess burden. For those with $a_k < z < a_{k+1}$, the welfare change is, as obtained above, given by $z_i - a_k$. Thus, writing $\gamma_k = \bar{z}_k / \left(\bar{z}_k - a_k\right)$, aggregate marginal excess burden is similar to the earlier result that:

$$MEB_k = N_k \left(\bar{z}_k - a_k\right) \frac{\eta_k \gamma_k \tau_k}{1 - \tau_k} \tag{12.46}$$

However, the marginal welfare cost becomes:

$$MWC_k = \frac{\eta_k \gamma_k \tau_k}{1 - \tau_k - \eta_k \gamma_k \tau_k + D_k} \tag{12.47}$$

where:

$$D_k = \frac{N_{k+1}^{+}}{N_k} \left(\frac{a_{k+1} - a_k}{\bar{z}_k - a_k}\right) \left(1 - \tau_k\right) \tag{12.48}$$

and substitution gives:

$$D_k = \frac{(1-\tau_k)(a_{k+1}-a_k)\{1-F(a_{k+1})\}}{\bar{z}\{F_1(a_{k+1})-F_1(a_k)\}-a_k\{F(a_{k+1})-F(a_k)\}} \tag{12.49}$$

The result for the top marginal rate is thus simply the special case where $a_{K+1} = \infty$ and $F(a_{K+1}) = F_1(a_{K+1}) = 1$, so that $D_K = 0$. If there is no tax-free threshold in the income tax structure, so that $a_1 = 0$, it can be seen that $\gamma_1 = 1$ and $D_1 = [(1-\tau_1)a_2\{1-F(a_2)\}] / \{\bar{z}F_1(a_2)\}$. Consider the effect of changing the tax rate in the kth bracket. This gives rise to an elasticity, $\varepsilon_{MWC_k,\tau_k}$, of:

$$\varepsilon_{MWC_k,\tau_k} = \left\{1 + \left(\frac{1+\eta\gamma_k-\xi_k}{\eta\gamma_k}\right) MWC_k\right\} \tag{12.50}$$

where $\xi_k = (a_{k+1}-a_k)\{1-F(a_{k+1})\}$. This suggests that changes in welfare costs resulting from increases in marginal tax rates are proportionately smaller for the lower tax brackets, because a larger proportion of the population, $\{1-F(a_{k+1})\}$, is above the upper threshold of the lower brackets.

To give an idea of variations, consider a tax structure having four (positive) tax brackets, with thresholds of \$5,000, \$15,000, \$50,000 and \$75,000 and marginal rates of 0.15, 0.20, 0.30 and 0.35. Unlike the case where only the top marginal rate is considered, where a value of γ_K can simply be specified, it is necessary to have information about the nature of the income distribution over the whole range of incomes. Suppose for illustrative purposes that the distribution of taxable income is lognormally distributed with mean and variance of logarithms of 10 and 0.7 respectively. The latter value of 0.7 is the order of magnitude typically found for industrialised countries. The marginal welfare cost is given in Table 12.2 for each marginal tax rate, for values of the elasticity, η_k, varying from 0.1 to 0.9. The zero values for the top marginal rate appear because, for those values of η_k, a small increase in the tax rate actually reduces revenue. The effect of D_k in reducing the marginal welfare cost in the lower tax brackets – because it raises extra rev-

Table 12.2: Marginal Welfare Cost for Tax Brackets

Bracket	$\bar{z}_k$	γ_k	η_k	D_k	MWC_k
1	10201	1.961	0.1	3.884	0.006
			0.3		0.019
			0.5		0.032
			0.7		0.045
			0.9		0.059
2	27972	2.156	0.1	0.688	0.030
			0.3		0.095
			0.5		0.169
			0.7		0.255
			0.9		0.353
3	60445	5.787	0.1	1.302	0.095
			0.3		0.352
			0.5		0.765
			0.7		1.545
			0.9		3.555
4	115821	2.837	0.1	0	0.180
			0.3		0.846
			0.5		3.235
			0.7		–
			0.9		–

enue from those above the relevant brackets, without an associated excess burden – can clearly be seen from these results.

As anticipated, there are again combinations of values where the MWC values are highly sensitive to parameters. In particular, for the third and fourth tax brackets, small increases in the elasticity of taxable income give rise to large changes in the welfare costs. The sensitivity to changes in the tax rate in the different tax brackets, mentioned above, is shown as follows. Suppose that the tax rate in the bottom tax bracket is increased by 0.02 (that is, by two percentage points), the welfare costs for each of the elasticities become 0.007, 0.022, 0.037, 0.053 and 0.095 for the five elasticities η_k varying from 0.1 to 0.9 respectively; these are only slightly larger than the values shown in Table 12.2. However, if the rate in the third tax bracket is increased by 0.02, the corresponding marginal welfare costs become 0.105, 0.400, 0.909, 1.999 and 5.991 respectively. These bigger differences arise not only because of the smaller proportion of people above the respective tax bracket, but also because of the wider spread between upper and lower income thresholds for the higher tax brackets, as both terms affect the value of ξ_k. However, an increase in each of the tax thresholds by $500 was found to have little effect on the welfare costs, for each of the tax brackets.

Furthermore, the effect of varying the variance of logarithms is not obvious. Calculations (not reported here) show that if the variance of logarithms of income is instead 0.5, rather than 0.7, most values are similar to those in the table except that the marginal welfare cost in the top tax bracket for $\eta = 0.5$ becomes very high at 33.422.

Finally, if a proportion, s, of the income reduction is actually shifted to another source which attracts a tax rate of t, the marginal welfare cost becomes:

$$MWC_k = \frac{\eta_k \gamma_k (\tau_k - st)}{1 - \tau_k - \eta_k \gamma_k (\tau_k - st) + D_k} \tag{12.51}$$

with D_k as defined above.

12.5 Estimation Methods

This section turns to methods of estimating the taxable income elasticity. Here it is important to recognise that some changes in declared income may have arisen from a variety of non-tax-related dynamic factors, but there is a danger of attributing all changes in declared income to marginal tax changes and supply-side adjustments. In addition, some observed responses to tax changes may involve mainly the timing of declarations, particularly in anticipation of announced changes taking effect.

The following discussion is in the context of the commonly used reduced form discussed above, in which the elasticity is constant. Let z_{it} and z_{0it} denote declared income of person i at time t and the income which would be declared in the absence of taxation. Furthermore, τ_{it} is the marginal tax rate facing individual i at time t, given by $dT(z_{it})/dz_{it}$ where $T(z)$ is the tax function. Thus:

$$z_{it} = z_{0it}(1 - \tau_{it})^{\eta} \tag{12.52}$$

The further assumption is made that the elasticity η is the same for all individuals in the relevant population group considered. Given information about z_{it} and τ_{it} for a group of individuals, a simple regression of $\log z_{it}$ on $\log(1 - \tau_{it})$ and a constant, thereby omitting the unobservable z_{0it}, cannot be expected to provide a useful estimate of η, since the omitted variable is correlated with τ_{it}.

Subsection 12.5.1 considers estimation using information about declared incomes and marginal tax rates before and after a policy change. Some individuals also experience marginal rate changes as a result of 'fiscal drag', when the lack of adjustment to income tax thresholds during periods of inflation means that they move into higher tax brackets. The use of this kind of information to estimate the elasticity of taxable income is discussed in subsection 12.5.2.

12.5.1 Policy Changes

One approach is to consider actual policy changes in the tax structure, and situations in which a relatively small group of individuals is affected by the tax change, using information before and after the policy change. For example, suppose there is a change in only one marginal rate, say the top marginal income tax rate, which has no effect on individuals subject to lower rates. Let P_t denote the share of income of the affected group at time t, and their average marginal tax rate at t is τ_{Pt}. Let $t = 0$ and $t = 1$ denote pre- and post-change periods. Assuming that in the absence of the tax change the share of income in the relevant group would have remained constant, an estimate, $\hat{\eta}$, can be obtained using:

$$\hat{\eta} = \frac{\log P_1 - \log P_0}{\log(1 - \tau_{P1}) - \log(1 - \tau_{P0})} \tag{12.53}$$

However, results have been found to be sensitive to the period and tax reform examined. Given a time series of cross-sections over a longer period, an alternative estimate can be obtained by running the regression:

$$\log P_t = \eta \log(1 - \tau_{Pt}) + \varepsilon_t \tag{12.54}$$

where ε_t is assumed to have the usual properties. However, income shares may change over time for non-tax-related reasons. This difficulty may be overcome in some cases by including a time trend on the right hand side of (12.54).

A further approach involves using a difference-in-difference framework with panel data. However, the 'control' and 'treatment' groups cannot be identified in the usual way since in the present context they are defined by income. Suppose that the treatment group, T, comprises the top $P1$ percentile of the income distribution and the control group, C, is made up of individuals in the next $P2$ percentile. Being in the treatment group clearly depends on the behaviour and characteristics of taxpayers. The tax policy change is from period 0 to period 1, and let $E(.)$ denote the respective sample average. The appropriate difference between groups in the differences between average log-taxable income from one period to the next, denoted $\Delta \log z$, is given by:

$$\Delta \log z = \{E(\log z_{i1}| T) - E(\log z_{i0}| T)\} - \{E(\log z_{i1}| C) - E(\log z_{i0}| C)\} \tag{12.55}$$

The difference between groups in the differences between the logarithm of average net-of-tax rates from one period to the next, denoted $\Delta \log(1 - \tau)$, is given by:

$$\begin{aligned}\Delta \log(1-\tau) &= \{E(\log(1-\tau_{i1})|T) - E(\log(1-\tau_{i0})|T)\} \\ &\quad - \{E(\log(1-\tau_{i1})|C) - E(\log(1-\tau_{i0})|C)\}\end{aligned} \tag{12.56}$$

The estimate of the elasticity of taxable income, $\hat{\eta}$, can be obtained using:

$$\hat{\eta} = \frac{\Delta \log z}{\Delta \log(1-\tau)} \tag{12.57}$$

Again, this involves an assumption that without the policy change the incomes of the two groups would have grown at the same rate. In addition, the elasticity of taxable income is assumed to be the same for both groups. In practice, income changes occur for non-tax reasons, in particular the process of relative income changes from year to year may well display some 'regression towards the mean'.[10]

12.5.2 Fiscal Drag and Marginal Rate Changes

The difference-in-difference approach has also been applied in situations where there is no explicit policy change affecting the marginal tax rate faced by some individuals.[11] In particular, fiscal drag – whereby income tax thresholds are not adjusted in line with nominal income growth – gives rise to a general increase in average tax rates.[12] For those who are initially close to the upper income threshold of a marginal tax bracket, fiscal drag can shift

[10]If a long panel dataset is available, one approach is to regress $\log(z_{it+1}/z_{it})$ on $\log\{(1-\tau_{it+1})/(1-\tau_{it})\}$, the coefficient on this being η, along with controls to handle income movements.

[11]Saez (2009) has suggested another method using information about the bunching of individuals at the kinks of piecewise-linear budget constraints, created by increases in marginal rates at income thresholds. However, such kinks need not necessarily produce bunching, even if labour supply responses are significant, and modes in the distribution of income can occur at places other than kinks: see Creedy (2001b).

[12]In addition to income tax thresholds, the real value of other tax parameters (such as allowance and deduction limits) can fall during inflation, as examined by Onrubia and Sanz-Sanz (2009).

them into the next bracket and thus subject them to a higher marginal rate. Such individuals are regarded as being in the 'treatment' group. Those in the lower section of an income range do not face a higher marginal rate, as they do not cross a threshold, and are regarded as being in the 'control' group. The expression for $\hat{\eta}$ can thus be used in this context. This method can be used for each tax bracket.

Consider the situation where income growth differs between treatment and control groups. Suppose the incomes of the members of the control group (those who do not move into a higher tax bracket) grow at the rate, θ_C, while those of the treatment group (those who move into the next bracket) grow at the rate, θ_T. The two marginal tax rates in the respective tax brackets are τ_1 and τ_0. Hence the first term in the denominator of (12.57) is simply $\log\{(1-\tau_1)/(1-\tau_0)\}$ while the second term in the denominator is zero. Declared income is, as before, assumed to be generated by the reduced-form expression, $z = z_0(1+\tau)^\eta$. The income that would be declared in the absence of taxation, z_0, remains unchanged, by assumption. The second term in the numerator of (12.57) becomes $\log(1+\theta_C)$ because there is no change in the tax rate facing members of that group. The first term in the numerator becomes $\eta\log\{(1-\tau_1)/(1-\tau_0)\} + \log(1+\theta_T)$. Thus, substituting in (12.57) gives:

$$\hat{\eta} = \eta + \frac{\log\{(1+\theta_T)/(1+\theta_C)\}}{\log\{(1-\tau_1)/(1-\tau_0)\}} \tag{12.58}$$

This shows that $\hat{\eta}$ provides an unbiased estimate of η only if $\theta_C = \theta_T$, so that the incomes of all members of the tax bracket grow at the same rate. The bias arises because any difference in growth rates in the different income ranges is attributed to the effects of the difference in marginal tax rates. Hence where $\theta_T > \theta_C$, the larger growth of the target group (those crossing the tax threshold) leads to a negative bias in estimating the elasticity of taxable income. Conversely, if the incomes in the higher ranges of the tax bracket grow more slowly than in the lower ranges, too much of the change is attributed to the higher marginal tax rate and there is a positive bias.

Some illustrative examples are shown in Table 12.3, showing that the bias is higher, the smaller is the difference between the marginal tax rates and the larger is the proportional difference between growth rates. The bias can be substantial, bearing in mind the sensitivity of excess burdens to the value of η. In practice there is a dispersion of growth rates among individuals. Any independent evidence regarding differences in relative income movements over time can therefore be helpful in obtaining some idea of the size of the second term in (12.58).

Table 12.3: Fiscal Drag and Bias in Estimation of Elasticity η

θ_C	$\theta_T - \theta_C$	τ_0	$\tau_1 - \tau_0$	Bias
0.10	0.01	0.35	0.05	−0.113
0.10	0.03	0.35	0.05	−0.336
0.05	0.01	0.35	0.05	−0.118
0.05	0.03	0.35	0.05	−0.352
0.10	0.01	0.35	0.15	−0.034
0.10	0.03	0.35	0.15	−0.103
0.05	0.01	0.35	0.15	−0.036
0.05	0.03	0.35	0.15	−0.107
0.10	0.01	0.30	0.05	−0.122
0.10	0.03	0.30	0.05	−0.363
0.05	0.01	0.30	0.05	−0.128
0.05	0.03	0.30	0.05	−0.380
0.10	0.01	0.30	0.15	−0.038
0.10	0.03	0.30	0.15	−0.112
0.05	0.01	0.30	0.15	−0.039
0.05	0.03	0.30	0.15	−0.117

12.6 Conclusions

This chapter has provided an introduction to the concept of the elasticity of taxable income, with respect to changes in the net-of-tax marginal tax rate. This involves a reduced-form approach to modelling behavioural responses to income taxation, in which all the potential types of adjustment (in addition to the familiar labour supply response) are summarised by the elasticity of taxable income. This approach appears to offer a great deal. Without any need to consider, for example, the highly complex nonlinear tax and transfer systems in operation and the associated corner solutions, the often complex rules regarding the use of different tax schedules (relating to different income sources) and the nature of individuals' preferences which are likely to display considerable heterogeneity, the responses are described by a single parameter. Furthermore, a simple expression can be obtained for the marginal welfare cost of taxation, applying to a group of individuals without any aggregation complexities.

The attraction of a reduced-form specification of taxable income in terms of the marginal tax rate, and very few other variables, is clear. It means that, if interest relates only to aggregate responses, there is no need to invest in the production of large-scale tax models allowing for endogenous labour supply. Such models require large data sets and deal with the full complexity of tax and transfer systems and population heterogeneity, along with the estimation of preference functions. They need to overcome the complexities of producing welfare change measures. In contrast, the elasticity approach offers the simplicity of dealing with all adjustment margins in one single elasticity and produces a simple measure of marginal welfare cost per dollar.

However, much care is needed. In this introduction, emphasis has been placed on the assumptions underlying the approach, particularly with regard to welfare measurement, and the sensitivity of results to changes in some of the underlying parameters. It has been seen that very strong assumptions are needed to obtain the convenient welfare results: in particular it is necessary to assume that there are no income effects arising from tax changes and that, with the group examined, all individuals have the same elasticity. In using a constant elasticity reduced-form specification, a particular quasi-linear utility specification is needed. In addition, when estimating the elasticity, it was suggested that it is often very difficult to isolate those income changes, resulting from adjustments to tax rate changes, from changes which may arise for other reasons. Care is also needed when making inferences about welfare costs, in view of the considerable sensitivity of those costs, over certain ranges, to values of the elasticity of taxable income.

A further word of caution is also needed regarding the use of the elasticity concept. While labour supply responses can be regarded as depending on individuals' preferences and their personal circumstances, it is important to recognise that many features involved in the other components of the elasticity of taxable income are substantially affected by the details of tax regulations. These clearly differ among countries. This dependence on tax regulations also means that policy changes affecting tax rules can have important implications for the elasticity of taxable income, and hence also for optimal tax rates. For example, the finding that welfare costs are high may lead to modification of certain tax regulations, which make income shifting relatively easy, rather than changes in the tax rate structure. The elasticity should not therefore be regarded as a fixed parameter, but one which is itself subject to modification through careful policy design.

Chapter 13

Changes in Income Tax Revenue

The aim of this chapter is to show how the change in income tax revenue – at individual and aggregate levels – as a consequence of a marginal rate change can be decomposed into several effects. The decomposition is useful for revenue forecasting purposes and in contexts where revenue changes form one component of a larger economic model. First, in elasticity terms there is the obvious *ceteris paribus* positive revenue effect of a rate rise which depends (at the individual level) only on the tax structure: this is the *partial* elasticity of revenue with respect to the relevant tax rate. Second there is a negative effect arising from behavioural responses. This latter effect can itself be divided into two multiplicative influences. The elasticity of taxable income – the response of taxable income to a change in the marginal net-of-tax rate (one minus the marginal rate) – captures the net effect of all incentive effects associated with the marginal rate change: this was examined in chapter 12. In addition, the tax revenue elasticity – the elasticity of tax revenue with respect to a change in income – determines the consequent effect on revenue of the behavioural response: this was discussed in chapter 11.

The recognition of two basic effects of a rate rise is not of course new. Reference has long been made to 'tax base' and 'tax rate' effects of rate changes and, for example, behavioural and 'mechanical' effects of an increase in the top marginal tax rate in a multi-rate structure were distinguished by Saez (2004).[1] However, when discussing revenue changes resulting from marginal rate changes, the literature on the elasticity of taxable income has not identified the specific role of the revenue elasticity. The latter is the central concept in the literature on 'fiscal drag', which is concerned with the extent to which the non-indexation of tax thresholds leads to increasing average tax rates over time. In this context, the change in gross income is considered to be exogenous and any consequent feedback disincentive effect on income arising from the change in the average tax rate is ignored. Indeed, at the individual level the literature concentrates on changes which do not involve a movement across tax thresholds, which would otherwise lead to a change in the marginal tax rate.[2]

Hence, in addition to the partial elasticity of revenue with respect to the relevant tax rate, one elasticity concerns the way tax revenue changes in response to exogenous income changes while the other elasticity measures the extent to which income declared for tax purposes adjusts when the income tax rate varies. The revenue elasticity is concerned only with the nature of the income tax structure itself and, when considering aggregation over individuals, the form of the income distribution. The elasticity of taxable income is concerned with a wide range of behavioural adjustments associated with tax rate changes, captured in a single measure. Hence there is no direct connection between the two elasticity concepts. It is shown below how the revenue elasticity has a clear role at the individual level in influencing the change in tax resulting from a rate change. In considering aggregate revenue

[1]Changes in total tax obtained from the top marginal rate are also examined in Saez *et al.* (2009), in the course of deriving the aggregate excess burden. Following Saez, the two components were also discussed by, for example, Giertz (2009).

[2]In simulations generating aggregate elasticities from individual elasticities, care is also needed to avoid such movements because they can involve huge individual revenue elasticities for tiny changes in gross income. Labour supply incentive effects, in the context of the revenue elasticity with respect to wage rate changes, are examined by Creedy and Gemmell (2005).

over all individuals, changes are shown to depend on the revenue elasticity at the arithmetic mean income level within each tax bracket in a multi-rate income tax structure. The restriction of previous analyses to the top marginal rate also involves a substantial simplification. The present paper extends the treatment to deal with changes resulting from any tax rate, and thereby also deals with simultaneous changes in all tax rates.

The aim of this chapter is to explore the precise relationships among the various elasticities for the tax functions mentioned above. Section 13.1 examines the individual tax revenue elasticity and the individual elasticity of taxable income. It explores the way in which these elasticities combine to determine the elasticity of tax with respect to a change in the marginal tax rate. Section 13.2 looks at aggregation over individuals when a single marginal rate changes in a multi-rate tax structure. To illustrate the orders of magnitude involved section 13.2 applies the aggregate analysis to the New Zealand income tax system. The New Zealand government's May 2010 Budget involved changes to all marginal income tax rates while holding all thresholds constant. Analytical results for the effects of changes in income thresholds are examined in section 13.3.

13.1 Relationships Among Elasticities

This section demonstrates, at the individual level, how the revenue elasticity and the elasticity of taxable income combine to generate the elasticity of tax with respect to the marginal rate. In this section, the distinction between gross income and taxable income is ignored, though this distinction is likely to be important for countries with extensive income tax deductions.[3]

The literature on the tax revenue elasticity concentrates on the effects

[3] For discussion of the empirical importance of income-related deductions in personal income tax regimes in OECD countries, see Caminada and Goudswaard (1996) and Wagstaff and van Doorslaer (2001). For the US, Feldstein (1999, p. 675) estimated that total income tax deductions in 1993 amounted to about 60 per cent of estimated taxable income.

of changes in taxation resulting from exogenous changes in taxable income, with tax rates and thresholds held constant.[4] Furthermore, it is usual to assume that the exogenous change in income does not cause the individual to move into a higher tax bracket. Such a movement, where the tax function involves discrete changes in marginal rates, gives rise to a large jump in the elasticity, and this can – when carrying out appropriately tax-share weighted aggregation – distort the aggregate elasticity.

Suppose the multi-step tax function depends on a set of income threshold, $a_k, ..., a_K$, and a corresponding set of marginal tax rates $\tau_k, ..., \tau_K$. The tax paid by an individual with income of y is $T(y) = T(y|\, \tau_1, ..., \tau_K, a_1, ..., a_K)$. The individual revenue elasticity, $\eta_{T,y}$, is thus defined as:

$$\eta_{T,y} = \frac{dT}{dy}\frac{y}{T} \tag{13.1}$$

and is given by the ratio of the marginal tax rate to the average tax rate faced by the individual. The following uses the general notation, $\eta_{b,a} = \frac{a}{b}\frac{db}{da}$, to denote a 'total' elasticity, and $\eta'_{b,a} = \frac{a}{b}\frac{\partial b}{\partial a}$, to denote a partial elasticity. The revenue elasticity (where a tax threshold is not crossed) thus has the property that $\eta_{T,y} = \eta'_{T,y}$.

The above multi-step function can be written as:[5]

$$\begin{aligned} T(y) &= \tau_1 (y - a_1) & & a_1 < y \leq a_2 \\ &= \tau_1 (a_2 - a_1) + \tau_2 (y - a_2) & & a_2 < y \leq a_3 \end{aligned} \tag{13.2}$$

and so on. If y falls into the kth tax bracket, so that $a_k < y \leq a_{k+1}$, $T(y)$ can be expressed for $k \geq 2$ as:

$$T(y) = \tau_k (y - a_k) + \sum_{j=1}^{k-1} \tau_j (a_{j+1} - a_j) \tag{13.3}$$

[4]The restriction to exogenous income changes is easily controlled in considering individual elasticity values but of course the nature of the overall distribution of income, which is needed to obtain aggregate values, may well be influenced by the incentive effects of the consequent tax changes.

[5]The revenue elasticity properties of this function are examined in more detail in chapter 11 and in Creedy and Gemmell (2006).

This can be rewritten as:

$$T(y) = \tau_k (y - a_k^*) \tag{13.4}$$

where:

$$a_k^* = \frac{1}{\tau_k} \sum_{j=1}^{k} a_j (\tau_j - \tau_{j-1}) \tag{13.5}$$

and $\tau_0 = 0$. Thus the tax function facing any individual taxpayer in the kth bracket is equivalent to a tax function with a single marginal tax rate, τ_k, applied to income measured in excess of a single threshold, a_k^*. Therefore, unlike a_j, a_k^* differs across individuals depending on the marginal income tax bracket into which they fall. For this structure, and supposing that the income thresholds, a_k, remain fixed, the revenue elasticity is:

$$\begin{aligned} \eta_{T,y} &= \frac{y}{y - a_k^*} \\ &= 1 + \frac{a_k^*}{y - a_k^*} \end{aligned} \tag{13.6}$$

and the individual partial elasticity must exceed unity. Within each threshold (for which the marginal rate is fixed) the elasticity declines as income increases. As an individual crosses an income threshold, the revenue elasticity takes a discrete upward jump, before gradually declining again, as shown by the saw-tooth pattern in Figure 11.2.

For the multi-step function the partial individual elasticity, η'_{T,τ_j}, for $j < k$ (that is, for changes in marginal tax rates below the tax bracket in which the individual falls) is given by:

$$\eta'_{T,\tau_j} = \frac{\tau_j (a_{j+1} - a_j)}{T(y)} \tag{13.7}$$

which is simply the tax paid at the rate, τ_j, divided by total tax paid by the individual. Furthermore:

$$\eta'_{T,\tau_k} = \frac{\tau_k (y - a_k)}{T(y)} \tag{13.8}$$

Hence $\sum_{j=1}^{k} \eta'_{T,\tau_j} = 1$.

The individual elasticity of taxable income, $\eta_{y,1-\tau}$, measures the behavioural response of taxable income to a change in a marginal net-of-tax rate, $1-\tau$, facing the individual. This can be applied to any particular tax rate (not simply the rate corresponding to the tax bracket in which the individual's income falls), and a subscript is omitted here for convenience. This elasticity is positive, because increases in the net-of-tax rate are expected to lead to increases in y. In terms of the elasticity of taxable income with respect to the *tax rate*, this is:

$$\eta_{y,1-\tau} = -\left(\frac{1-\tau}{\tau}\right)\eta_{y,\tau} \tag{13.9}$$

Consider a change in the individual's tax liability resulting from an exogenous increase in one of the marginal tax rates (with other rates and the thresholds unchanged). This gives rise to a behavioural response, so that:

$$dT = \frac{\partial T}{\partial y}dy + \frac{\partial T}{\partial \tau}d\tau \tag{13.10}$$

From (13.10), dividing by $d\tau$ gives:

$$\frac{dT}{d\tau} = \frac{\partial T}{\partial \tau} + \frac{\partial T}{\partial y}\frac{dy}{d\tau} \tag{13.11}$$

and in terms of elasticities, this becomes:

$$\begin{aligned} \eta_{T,\tau} &= \eta'_{T,\tau} + \eta_{T,y}\eta_{y,\tau} \\ &= \eta'_{T,\tau} - \left(\frac{\tau}{1-\tau}\right)\eta_{T,y}\eta_{y,1-\tau} \end{aligned} \tag{13.12}$$

The first term may be said to reflect a pure 'tax rate' effect of a rate change, with unchanged incomes, while the second term reflects the combined 'tax base' effect, resulting from the incentive effects on taxable income, and the revenue consequences of that income change. When discussing the effect on total revenue of a change in the top income tax rate, Saez *et al.* (2009) refer to the tax rate effect as 'mechanical' and the second term as the 'behavioural' effect respectively. Thus, their 'behavioural effect' combines the revenue elasticity and elasticity of taxable income effects.[6]

Tax paid by the individual increases, when the marginal rate increases, only if:

$$\frac{1-\tau}{\tau} > \frac{\eta_{T,y}\eta_{y,1-\tau}}{\eta'_{T,\tau}} \tag{13.13}$$

Or, in terms of $\eta_{y,\tau}$, tax increases if:

$$\left(\eta_{T,y}\right)\left|\eta_{y,\tau}\right| < \eta'_{T,\tau} \tag{13.14}$$

In any progressive income tax structure, the revenue elasticity, $\eta_{T,y}$ exceeds 1, unless (as shown in the following section) allowances vary sufficiently with income. Equation (13.14) shows that, for the individual's tax liability to increase when τ increases, the combination of (absolute) elasticities must lie to the south west of a rectangular hyperbola, as shown in Figure 13.1. The nature of the tax structure determines the position of the byperbola (via the elasticity, $\eta'_{T,\tau}$) and the revenue elasticity (which in turn depends on the individual's income). It is of course expected that $\left|\eta_{y,\tau}\right|$ is non-zero only for a change in the marginal rate corresponding to the bracket in which the individual falls, otherwise a rate change affects only the average tax rate faced by the individual.

For the tax function considered here, appropriate substitution gives the result that the elasticity of revenue with respect to the marginal rate faced by an individual in the kth tax bracket is given by:

$$\eta_{T,\tau_k} = \eta'_{T,\tau_k} - \left(\frac{y}{y-a_k^*}\right)\left(\frac{\tau_k}{1-\tau_k}\right)\eta_{y,1-\tau_k} \tag{13.15}$$

The first term, $\eta'_{T,\tau_k} = \tau_k\left(y-a_k\right)/T\left(y\right)$, is the partial or mechanical 'tax rate effect' of the rate change, while the second term combines the behav-

[6] Saez *et al.* (2009, p. 5) do not discuss the separate role of the revenue elasticity in this context. Discussion of the rate and base effects is often discussed in the context of a simple proportional tax structure, with constant average and marginal rate, t, where the revenue elasticity is everywhere unity. Thus if $\bar{y}$ is arithmetic mean income, $\frac{dT}{dt} = \bar{y} + \frac{td\bar{y}}{dt}$ and in terms of elasticities, $\eta_{T,t} = 1 + \eta_{\bar{y},t}$.

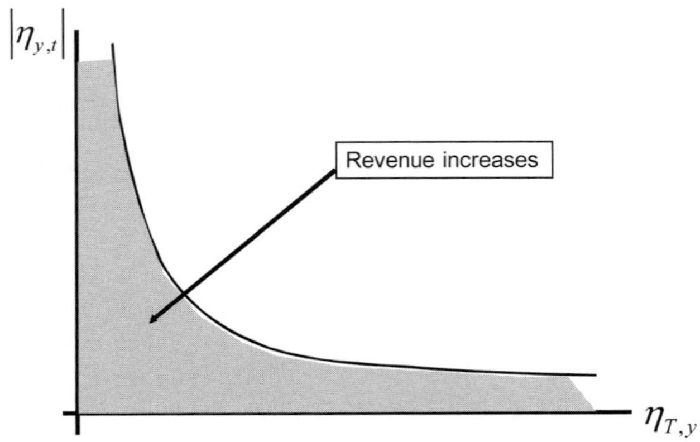

Figure 13.1: Revenue-Increasing Elasticity Combinations

ioural reduction in the tax base (via the individual elasticity of taxable income) with structural effect (via the individual revenue elasticity) to give the consequent effect on revenue.

13.1.1 Endogenous Allowances

Suppose that, instead of having only fixed income thresholds, there is a range of deductions which are income related. In the case of the multi-rate tax schedule discussed in the previous subsection, the deductions can be integrated into the income thresholds, a_k, which are then considered to adjust when income varies.

Consider first the revenue elasticity. In this case, again assuming that the individual does not cross into a higher-rate tax bracket when income increases, it can be shown that the total revenue elasticity is given by:

$$\eta_{T,y} = \eta'_{T,y} + \eta'_{T,a^*}\eta_{a^*,y} \tag{13.16}$$

where $\eta_{a^*,y}$ measures the extent to which the 'effective threshold', a^*, varies when income changes (a k subscript is suppressed here for convenience). In the case of the multi-rate schedule, the elasticity of tax with respect to the effective threshold, η'_{T,a^*}, is given by:

$$\eta'_{T,a^*} = -\frac{a^*}{y - a^*} \tag{13.17}$$

Hence:

$$\eta_{T,y} = \eta'_{T,y} \left(1 - \frac{a^*}{y}\eta_{a^*,y}\right) \tag{13.18}$$

Next, consider the elasticity of taxable income. With endogenous deductions, a modification must also be made to the expression given above for $\eta_{T,\tau}$, such that:

$$\begin{aligned} \eta_{T,\tau} &= \eta'_{T,\tau} + \eta'_{T,y}\eta_{y,\tau} + \eta'_{T,a^*}\eta_{a^*,\tau} \\ &= \eta'_{T,\tau} + \left(\eta'_{T,y} + \eta'_{T,a^*}\eta_{a^*,y}\right)\eta_{y,\tau} \end{aligned} \tag{13.19}$$

and using (13.9):

$$\eta_{T,\tau} = \eta'_{T,\tau} - \left(\frac{\tau}{1-\tau}\right)\left(\eta'_{T,y} + \eta'_{T,a^*}\eta_{a^*,y}\right)\eta_{y,1-\tau} \tag{13.20}$$

Hence the total effect on revenue as a result of a change in the marginal tax rate is modified by the endogenous effect of an income change on the deductions from gross income. Indeed, to the extent that an increase in the marginal tax rate reduces declared income, it also reduces the level of deductions claimed, so that the fall in tax revenue is not as large as it otherwise would be if deductions were fixed.

For the multi-rate schedule, appropriate substitution gives (again neglecting the k subscript), for the individual elasticity:

$$\eta_{T,\tau} = \eta'_{T,\tau} - \left(\frac{y}{y-a^*}\right)\left(\frac{\tau}{1-\tau}\right)\left(1 - \frac{a^*}{y}\eta_{a^*,y}\right)\eta_{y,1-\tau} \tag{13.21}$$

This can alternatively be expressed in terms of responses of ‘taxable income’,

$y_T = y - a^*$, as follows:

$$\begin{aligned}\eta_{T,\tau} &= \eta'_{T,\tau} - \left(\frac{\tau}{1-\tau}\right)\left(\frac{y}{y-a^*}\right)\left(\frac{d(y-a^*)}{dy}\right)\eta_{y,1-\tau} \\ &= \eta'_{T,\tau} - \left(\frac{\tau}{1-\tau}\right)\eta_{y_T,y}\eta_{y,1-\tau} \\ &= \eta'_{T,\tau} - \left(\frac{\tau}{1-\tau}\right)\eta_{y_T,1-\tau} \qquad (13.22)\end{aligned}$$

Hence the elasticity of interest, $\eta_{T,\tau}$, can be expressed simply in terms of the marginal tax rate, τ, and the responsiveness of *taxable* income, y_T, to the net-of-tax rate, $1 - \tau$.

13.2 Aggregate Revenue

For tax policy purposes attention is often devoted to aggregate revenue and its variation as component tax rates are changed. This section therefore examines aggregation over individuals. Emphasis is on the effect on total income tax revenue of a change in a single tax rate, and the effect of a simultaneous similar change in all rates. In order to obtain clear results, attention is restricted to the case of the multi-rate tax function. It is assumed that all individuals face the same income thresholds, so that endogenous allowances are not considered here. First, components of total revenue are examined in subsection 13.2.1. Aggregate elasticities are derived in subsection 13.2.2 and, in subsection 13.2.3, these are compared with an earlier result produced by Saez *et al.* (2009). The potential orders of magnitude involved are then examined in subsection 13.2.4.

13.2.1 Components of Total Revenue

When dealing with population aggregates it is necessary to distinguish various tax and revenue terms, for both clarity and succinctness. In the previous section, the tax liability facing an individual with an income of y was denoted by $T(y)$. In the multi-tax form, if y is in the kth tax bracket a distinction can be made between $T(y) = \tau_k (y - a_k^*)$ and the tax paid by the individual at the marginal rate, τ_k, thereby ignoring tax paid on income falling into lower thresholds.

For aggregate revenue amounts defined over populations, or population sub-groups, R is used. Thus in this section R represents aggregate revenue, while R_k refers to the aggregate revenue obtained from all individuals whose incomes fall in the kth tax bracket: that is, R_k is the aggregate over individuals in the kth bracket of $\tau_k (y - a_k^*)$ values. Let $R_{(k)}$ denote the aggregate amount raised only at the rate k from individuals who fall into the kth bracket: that is, $R_{(k)}$ is the sum over individuals in the kth bracket of $\tau_k (y - a_k)$ values. Furthermore, $R_{(k)}^+$ refers to the aggregate revenue obtained at the kth rate from individuals whose incomes fall into higher tax brackets: that is, $R_{(k)}^+$ is the number of all individuals in higher tax brackets multiplied by $\tau_k (a_{k+1} - a_k)$.

In the multi-step tax function with K brackets, suppose P_k people are in each bracket, for $k = 1, ..., K$, and the arithmetic mean income in each bracket is $\bar{y}_k$. Then aggregate revenue is:

$$
\begin{aligned}
R &= \sum_{k=1}^{K} R_k \\
&= \tau_1 (\bar{y}_1 - a_1) P_1 \qquad (13.23) \\
&\quad + \{\tau_2 (\bar{y}_2 - a_2) + \tau_1 (a_2 - a_1)\} P_2 \\
&\quad + \{\tau_3 (\bar{y}_3 - a_3) + \tau_1 (a_2 - a_1) + \tau_2 (a_3 - a_2)\} P_3 \\
&\quad + \text{and so on} \qquad (13.24)
\end{aligned}
$$

Let $P_k^+ \equiv \sum_{j=k+1}^{K} P_j$ denote the number of people above the kth tax bracket. For the top marginal rate, where $k = K$, clearly $P_K^+ = 0$. Thus aggregate revenue can be written more succinctly as:

$$R = \sum_{k=1}^{K} \tau_k (\bar{y}_k - a_k) P_k + \sum_{k=1}^{K-1} \tau_k (a_{k+1} - a_k) P_k^+ \qquad (13.25)$$

Thus, using $R^+_{(K)} = 0$:

$$R = \sum_{k=1}^{K} R_{(k)} + \sum_{k=1}^{K-1} R^+_{(k)} = \sum_{k=1}^{K} \left(R_{(k)} + R^+_{(k)} \right) \tag{13.26}$$

In this expression, $R_{(k)} + R^+_{(k)} \neq R_k$, although their sums over $k = 1, ..., K$ are equal.

13.2.2 Changes in Aggregate Revenue

First, it is useful to clarify the general relationship between the elasticity of aggregate revenue with respect to a single marginal rate change, and the elasticity with respect to changes in all rates. Suppose all marginal tax rates change, but income thresholds remain fixed. Totally differentiating R gives:

$$dR = \sum_{k=1}^{K} \frac{\partial R}{\partial \tau_k} d\tau_k \tag{13.27}$$

Hence if all rates change by the same proportion, $\partial \tau_k / \tau_k = d\tau / \tau$ for all k and:

$$\eta_{R,\tau} \equiv \frac{\tau}{R} \frac{dR}{d\tau} = \sum_{k=1}^{K} \frac{\tau_k}{R} \frac{\partial R}{\partial \tau_k} = \sum_{k=1}^{K} \eta'_{R,\tau_k} \tag{13.28}$$

Thus the elasticity of aggregate revenue with respect to a simultaneous equal proportional change in all tax rates is the sum of the separate elasticities, η'_{R,τ_k}, over all $k = 1, ..., K$.

Consider next the response of aggregate revenue to a change in the kth marginal tax rate. This has two basic components. First, there is the direct effect of the change in the kth tax rate on tax from that bracket alone. From previous sections above, this is made up of the behavioural effect of the tax rate change on the incomes of those in the kth bracket, along with the revenue elasticity effect (which is not a reflection of behaviour but depends on the tax structure). Second, there is an indirect effect on individuals in higher tax brackets, as a result of the term $\tau_k (a_{k+1} - a_k)$. Assume first that there are no behavioural responses. It can be seen that, letting $\eta'_{R,\tau_k} \equiv \frac{\tau_k}{R}\frac{\partial R}{\partial \tau_k}$:

$$\eta'_{R,\tau_1} = \frac{\tau_1}{R}\left\{(\bar{y}_1 - a_1) P_1 + (a_2 - a_1) P_1^+\right\} \tag{13.29}$$

$$\eta'_{R,\tau_2} = \frac{\tau_2}{R}\left\{(\bar{y}_2 - a_2) P_2 + (a_3 - a_2) P_2^+\right\} \tag{13.30}$$

and so on. Hence in general:

$$\eta'_{R,\tau_k} = \frac{\tau_k}{R}\left\{(\bar{y}_k - a_k) P_k + (a_{k+1} - a_k) P_k^+\right\} \tag{13.31}$$

For this 'no behavioural response' case, these elasticities sum to:

$$\eta_{R,\tau} = \sum_{k=1}^{K} \eta'_{R,\tau_k} = 1 \tag{13.32}$$

and the elasticity of total revenue with respect to an equal proportional change in all rates, in (13.28), is unity. Any behavioural response clearly reduces the elasticity below 1, as shown below.

In the case where there are behavioural effects of marginal rate changes, it is convenient to assume that all those in a given bracket have the same elasticity, η_{y,τ_k}. In this case, it can be shown that an appropriate adjustment to the average income level within the tax bracket gives:

$$\eta'_{R,\tau_k} = \frac{\tau_k}{R}\left[\left\{\bar{y}_k\left(1 + \eta_{y,\tau_k}\right) - a_k\right\} P_k + (a_{k+1} - a_k) P_k^+\right] \tag{13.33}$$

The expression in (13.33), while quite straightforward, does not bring out the separate elements influencing η'_{R,τ_k} in a transparent way. First, rewrite this as:

$$\eta'_{R,\tau_k} = \frac{\tau_k P_k}{R}\left[(\bar{y}_k - a_k) - \bar{y}_k\left(\frac{\tau_k}{1-\tau_k}\right)\eta_{y,1-\tau_k} + (a_{k+1} - a_k)\frac{P_k^+}{P_k}\right] \tag{13.34}$$

Then multiplying and dividing by $(\bar{y}_k - a_k^*)$ gives:

$$\eta'_{R,\tau_k} = \frac{R_k}{R}\left[\frac{R_{(k)} + R_{(k)}^+}{R_k} - \left(\frac{\bar{y}_k}{\bar{y}_k - a_k^*}\right)\left(\frac{\tau_k}{1-\tau_k}\right)\eta_{y,1-\tau_k}\right] \tag{13.35}$$

Hence, in the case where $\eta_{y,1-\tau_k} = 0$, the sum $\sum_{k=1}^{K} \eta'_{R,\tau_k}$ is, using (13.26), equal to 1, as in (13.32).

From equation (13.6), $\bar{y}_k / (\bar{y}_k - a_k^*)$ is the revenue elasticity at arithmetic mean income in the kth bracket. This expression therefore shows how the elasticity, η'_{R,τ_k}, depends on the elasticity of taxable income of those in the kth tax bracket, $\eta_{y,1-\tau_k}$, along with the revenue elasticity at $\bar{y}_k$, and various tax-share terms. Furthermore, it can be shown that $\eta'_{R,\tau_k} > 0$ if:

$$\eta_{y,1-\tau_k} < \left(\frac{1-\tau_k}{\tau_k}\right) \left[\bar{y}_k - a_k \left(1 + \frac{P_k^+}{P_k}\right) + a_{k+1} \left(\frac{P_k^+}{P_k}\right)\right] \frac{1}{\bar{y}_k} \qquad (13.36)$$

For the top bracket, the final term within square brackets in equation (13.36) is zero and the elasticity is positive if:

$$\eta_{y,1-\tau_K} < \left(\frac{1-\tau_K}{\tau_K}\right) \left(\frac{\bar{y}_K - a_K}{\bar{y}_K}\right) \qquad (13.37)$$

and although the first term in brackets exceeds 1 as long as the tax rate, τ_K, is less than 0.5, the second term in brackets is likely to be well below 1. Hence the elasticity of taxable income must be relatively low for a tax rate increase to increase aggregate revenue.

13.2.3 Comparison with Earlier Results

The above result for any tax rate in a multi-rate structure may be compared with that given by Saez *et al.* (2009, p. 5, equation 4) for the top marginal rate. They consider changes in taxation paid at the top rate only. When converted to the present notation and written in elasticity form, their result thus refers not to actual tax paid but to the elasticity of tax paid at the rate τ_K, which can be defined as $\eta'_{R(K),\tau_K}$. Hence:

$$\eta'_{R(K),\tau_K} = \left[1 - \left(\frac{\bar{y}_K}{\bar{y}_K - a_K}\right) \left(\frac{\tau_K}{1-\tau_K}\right) \eta_{y,1-\tau_K}\right] \qquad (13.38)$$

Saez *et al.* (2009) discuss the term $\bar{y}_K / (\bar{y}_K - a_K)$, which is constant if the income distribution above the top threshold follows the Pareto form. Their expression therefore does not indicate the separate role for the revenue elasticity at $\bar{y}_K$. Furthermore, their 'behavioural response' actually includes both the behavioural response and the revenue elasticity effect, which depends on the full tax structure as well as average income above the top threshold. It is useful to convert (13.38) into an expression which does separate these two elasticity effects, by writing:

$$\eta'_{R_{(K)},\tau_K} = \frac{R_K}{R_{(K)}} \left[\frac{R_{(K)}}{R_K} - \left(\frac{\bar{y}_K}{\bar{y}_K - a_K^*} \right) \left(\frac{\tau_K}{1-\tau_K} \right) \eta_{y,1-\tau_K} \right] \tag{13.39}$$

and remembering that $\bar{y}_K / (\bar{y}_K - a_K^*)$ is the revenue elasticity at $\bar{y}_K$.

From the general result above, the value of η'_{R,τ_K} is given by:

$$\eta'_{R,\tau_K} = \frac{R_K}{R} \left[\frac{R_{(K)}}{R_K} - \left(\frac{\bar{y}_K}{\bar{y}_K - a_K^*} \right) \left(\frac{\tau_K}{1-\tau_K} \right) \eta_{y,1-\tau_K} \right] \tag{13.40}$$

For comparison with (13.39), it is necessary to use the general relationship between $\eta'_{R_{(K)},\tau_K}$ and η'_{R,τ_K}. For the top rate, this takes the simple form:

$$\eta'_{R_{(K)},\tau_K} = \left(\frac{R}{R_{(K)}} \right) \eta'_{R,\tau_K} \tag{13.41}$$

Thus multiplication of (13.40) by $R/R_{(K)}$ gives the rearranged form of the Saez *et al.* result in (13.39). Hence, as expected, the Saez result is a special case of the more general result derived above. But instead of focussing on a term such as $\bar{y}_K / (\bar{y}_K - a_K)$, which depends purely on the form of the distribution of income, the present formulation emphasises the *joint* role of the elasticity of taxable income and the appropriate revenue elasticity (at the income level, $\bar{y}_K$), which depends on the nature of the tax function (the lower rates and thresholds, not simply the top threshold) as well as the income distribution (which, together with a_K, affects $\bar{y}_K$).

13.2.4 Illustrative Examples

In order to provide an illustration of the nature of the relationships involved and the sensitivity to variations in the elasticity of taxable income, it is useful to consider the change to the income tax structure in New Zealand, made in the 2010 Budget. Table 13.1 provides summary information regarding the distribution of annual personal taxable incomes in the 2008/09 tax year, the most recent year for which data are available.[7] For comparison purposes the tax rates and thresholds shown in the table relate to the structure in 2009/10. The overall arithmetic mean taxable income is $35,507.

Table 13.1: The Distribution of Taxable Income in New Zealand: 2008/09 Tax Year

k	a_k	$\bar{y}_k$	Prop. of people	Prop. of income
1	1	6,748.82	0.241	0.046
2	14,000	24,080.76	0.434	0.294
3	48,000	52,414.34	0.224	0.331
4	70,000	115,480.70	0.101	0.329

Table 13.2 provides summary information about the pre- and post-2010 Budget tax structures, for the taxable income distribution of Table 13.1. In the 2010 Budget, all the income thresholds were left unchanged, but the marginal tax rates were reduced, in particular the top marginal rate. Given the relatively low value of the income threshold above which the top rate applies, this tax bracket contributes a higher proportion of total income tax revenue than the other brackets, even though it contains only 10 per cent of taxpayers. This compares with the second tax bracket, which contains over 40 per cent of all taxpayers. The final column of the table reports the revenue elasticity, $\eta_{T,y}$, in each tax bracket, evaluated at arithmetic mean income within the bracket. For each tax structure, this elasticity is highest in the third tax bracket because the value of $\bar{y}_3$ is relatively closer to the effective income threshold, a_3^* than for the other brackets. For those in the first tax bracket, the average and marginal tax rates are equal and hence the revenue elasticity is unity. The Budget change in the marginal tax rates has

[7] The table is obtained from unpublished Inland Revenue Department data covering 3,304,210 individuals.

little effect on the revenue elasticities.

Table 13.2: The New Zealand Income Tax Structure Before and After the 2010 Budget

k	τ_k	a_k^*	R_k/P_k	R_k/R	$\eta_{T(\bar{y}_k),y}$
Tax rates pre-2010 Budget					
1	0.125	1.00	843.48	0.027	1.000
2	0.210	5667.26	3866.83	0.222	1.308
3	0.330	21060.99	10346.61	0.306	1.672
4	0.380	27500.33	33432.53	0.446	1.313
Tax rates post-2010 Budget					
1	0.105	1.00	708.52	0.026	1.000
2	0.175	5600.60	3234.03	0.217	1.303
3	0.300	23267.02	8744.20	0.303	1.798
4	0.330	27515.47	29028.52	0.454	1.313

Figures 13.2 and 13.3 show the variations in the elasticity, η'_{R,τ_k}, for each tax bracket, as the elasticity of taxable income, $\eta_{y,1-\tau}$, increases. As demonstrated above, the value of each η'_{R,τ_k} falls linearly with $\eta_{y,1-\tau}$, but the rate of decrease is less in the post-2010 Budget structure. In each case the elasticity, η'_{R,τ_k}, for the lowest income tax bracket remains approximately constant. Although the elasticity $\eta_{T(\bar{y}),y}$ is highest in the third tax bracket, the value of η'_{R,τ_k} falls slightly faster in the top marginal rate bracket. This is because the value of $\tau/(1-\tau)$ is higher for the higher marginal tax rate, along with the fact that the top-rate bracket contributes a higher proportion of aggregate tax revenue. The reduction in the higher marginal tax rates, resulting from the 2010 Budget, implies that the revenue elasticity, η'_{R,τ_k}, continues to be positive, for higher values of the elasticity of taxable income.

Some evidence regarding the elasticity of taxable income of New Zealand taxpayers is reported in Claus *et al.* (2010). They found that for those in the lower tax brackets, the estimated elasticities were very small, but for the top marginal tax rate the responses were substantial. For top-rate taxpayers, the values were mainly in the range 0.5 to 1.2.

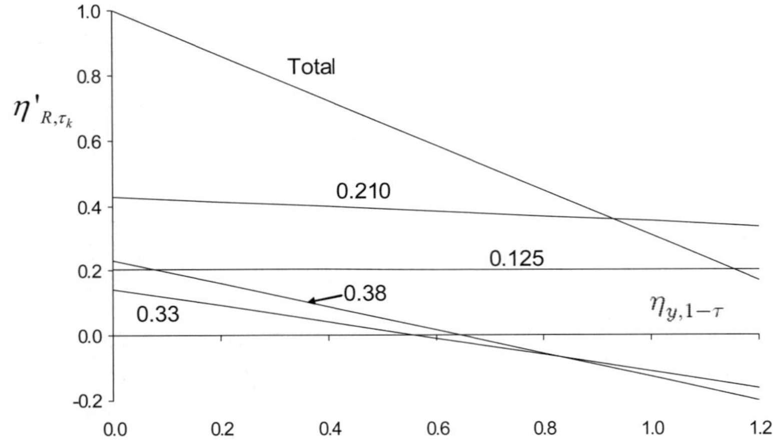

Figure 13.2: Elasticity of Total Tax Revenue wrt Tax Rates: Pre-2010 Budget

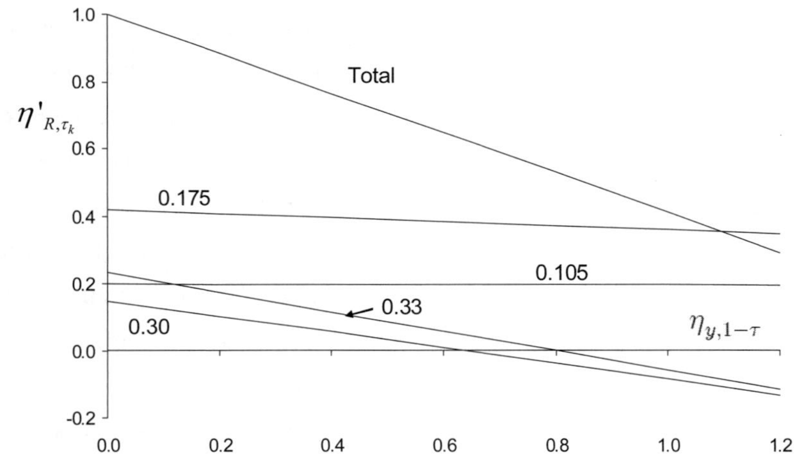

Figure 13.3: Elasticity of Total Tax Revenue wrt Tax Rates: Post-2010 Budget

13.3 Changes in Income Thresholds

This section considers the effect on total revenue of a small change in one of the thresholds. Differentiating (13.25) with respect to a_k gives:

$$\begin{aligned}\frac{\partial R}{\partial a_k} &= \tau_k\left(\bar{y}_k - a_k\right)\frac{\partial P_k}{\partial a_k} + \tau_k P_k\left(\frac{\partial \bar{y}_k}{\partial a_k} - 1\right) - \tau_k P_k^+ \\ &+\tau_{k-1}\left(\bar{y}_{k-1} - a_{k-1}\right)\frac{\partial P_{k-1}}{\partial a_k} + \tau_{k-1}P_{k-1}\frac{\partial \bar{y}_{k-1}}{\partial a_k} \\ &+\tau_{k-1}\left(a_k - a_{k-1}\right)\frac{\partial P_{k-1}^+}{\partial a_k} \end{aligned} \quad (13.42)$$

After some rearrangement, this can be expressed as:

$$\begin{aligned}\eta'_{R,a_k} &= -\frac{\tau_k a_k\left(P_k + P_k^+\right)}{R} + \frac{\tau_{k-1}\left(a_k - a_{k-1}\right)P_{k-1}^+}{R}\eta_{P_{k-1}^+,a_k} \\ &+\frac{\tau_k(\bar{y}_k - a_k)P_k}{R}\left[\eta_{P_k,a_k} + \frac{\bar{y}_k}{\bar{y}_k - a_k}\eta_{\bar{y}_k,a_k}\right] \\ &+\frac{\tau_{k-1}(\bar{y}_{k-1} - a_{k-1})P_{k-1}}{R}\left[\eta_{P_{k-1},a_k} + \frac{\bar{y}_{k-1}}{\bar{y}_{k-1} - a_{k-1}}\eta_{\bar{y}_{k-1},a_k}\right] \end{aligned} \quad (13.43)$$

where the various elasticities on the right hand side are understood to be partial elasticities. Using the various definitions of revenue terms, η'_{R,a_k} can be expressed as:

$$\begin{aligned}\eta'_{R,a_k} &= -\frac{\tau_k a_k\left(P_k + P_k^+\right)}{R} + \frac{R_{(k-1)}^+}{R}\eta_{P_{k-1}^+,a_k} \\ &+\frac{R_{(k)}}{R}\left[\eta_{P_k,a_k} + \left(\frac{\bar{y}_k}{\bar{y}_k - a_k}\right)\eta_{\bar{y}_k,a_k}\right] \\ &+\frac{R_{(k-1)}}{R}\left[\eta_{P_{k-1},a_k} + \left(\frac{\bar{y}_{k-1}}{\bar{y}_{k-1} - a_{k-1}}\right)\eta_{\bar{y}_{k-1},a_k}\right] \end{aligned} \quad (13.44)$$

The term, $\tau_k a_k\left(P_k + P_k^+\right)$ can be interpreted as the tax that would be raised on an income equal to $y = a_k$, at the rate τ_k, from those in and above tax bracket k, considered as a proportional tax. Alternatively, this term can be rewritten as:

$$\tau_k a_k\left(P_k + P_k^+\right) = R_{(k)} + R_{(k)}^+ - \tau_k\left(\bar{y}_k P_k + a_{k+1}P_k^+\right) \quad (13.45)$$

where the term $\tau_k\left(\bar{y}_k P_k + a_{k+1} P_k^+\right)$ is the tax that would be raised at the rate, τ_k, from all those in and above the kth bracket, if the tax is considered to be proportional for $y < a_{k+1}$. The term $\frac{\bar{y}_k}{\bar{y}_k - a_k}$ is the revenue elasticity at $\bar{y}_k$ if the tax is considered to have a single threshold at a_k. When the threshold, a_k, is increased, the number of those in the kth bracket falls as a result of some individuals near the threshold moving into the lower tax bracket, where the marginal tax rate is lower. The second line of the expression above is the change in revenue due to those shifting out of the bracket above a_k, as a result of the change in a_k, and the third line is the change in revenue due to those shifting into the bracket below a_k.

Yet another way to write this is:

$$\begin{aligned}
\eta'_{R,a_k} = & -\frac{\tau_k a_k P_k}{R} - \frac{\tau_k a_k P_k^+}{R} \\
& + \frac{R^+_{(k-1)}}{R} \eta_{P^+_{k-1},a_k} \\
& + \frac{R_{(k)}}{R}\left[\eta_{P_k,a_k} + \left(\frac{\bar{y}_k}{\bar{y}_k - a_k}\right)\eta_{\bar{y}_k,a_k}\right] \\
& + \frac{R_{(k-1)}}{R}\left[\eta_{P_{k-1},a_k} + \left(\frac{\bar{y}_{k-1}}{\bar{y}_{k-1} - a_{k-1}}\right)\eta_{\bar{y}_{k-1},a_k}\right]
\end{aligned} \tag{13.46}$$

The first line represents simple 'direct' effects on those in the kth bracket and above it. If the numbers of people were actually unchanged, these terms reflect the fact that less income is subject to τ_k. The units of the numerators in each term are revenue, so the terms are 'unit free' as required of an elasticity. The second line reflects the fact that fewer people are above the $(k-1)$th tax bracket: all those people pay tax at the rate τ_{k-1} on their income that lies between the income thresholds, so their actual income (which does not change, on the assumption that it responds only to marginal rate changes, and not average rate changes) is not relevant. The third line reflects the fact that there is movement out of the bracket, and that the average income of those remaining in the kth bracket changes (as a result of the reduced number of people in the bracket as those close to the threshold move into the lower bracket). The final line reflects the increased number of people in the $(k-1)$th tax bracket and the change in average income in that bracket. The latter results not only from the extra people who were previously just above the threshold, but from a behavioural response as they experience a lower marginal tax rate.

Finally, it is possible to express the various terms, involving changes in the Ps, in terms of the distribution of taxable income. Let $f(y)$ denote the density function of income, and let $F(y)$ denote the corresponding distribution function. Then:

$$P_k = N \int_{a_k}^{a_{k+1}} f(y)\,dy = N\{F(a_{k+1}) - F(a_k)\} \tag{13.47}$$

$$P_{k-1} = N \int_{a_{k-1}}^{a_k} f(y)\,dy = N\{F(a_k) - F(a_{k-1})\} \tag{13.48}$$

$$P_{k-1}^{+} = N \int_{a_k}^{\infty} f(y)\,dy = N\{1 - F(a_k)\} \tag{13.49}$$

Hence the required derivatives are $\frac{\partial P_k}{\partial a_k} = -Nf(a_k)$, $\frac{\partial P_{k-1}}{\partial a_k} = Nf(a_k)$ and $\frac{\partial P_{k-1}^{+}}{\partial a_k} = -Nf(a_k)$. Appropriate substitution gives the elasticities as:

$$\eta_{P_k,a_k} = \frac{-a_k f(a_k)}{F(a_{k+1}) - F(a_k)} \tag{13.50}$$

$$\eta_{P_{k-1},a_k} = \frac{a_k f(a_k)}{F(a_k) - F(a_{k-1})} \tag{13.51}$$

$$\eta_{P_{k-1}^{+},a_k} = \frac{-a_k f(a_k)}{1 - F(a_k)} \tag{13.52}$$

Furthermore, the arithmetic mean taxable income in the kth tax bracket, $\bar{y}_k$, is given by:

$$\bar{y}_k = \frac{\int_{a_k}^{a_{k+1}} y f(y)\,dy}{\int_{a_k}^{a_{k+1}} f(y)\,dy} = \frac{\bar{y}\{F_1(a_{k+1}) - F_1(a_k)\}}{F(a_{k+1}) - F(a_k)} \tag{13.53}$$

Hence:

$$\frac{\partial \bar{y}_k}{\partial a_k} = \frac{-\bar{y} a_k f(a_k)}{F(a_{k+1}) - F(a_k)} + \frac{\bar{y} f(a_k)\{F_1(a_{k+1}) - F_1(a_k)\}}{\{F(a_{k+1}) - F(a_k)\}^2} \tag{13.54}$$

and the elasticity is given by:

$$\eta_{\bar{y}_k,a_k} = -\frac{-a_k f(a_k)}{F(a_{k+1}) - F(a_k)} \left[a_k \left(\frac{\bar{y}}{\bar{y}_k} \right) - \frac{\bar{y} \{ F_1(a_{k+1}) - F_1(a_k) \}}{\{ F(a_{k+1}) - F(a_k) \}} \right] \quad (13.55)$$

Hence:

$$\eta_{\bar{y}_k,a_k} = -\eta_{P_k,a_k} \left[a_k \left(\frac{\bar{y}}{\bar{y}_k} \right) - \bar{y}_k \right] \quad (13.56)$$

Similarly, it can be shown that:

$$\eta_{\bar{y}_{k-1},a_k} = \eta_{\bar{y},a_k} + \eta_{P_{k-1},a_k} \left[a_k \left(\frac{\bar{y}}{\bar{y}_{k-1}} \right) - \bar{y}_{k-1} \right] \quad (13.57)$$

The first term here allows for the possibility that $\bar{y}$ changes as a result of the fact that those who move into the lower tax bracket, when a_k increases, may respond to the lower marginal tax rate. This is likely to be very small, particularly for a small threshold change.

13.4 Conclusions

This chapter has examined the joint role of the elasticity of taxable income (which refers to the effect on taxable income of a marginal tax rate rise) and the revenue elasticity (which reflects the effect on revenue of a change in taxable income) in influencing the revenue effects of tax rate changes. Traditionally, the revenue elasticity has been the central concept in examining fiscal drag, and obtaining local measures of tax progressivity. But it has an additional role in the context of the revenue effects of tax changes when incomes respond to rate changes. This separate effect has not previously been discussed explicitly. The elasticity of tax revenue with respect to a rate change was examined at both the individual and aggregate level.

When a single marginal tax rate in a multi-rate income tax structure is changed, those in the relevant tax bracket adjust their incomes in accordance with the elasticity of taxable income, and this affects the tax paid via the revenue elasticity. There is also a revenue effect on those individuals who are in higher tax brackets, since marginal rate changes in lower tax brackets imply a change in their effective income threshold. But there are no incentive effects on higher-rate taxpayers because only their average tax rate changes. If there were no incentive effects, an equal proportional change in all marginal tax rates would produce the same proportional increase in total revenue – the elasticity is unity. However, this rapidly falls at a linear rate as the elasticity of taxable income increases.

Illustrations were provided using the New Zealand income tax structures before and after the 2010 Budget. This reduced all rates while leaving income thresholds unchanged and, in particular, reduced the top marginal rate substantially. The elasticity of total tax revenue with respect to a single tax rate change was found to be particularly sensitive to the elasticity of taxable income in the top two tax brackets. In the pre-Budget structure, an elasticity of taxable income in excess of about 0.6 was found to produce a negative tax response to an increase in the top two marginal rates. When these rates are lower, as in the post-Budget structure, the elasticity of taxable income needs to be over 0.8 before tax revenue in the highest tax bracket is expected to fall in response to an increase in the marginal rate. However, recent estimates of the elasticity of taxable income in the top tax bracket in New Zealand are in the range (with some estimates in excess of 1) where tax revenue may fall. For New Zealand in particular, these results therefore suggest that further detailed empirical investigation of the elasticity of taxable income for taxpayers at different income levels may be warranted to assess whether cuts in some marginal tax rates are likely to be revenue enhancing.

Chapter 14

Tax Revenue and Lorenz Curves

The previous chapter introduced a diagrammatic representation of total tax revenue for a multi-rate income tax structure. The two-quadrant diagram had various amounts of income and numbers of people on axes. The present chapter considers an alternative diagrammatic approach based on the well-known Lorenz curve of taxable income. This curve traces the relationship between the (incomplete) first moment distribution function (average income of those below a given level divided by arithmetic mean over the whole population) and the distribution function of income (proportion of people below the given income level). First, section 14.1 considers the simplest case of a single tax rate applying to income measured above a tax-free threshold. Tax revenue is related to vertical distances in the Lorenz curve diagram, and the effects of a mean-preserving spread in the income distribution are examined diagrammatically. The approach is extended to the multi-step tax function in section 14.2.

14.1 A Tax-Free Threshold

Consider a simple income tax structure having a single rate of t applying to taxable income, x, measured above a threshold of a. Thus for $x > a$:

$$T(x) = t(x - a) \tag{14.1}$$

For a population of size N where incomes are continuously distributed with distribution function, $F(x)$, for $0 < x < \infty$, total revenue is equal to:

$$R = Nt \int_a^\infty (x - a)\, dF(x) \tag{14.2}$$

and:

$$\begin{aligned} R &= Nt \left[\int_a^\infty x dF(x) - a \int_a^\infty dF(x) \right] \\ &= Nt\bar{x} \left[\{1 - F_1(a)\} - \frac{a}{\bar{x}} \{1 - F(a)\} \right] \end{aligned} \tag{14.3}$$

where $F_1(x)$ denotes the first (incomplete) moment distribution function, equal to the proportion of total income obtained by those with incomes less than x. Therefore $F_1(x) = \int_0^x u dF(u) / \int_0^\infty u dF(u)$ or $F_1(x) = \int_0^x u dF(u) / \bar{x}$.

It is useful to define the function, $G(a)$ as the term in square brackets in (14.3), so that:

$$G(a) = \{1 - F_1(a)\} - \frac{a}{\bar{x}} \{1 - F(a)\} \tag{14.4}$$

This function, with its further modifications, is discussed further in Creedy (1996). Revenue can thus be written as:

$$R = Nt\bar{x}G(a) \tag{14.5}$$

Hence changes in revenue arising from changes in the tax parameters are given by:

$$dR = \bar{x}G(a)\, dt + t\bar{x} \left(\frac{\partial G(a)}{\partial a} \right) da \tag{14.6}$$

where:

$$\frac{\partial G(a)}{\partial a} = -\frac{\partial F_1(a)}{\partial a} - \frac{1 - F(a)}{\bar{x}} + \frac{a}{\bar{x}} \frac{\partial F(a)}{\partial a} \tag{14.7}$$

and since $\partial F(a)/\partial a = f(a)$ and $\partial F_1(a)/\partial a = af(a)/\bar{x}$, the first and last terms cancel and:

$$\frac{\partial G(a)}{\partial a} = -\frac{1 - F(a)}{\bar{x}} \tag{14.8}$$

These results are not new, but the remainder of this section relates the various components of total tax revenue to slopes and distances in the Lorenz curve diagram.

14.1.1 Diagrammatic Illustration

An alternative expression for total revenue is obtained from (14.3) by writing $N_T = N\{1 - F(a)\}$ as the number of individuals who pay positive tax, that is those who have $x > a$, so that:

$$R = t\bar{x}N_T \left\{ \frac{1 - F_1(a)}{1 - F(a)} - \frac{a}{\bar{x}} \right\} \tag{14.9}$$

The ratio $\{1 - F_1(a)\} / \{1 - F(a)\}$ has a simple interpretation in terms of the Lorenz curve of taxable income. Figure 14.1 shows the Lorenz curve in the top section, and the distribution function in the lower section. The ratio $\{1 - F_1(a)\} / \{1 - F(a)\}$ is the slope of the line AB, which must exceed 45 degrees. The point C corresponds to the arithmetic mean income, where the Lorenz curve has a slope of 45 degrees. Hence the vertical distance from point C to the Lorenz curve is the maximum distance from the curve to the line of equality, and is referred to as the Schutz index, S, given by:

$$S = F(\bar{x}) - F_1(\bar{x}) \tag{14.10}$$

On this measure and its interpretation see, for example, Lambert (1993, pp. 35–45). The effect of a mean-preserving spread in the distribution of taxable income is illustrated in Figure 14.2. The change in the distribution function, as shown in the lower section of the figure, involves a fixed arithmetic mean income. The mean is associated with the new Lorenz curve (at the point where that curve has a slope of 45 degrees), having a lower value of $F(\bar{x})$

than with the initial Lorenz curve. With a fixed value of the threshold, a, the value of $F(a)$ must be higher after the mean-preserving spread. Hence the slope of the line drawn from the point on the Lorenz curve, $(F_1(a), F(a))$, to the top right hand corner must be steeper than with the original distribution.

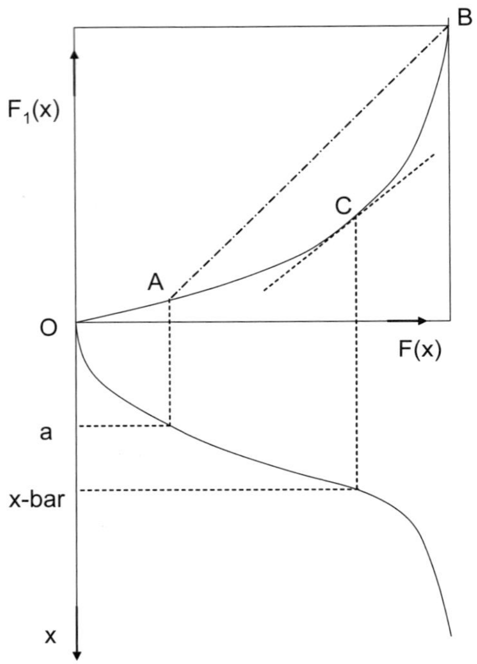

Figure 14.1: Tax Revenue and the Lorenz Curve

At the same time, the number of taxpayers, $N_T = N\{1 - F(a)\}$, must fall. Hence Figure 14.2 needs augmenting. Suppose new values are denoted by a prime. Using the function, G, it can be seen that revenue increases if:

$$\frac{F_1(a) - F_1'(a)}{\{1 - F'(a)\} - \{1 - F(a)\}} > \frac{a}{\bar{x}} \tag{14.11}$$

Consider Figure 14.3, which shows a further quadrant in the bottom left hand corner where, using a 45 degree line, $\bar{x}$ is translated to the new horizontal axis. Hence the right hand side of (14.11) is represented by the slope of the

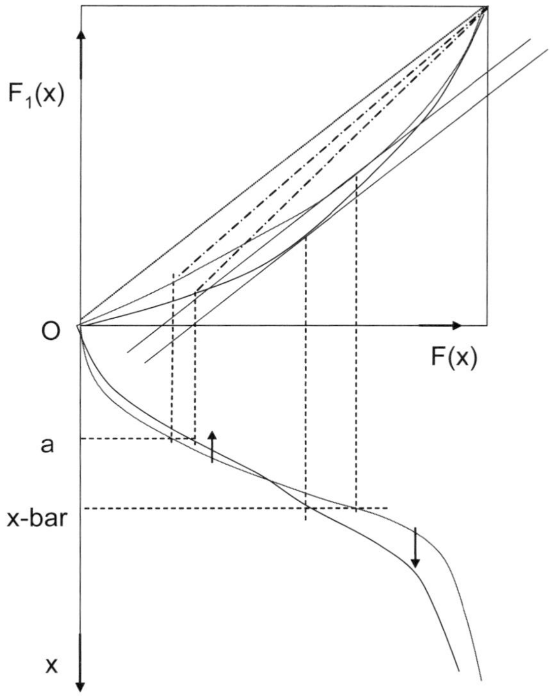

Figure 14.2: An Increase in Inequality: Fixed Mean Income

line CD. The left hand side is represented by the slope AB. Comparison of total revenue thus requires a comparison of the two slopes.

Hence there is not an unambiguous result regarding total tax revenue. Hence for two distributions with the same arithmetic mean and population size, if distribution A 'Lorenz dominates' distribution B – that is, if the Lorenz curve of A lies inside that of B – the income tax revenue from a structure having a single rate above a tax-free threshold is not necessarily lower in A than in B.

From the same kind of diagram as Figure 14.2, it can also be seen that if the Lorenz curve of B were to display less inequality than that of A in the income ranges up to and including the threshold, a, but more inequality

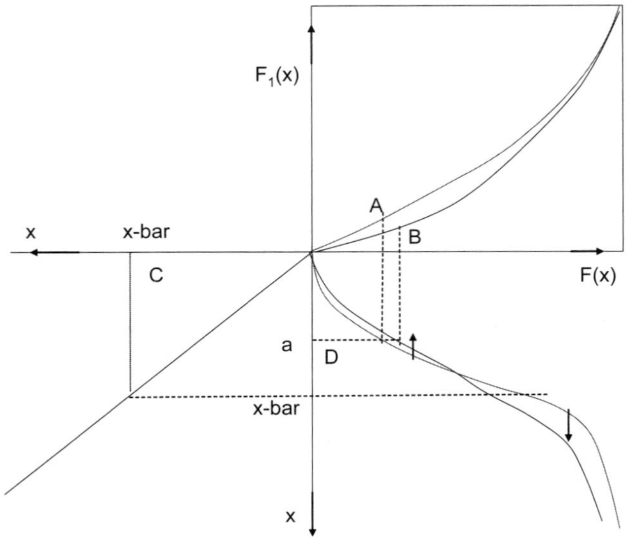

Figure 14.3: Tax Revenue and Mean-Preserving Spread

elsewhere (so that the Lorenz curve of B intersects that of A from above, when moving from left to right), the slope of the line from $(F_1(a), F(a))$ to the top right hand corner at $(1,1)$ is flatter in B. But, in addition, the number of taxpayers, N_T, must increase. Hence intersecting Lorenz curves, with fixed $\bar{x}$, also means that tax revenue comparisons are ambiguous.

A further rearrangement of the function, $G(a)$ gives:

$$G(a) = \{F(a) - F_1(a)\} - \left(1 - \frac{a}{\bar{x}}\right)\{1 - F(a)\} \tag{14.12}$$

The terms in this expression also have simple interpretations in terms of the Lorenz curve, as shown in Figure 14.4. This illustrates $\{F(a) - F_1(a)\}$ as the vertical distance from the Lorenz curve (corresponding to a) to the line of equality. The term $\{1 - F(a)\}$ is the horizontal distance to the right of the appropriate point on the Lorenz curve, and the term $1 - \frac{a}{\bar{x}}$ is the slope of the line from C to a in the bottom left hand quadrant of the diagram. Hence it is possible to express the product $\left(1 - \frac{a}{\bar{x}}\right)\{1 - F(a)\}$ as a vertical distance,

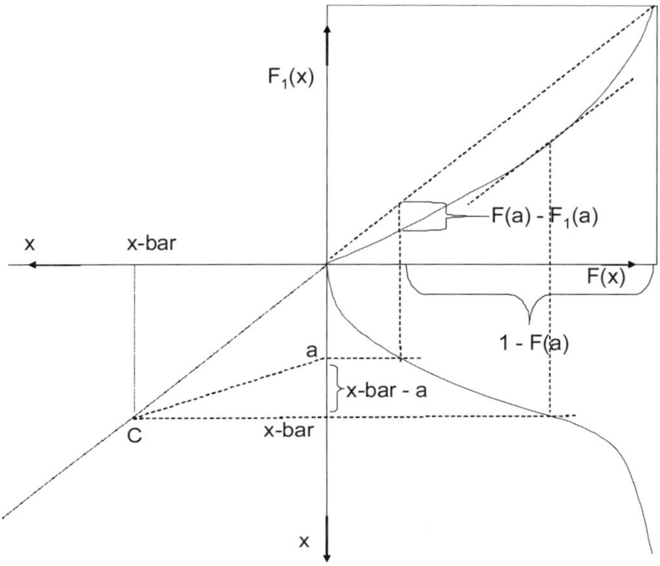

Figure 14.4: Components of $G(a)$

as in Figure 14.5, by drawing a line from the point $F(a)$ on the horizontal axis of the Lorenz curve which has the same gradient as the line from C to a. This has the effect of projecting the appropriate vertical distance on the right hand side of the box containing the Lorenz curve. Hence $G(a)$ is represented as the sum of two vertical distances.

Furthermore, noting that the second term in (14.12) can be written as $\{1 - F(a)\} - \frac{a}{\bar{x}}\{1 - F(a)\}$, and that the Gini inequality measure, $Gini$, can be written as:[1]

$$Gini = -\frac{2}{\bar{x}}Cov\{x, 1 - F(x)\} \tag{14.13}$$

the average value of the second term (using the fact that, for example, $Cov(x, y) = E(xy) - \bar{x}\bar{y}$) turns out to be simply half the Gini measure of inequality.

[1]See Creedy (1996, p. 20).

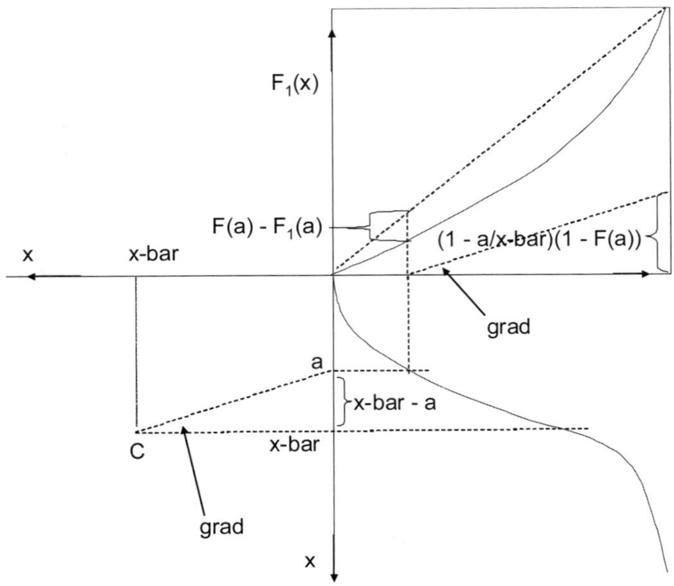

Figure 14.5: $G(a)$ as the Sum of Two Distances

14.2 A Multi-step Tax Function

The most common form of income tax function used in practice is the multi-step function, which is described by a series of marginal tax rates and income thresholds over which the rates apply.[2] Formally, the multi-step income tax function can be written as:

$$\begin{aligned} T(x) &= 0 & 0 < x \leq a_1 \\ &= t_1(x - a_1) & a_1 < x \leq a_2 \\ &= t_1(a_2 - a_1) + t_2(x - a_2) & a_2 < x \leq a_3 \end{aligned} \tag{14.14}$$

and so on.

If x falls into the kth tax bracket, so that $a_k < x \leq a_{k+1}$, and $a_0 = t_0 = 0$,

[2] For further discussion of the multi-step function, see Creedy (1996, pp. 54–6) and on the revenue elasticity properties, see chapter 11 above and Creedy and Gemmell (2006, pp. 25–32).

$T(x)$ can be written for $k \geq 1$ as:

$$T(x) = t_k (x - a_k) + \sum_{j=0}^{k-1} t_j (a_{j+1} - a_j) \tag{14.15}$$

The expression for $T(x)$ in (14.15) can be rewritten as:

$$T(x) = t_k x - \sum_{j=1}^{k} a_j (t_j - t_{j-1}) \tag{14.16}$$

Hence:

$$T(x) = t_k (x - a'_k) \tag{14.17}$$

where:

$$\begin{aligned} a'_k &= a_k - \sum_{j=0}^{k-1} \left(\frac{t_j}{t_k}\right) (a_{j+1} - a_j) \\ &= \frac{1}{t_k} \sum_{j=1}^{k} a_j (t_j - t_{j-1}) \end{aligned} \tag{14.18}$$

The implication of (14.17) and (14.18) is that the tax function facing any individual taxpayer is equivalent to a tax function with a single marginal tax rate, t_k, applied to income measured in excess of a single threshold, a'_k. The term, a'_k, is the effective threshold for individuals in the kth class, and is a weighted sum of the a_js, with weights, $(t_j - t_{j-1})/t_k$, determined by the structure of marginal rate progression.

Rewrite (14.17) as:

$$\begin{aligned} T(x) &= t_k x - t_k a'_k \\ &= t_k x - \sum_{j=1}^{k} a_j (t_j - t_{j-1}) \end{aligned} \tag{14.19}$$

The interpretation of the second term in (14.19) can be seen from Figure 14.6, which shows a section of the multi-step tax function. For threshold a_k, the value of $t_k a'_k$ is the sum of areas like A to the left of a_k. If all income were taxed at the rate t_k, too much tax would be paid, so the total area indicated

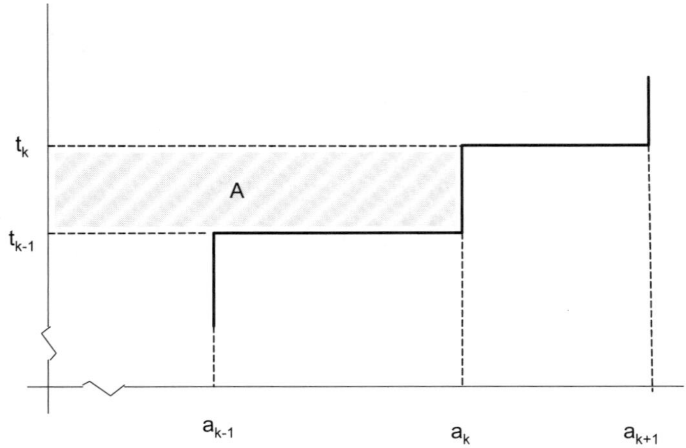

Figure 14.6: Multi-rate Thresholds and Rates

represents this excess tax over the actual tax from the multi-rate structure. The artificial threshold, a'_k, thus ensures that the correct revenue is obtained.

Using (14.17), aggregate tax revenue can be written, for K tax brackets with $a_{K+1} = \infty$, as:

$$R = N \sum_{k=1}^{K} \left[t_k \int_{a_k}^{a_{k+1}} (x - a'_k)\, dF(x) \right] \tag{14.20}$$

And using

$$\int_{a_k}^{a_{k+1}} dF(x) = F(a_{k+1}) - F(a_k) \tag{14.21}$$

and

$$\int_{a_k}^{a_{k+1}} x dF(x) = \bar{x} \{F_1(a_{k+1}) - F_1(a_k)\} \tag{14.22}$$

it is found that:

$$R = N\bar{x} \sum_{k=1}^{K} t_k \left[\{F_1(a_{k+1}) - F_1(a_k)\} - \frac{a'_k}{x} \{F(a_{k+1}) - F(a_k)\} \right] \tag{14.23}$$

The term in square brackets can be written more succinctly by modifying the function $G(a)$ defined earlier. Let $G_k(a_k)$ denote the term in square

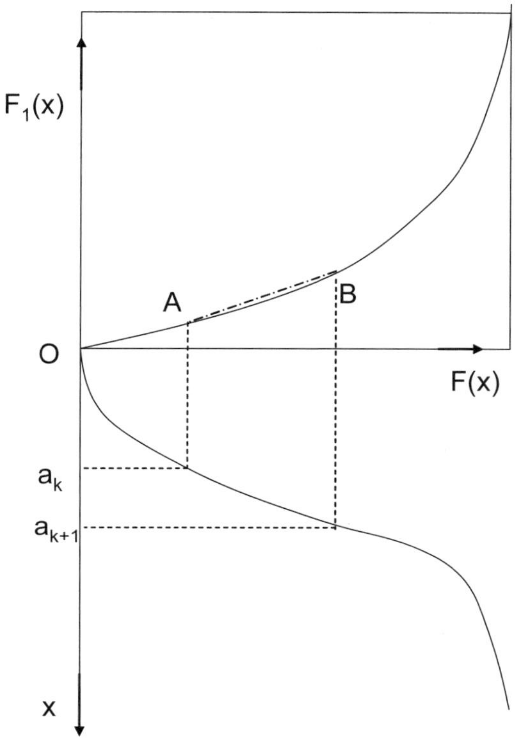

Figure 14.7: The Multi-step Tax Function

brackets, so that:

$$R = N\bar{x}\sum_{k=1}^{K} t_k G_k(a_k) \tag{14.24}$$

or, alternatively:

$$R = \bar{x}\sum_{k=1}^{K} t_k N_k \left[\frac{F_1(a_{k+1}) - F_1(a_k)}{F(a_{k+1}) - F(a_k)} - \frac{a_k'}{\bar{x}}\right] \tag{14.25}$$

where N_k is the number of taxpayers in the kth tax bracket. This result is thus a simple extension of equation (14.9), where there is just one threshold.

The first term in square brackets in (14.25) is the slope of the Lorenz curve between the two adjacent income thresholds. This is illustrated in Figure

14.7, as the slope AB. The term to be subtracted is not the actual threshold, but the effective threshold, a'_k, as a ratio of the arithmetic mean income. The effects of changes in population size, arithmetic mean income, the structure of marginal rates and thresholds, and of the dispersion of incomes (including a 'mean-preserving spread' – a change in the dispersion which leaves arithmetic mean unchanged), can thus easily be examined, given the Lorenz curve and using the expression given above. It must be remembered that a change in the structure of marginal rates, with income thresholds unchanged, nevertheless changes the a'_k values.

14.3 Conclusions

This chapter has shown how familiar expressions for total income tax revenue can be related to slopes and vertical distances in the popular Lorenz curve diagram, used to examine relative income inequality. This involves adding a quadrant showing the distribution function (the cumulative frequency density, or ogive curve). It is thereby possible to examine diagrammatically how income distribution changes can affect total tax revenue.

Part V

Tax Reviews

Chapter 15

The NZ Tax Working Group

The Report of the Victoria University of Wellington Tax Working Group (TWG), *A Tax System for New Zealand's Future* (2010), represents a unique collaboration among individuals from the New Zealand Treasury, the Inland Revenue Department and the Victoria University Centre for Accounting, Governance and Taxation Research (CAGTR), along with a range of other acknowledged tax experts. The Report has also been produced with remarkable speed and relatively cheaply. Favourable comparisons may, for example, be made with the reviews being carried out by the Australian Treasury (*Australia's Future Tax System*) and the Institute for Fiscal Studies (*Reforming the Tax System for the 21st Century*) in the UK.

Taxation is an area where strong disagreement and argument at cross purposes are notoriously present. The major strength of the Report is that it is an exercise in 'Rational Policy Analysis'. By this is meant that its aim is mainly to examine the implications, using a variety of measures, of a range of alternative policies. This involves a clear statement of the criteria against which a tax structure may be compared. It encourages an understanding of why different people may not agree about the best way to proceed, and therefore allows for rational discussion rather than heated argument. The Report is refreshingly free of the kind of rhetoric which is so often a part of taxation debates.

At times the Tax Working Group was unable to resist the pressure to make specific proposals for reform of the NZ tax structure, though in doing so it is careful to point out that its members are not always unanimous. The group was, it seems, responding to outside pressures to produce specific recommendations. But rational policy analysis at its best provides the information which enables others, using their own value judgements and views about likely orders of magnitude, to make up their own minds.

After briefly describing the reforms suggested by the Tax Working Group, in section 15.1, section 15.2 considers the way in which tax structures are evaluated. Some criticisms regarding the precision of concepts are made in section 15.3, and suggestions for further analyses are made in section 15.4. Brief conclusions are in section 15.5.

15.1 New Zealand Taxes and Reforms

Some distinctive features of the New Zealand tax structure may be briefly mentioned. The personal income tax has no tax-free threshold. There are few deductions, and the top marginal rate is 38 per cent. It has a very limited capital gains tax, a substantial difference between the corporate tax rate (of 30 per cent) and the top personal rate, and a Goods and Services Tax with a very broad base and low rate relative to European countries. The Report explains why changes are needed, arising from domestic and international changes since the previous major reforms of the 1980s, such as the increasing extent of international capital mobility. Motivated by the extent to which the tax rates applied to corporations, trusts and the top personal tax rate have become 'misaligned', it then considers a range of alternative methods of taxing corporations. These reforms include: reductions in personal income tax rates; methods to broaden the tax base, including the introduction of a Land Tax and extensions to the Capital Gains Tax; and changes to rules regarding depreciation allowances for property investment. The report stresses the need for changes which place less reliance on those taxes (such as personal income taxes and corporation taxes) where there are efficiency problems and where labour and capital are mobile. The report argues for the need to bring corporation, trust and personal tax rates into closer alignment. In each case the advantages and disadvantages are carefully discussed.

In considering changes, an important feature is that the Tax Working Group restricted its attention to reforms which are revenue neutral, so that total tax revenue is estimated to remain unchanged. The restriction to revenue-neutral changes is necessary because any change in revenue involves another unspecified policy, so that alternatives cannot properly be compared. Thus, for example, the argument that concerns about the future adequacy of tax revenue would disappear if only government expenditure were cut would be irresponsible, unless at the same time a detailed set of proposals for cutting expenditure were produced and their implications examined. Expenditure considerations were outside the scope of the review.

Any revenue-neutral change in the tax structure must of course involve some winners and some losers. Hence unanimity cannot be expected and distributional value judgements cannot be avoided. It is therefore important to attempt to make such value judgements explicit, since they are the source of many disputes about tax policy. Given the inevitability of there being some losers from a tax policy change, a strong desire on the part of policy makers to avoid losers clearly creates a bias towards the status quo.

Revenue-neutral changes examined by the Tax Working Group assume an absence of behavioural responses to tax changes, such as profit shifting by corporations and labour supply adjustments by individuals. Such behavioural responses may be substantial. To the extent that a policy change improves incentives and increases taxable incomes (including profits), post-reform tax revenue is likely to be understated.

15.2 Evaluating Tax Structures

This section discusses the Report's approach to the evaluation of tax structures. The basic principles adopted by the Tax Working Group are examined and this is followed by discussion of some features which, it is suggested, need some further elaboration and more clarity. The choice of tax base and the distinction between 'rules of thumb' and tax principles are then discussed.

15.2.1 Basic Tax Principles

The Report sets out six 'principles of a good tax system'. These are: efficiency and growth; equity and fairness; revenue integrity; fiscal cost; compliance and administration cost; and coherence (as part of a multi-tax and benefit structure). Any statement of tax principles inevitably brings to mind Adam Smith's famous 'four maxims', which are frequently discussed and extended. A fundamental problem is that, even if these principles were substantially elaborated, it would not be possible to treat them as axioms and from them derive an implied 'ideal' tax structure. The Tax Working Group appeared to recognise that even the production of a table, listing tax policies in the rows and the principles in columns, with ticks and crosses in appropriate boxes, would not in the present context provide sufficient information. The Report thus more usefully produced tables listing various advantages and disadvantages of each alternative. These features in fact include further criteria such as 'certainty regarding future taxes' (see pp. 28, 64 of the Report).

However, there are some important principles which are implicit in the Report, but which really need to be made explicit. Thus, only on p. 56 is mention made of the fact that 'value judgements are necessary to determine the priorities and respective weighting of these objectives'. The fact that value judgements play such an important role in tax policy decisions explains also why there is usually so much disagreement in tax policy debates. It is seldom clear if opponents disagree because they hold different value judgements, or because they form different views about the way people respond to tax changes (given that complete information is never available). This is precisely how rational policy analysis can help – by indicating the implications of adopting different values, so that readers can make up their own minds.

15.2.2 The Tax Base

A fundamental judgement taken – but not fully articulated in the Report – is that taxes should reflect 'ability to pay', rather than the 'benefits received' as a result of the subsequent public expenditure. Thus it is stated that, 'a good tax system should [ensure that] taxes paid reflect ability to pay' (p. 59). In considering ability to pay, a further important step is taken in suggesting that it 'should' be measured by 'comprehensive income'. Unfortunately the Report never states this explicitly, suggesting for example only that, 'taxing capital gain "on accrual" would bring the tax system closer to taxing comprehensive income' (p. 48) and referring to a capital gains tax as 'a more comprehensive option for base broadening' (p. 11).

The term 'comprehensive income' means simply that income is defined as the amount that can be consumed in a given period without reducing wealth. This 'maintaining capital intact' income concept is indeed widely used in economics, but its adoption as a tax base involves a value judgement. The important point here – not brought out sufficiently clearly in the Report – is that the use of this concept is the fundamental reason for attempting to tax capital gains. Such taxes obviously face problems in dealing with those gains which accrue but are not realised, and the Report recognises that a 'comprehensive capital gains tax' is impossible to impose. Nevertheless, there may be scope for extending CGT along the lines used in other countries.

In popular debates regarding the introduction of, or extension to, a tax there is perhaps a tendency to judge a proposal against a 'perfect' tax, when of course no existing tax is perfect. And there is always some resistance to a new tax. As the writer of the first English language full length treatise on public finance, John Ramsay McCulloch (1863), declared: 'it is sometimes better "to bear those ills we have, than to fly to others that we know not of".'[1] It is therefore likely that the discussion of extending CGT in New Zealand will meet with some resistance, even among those who may not expect to lose by such a change, but it provides a useful starting point for debate.

15.2.3 Rules of Thumb

An important position taken by the Report is that, 'the TWG considers that the broad-base low-rate [BB–LR] option is generally a sound principle to adopt' (pp. 16, 64). However, the adoption of BB–LR is not in fact a 'principle', but a rule of thumb. It is nevertheless a useful rule. It arises from recognition that the efficiency cost (in terms of the excess burden) of a tax is approximately proportional to the square of the tax rate. Hence it is useful, other things being equal, to keep the rate low, and this is achieved by keeping the tax base as broad as possible. But of course in evaluating a tax structure there are other considerations (as indeed are indicated in the Tax Working Group's own list of criteria), involving distributional value judgements, along with 'merit good' and externality arguments.

The BB–LR rule of thumb leads, in the Report, directly to the suggestion that the top marginal income tax rate should be reduced. But it is important to recognise that economic 'efficiency' criteria alone are not sufficient to determine policy – value judgements play an important role and more detailed information is required. For example, there is considerable heterogeneity in excess burdens, and many individuals below the top marginal rate face high burdens, depending on demographic and other characteristics. The preferred

[1] Here McCulloch is quoting from probably the most famous speech in Shakespeare (Hamlet, 'To be or not to be ...'), and so does not give the source.

policy depends on the judge's precise value judgements, including the degree of aversion to inequality.

Some ambivalence is also present in the discussion of the 'alignment' of the corporation tax rate, the rate applied to trusts and the top personal income tax rate. It sometimes appears that the Report treats alignment as a basic principle, while recognising that it would involve a loss of degrees of freedom in policy choices. Yet again it is more appropriate to consider it as a rule of thumb based on an assumed ease of shifting between income sources, rather than a principle. Starting from some specified objectives, and given other features (such as regulations regarding allowances and deductions, the costs of income shifting and the precise extent of behavioural responses to tax changes), it would be extremely difficult (as mentioned above) to produce an optimal structure: there is little reason a priori to expect identical rates to emerge from such a problem. And of course the relevant rates on trusts and corporations are proportional, while the average personal income tax rate is below the top marginal rate. However, there can be little doubt, as the Report argues, that the rates have now become seriously out of line and some movement towards alignment, if not necessarily to equality, is a high priority.

15.3 Precision Regarding Concepts

Perhaps surprisingly, one major concept is not defined by the Tax Working Group, leading to some potential misunderstanding. A tax structure is progressive if, over the relevant income range (where income is the tax base), the average tax rate increases with income. However, progressivity does not require 'marginal rate progression', which refers to an increasing marginal tax rate as income increases. Indeed, a considerable degree of progressivity can be achieved with a proportional tax, combined with a basic income (that is, a fixed and unconditional transfer payment).

This is relevant when considering a change in the tax mix – a shift from personal income taxes towards indirect taxation in the form of the GST. This can of course be achieved in a variety of ways, including reductions in all marginal income tax rates, or as part of a rate-flattening exercise with reduction in the top personal rate of taxation. A revenue-neutral tax shift must, as suggested earlier, involve losers as well as winners. However, the approach adopted clearly depends on the value judgements regarding income distribution. Where concern is largely with low-income groups, a cut in higher income tax rates can be combined with an increase in the GST rate, along with a suitable adjustment to benefit levels to maintain their real values. After all, this was done when GST was first introduced.

15.3.1 Taxes and Elasticities

The Report suggests that, 'taxing those bases that are least likely to be subject to significant behavioural change ... (inelastic bases) is also a sound principle to adopt when ... broadening the tax base' (p. 10). This is an allusion to the efficiency effects of taxes, concerning the distorting effect of non-uniform taxes on behaviour. Reference is made to a result obtained by Ramsey (1927). If the aim is to minimise a measure of the sacrifice arising from taxation, the appropriate tax structure turns out to be one that reduces the consumption of all goods by the same proportion. This implies a higher tax on inelastic goods and a lower tax on elastic goods. However, this result is severely limited because it refers to a single-person economy, and thus excludes any equity concerns.

Importantly, the most widely accepted modern measures of the efficiency effects (excess burdens) arising from taxation are based on 'compensating variations' and 'equivalent variations'. These measures depend not on market price or income elasticities, but on 'compensated' elasticities, where the 'income effects' of the price changes are excluded. This is not merely a pedantic point about definitions. In the context of labour supply and taxation, where income effects of tax changes can be significant, it is possible to observe high marginal welfare costs (excess burdens per dollar of extra revenue), even for those whose labour supply changes very little.

Here is the appropriate point to consider how the Tax Working Group's discussion of a Land Tax fits in with its list of tax principles. It is not in fact motivated by the use of a comprehensive income measure of ability to pay. Indeed, the comprehensive income concept gives no support to any kind of wealth (or net worth) tax – only tax on the income arising from assets (both human and non-human capital). The proposal for a Land Tax relies exclusively on the desire to find an additional tax base and, on the argument that the stock of land is fixed, uses the criterion relating to elasticity. Hence it is concerned only with efficiency, while transition, tax shifting and equity effects are important considerations which need further analysis.

15.4 Some Next Steps

The Report recognises that further analyses need to be carried out. Given the remarkably short time scale within which the Report was produced, and the low level of resources made available to the Tax Working Group, this is of course inevitable. One area mentioned concerns the transfer system and its integration with the personal income tax structure. In particular, the complex system of in-work benefits in New Zealand gives rise to substantial marginal tax rates applying to middle-income groups, and high levels of government expenditure. It also appears that there are unintended consequences whereby some individuals who are not in the 'target group' considered by the designers of the system are in receipt of transfer payments. It is suggested that a comprehensive review of the benefit system, to complement that of the tax side, needs to be given very high priority.[2]

Additional areas where further work is needed, not mentioned explicitly by the Report but undoubtedly supported by it, include behavioural responses. Despite the potential importance of foreign direct investment, and profit shifting by corporations (both real and that achieved by the exploitation of transfer pricing), very little solid empirical evidence is available regarding companies operating, or previously operating, in NZ. Similarly, there no longer exists a behavioural model in NZ that is capable of producing estimates of labour supply responses to tax changes and their associated efficiency (welfare) costs.

One suggestion made several times in the Report is that there should be some kind of review body, or organisation, charged with, and sufficiently equipped to carry out, the task of conducting regular independent evaluations of the tax structure in NZ. This, it seems, is not intended to propose yet another quasi non-governmental organisation, but presumably the Tax Working Group has in mind something like the role played (among other things) by the Institute for Fiscal Studies in London. The aim is to inform public 'rational debate', by investigating the detailed implications of tax policy changes. It is suggested that this could impose some constraints on politicians with a propensity to tinker with a tax structure in ways that have insufficient regard for the integrity of the complete system. It could also help to make the system less vulnerable to the inevitable special pleading by interest groups. The question of the funding and location of such a body was not discussed in the Report.

[2] A Welfare Working Group was indeed subsequently established and reported in February 2011: see http://ips.ac.nz/WelfareWorkingGroup/Index.html. However, this group did not follow the 'model' exemplified by the tax working group. Furthermore, it was unable to consider the scheme called 'Working for Families', which was identified by the tax working group as having serious problems.

15.5 Conclusions

In any discussion of taxation, it is important to recognise the inevitability of disagreement and a lack of consensus. There are simply too many value judgements involved and too many areas where only informed guesses must be made in the absence of direct information. It is certainly no weakness of the Report that it does not report unanimous support for various policy reform proposals. However, the members managed to agree on a broad framework for discussing reforms, and the need for some action. A Report which simply set out a dogmatic agenda for reform, using the kind of rhetoric that is familiar from the commentaries of special-interest groups, would have little value and would be read only by like-minded people.

The influence of the Tax Working Group on the tax debate, indeed in making taxation itself more prominent in public debate, is clear from even the most casual examination of the media in New Zealand. The suggestion that there are substantial revenue risks and that the distorting effects of some forms of taxation have growth effects as well as the less visible – but nonetheless substantial – excess burdens, has clearly influenced the government in its thinking about tax structure changes.

As mentioned earlier, the strength of the Report is in its attempt to contribute to rational policy debate by rehearsing the various arguments in a clear and dispassionate manner, so that those on different sides of the debate can come to understand just why they differ. That a disparate group of individuals from a range of backgrounds has established some common ground in a way of thinking about taxes is itself sufficient cause for praise. The Report can be read with interest and profit by all those interested in tax policy.

Chapter 16

The IFS and Tax Design

Tax By Design marks the completion of an extensive and comprehensive review of taxes and transfers, carried out under the aegis of the Institute for Fiscal Studies and chaired by James Mirrlees. Following the publication of *Dimensions of Tax Design*, a collection of commissioned technical or 'background' papers, along with commentaries, by a wide range of authors, *Tax By Design* sets out the final conclusions regarding tax design issues for open economies and policy recommendations for reforming the UK tax structure. Unlike the earlier volume, the conclusions are attributed not to particular authors but to an editorial committee, and thus give the impression of consensus among its members. In view of the high standing of these authors in the economics profession and the valued political independence of the IFS, the analysis and recommendations cannot fail to attract considerable interest. Broadly speaking, these recommendations include, among other things: the integration of income tax and employee National Insurance Contributions into a single tax, where all work-related expenses are deductible; the integration of as many benefits as possible into a single benefit, remaining separate from income tax; broadening the VAT base and moving towards a uniform rate; the taxation of income from savings based on returns in excess of a 'normal' rate; the introduction for corporate income tax of an 'Allowance for Corporate Equity' whereby a 'normal' return on equity-financed investments would be exempt;[1] the introduction of a Land Value Tax; and the introduction of a tax on lifetime receipts as part of the taxation of wealth. The specific policy recommendations are likely to be closely scrutinised in future months. Rather than add to such detailed discussions at this point, the limited purpose of the present chapter is to make some broad reflections on the nature of the volume and indeed of tax reviews in general.

16.1 Comparisons with Other Reviews

In a period when media attention in the area of public economics is concentrated largely on the question of aggregate public expenditure and government debt, it is interesting that this review is the third review of taxation to produce its conclusions in 2010. In Australia, a Review Panel, chaired by Ken Henry, the Secretary to the Treasury, published its report on *Australia's Future Tax System.*[2] The Review Panel consisted of just five individuals, including one industry representative and one academic economist. In New Zealand, a Tax Working Group was organised by the Centre for Accounting Governance and Taxation Research at Victoria University of Wellington, and was chaired by Professor Bob Buckle, the Pro Vice-Chancellor and Dean of the Faculty of Commerce and Administration. This consisted of a range of experts from the New Zealand academic and business communities (where not all of the latter were tax experts) and tax experts from the New Zealand Inland Revenue Department and the Treasury. While members of the Inland Revenue Department and Treasury contributed to the process and supported the Group in accessing and commissioning tax research, the Tax Working

[1] Considerations of international competition lead the authors to suggest that the consequent loss of tax revenue should not be recovered by raising the corporate tax rate.

[2] The review was unfortunately unable to consider the Goods and Services Tax, the Australian equivalent of VAT. For a critical overview of the Henry review, see especially Freebairn (2010) and other chapters in Evans, Krever and Mellor (2010). In addition, discussions of various aspects of the Review are provided in the 'Policy Forum' section of the December 2010 issue of the *Australian Economic Review*.

Group had independent authority to report on and recommend changes to the New Zealand tax system. The Tax Working Group received ministerial support for the discussion of major tax issues, and was encouraged to inform public debate.[3] The report, *A Tax System for New Zealand's Future, Report of the Victoria University of Wellington Tax Working Group*, was released in January 2010, and discussed in the previous chapter.[4]

The three tax reviews are very different and present interesting contrasts. The New Zealand review was undoubtedly the quickest and the cheapest of all, and produced the shortest final report. There is some irony in the contrast between that report and that of the Henry review. Gemmell (2010, p. 82) has pointed to a major difference, stating that, 'the New Zealand review was probably more weighted towards generating and influencing public debate around tax reform while the Henry review had a primary remit of making recommendations to government'. Nevertheless, while the TWG was indeed highly successful in stimulating widespread public debate, some of its recommendations have in fact already been adopted by the present government, in what were described as the biggest tax changes in nearly 25 years.[5] By contrast, the policy influence of the Henry review seems to have been negligible and its longevity is doubtful. Freebairn (2010, p. 57), after discussing the recommendations of that review, concluded that it, 'may be many years before there is a political will and consensus to turn these or modified proposals into actual reforms'.

Comparisons with *Tax By Design* are interesting from several points of view. The Mirrlees review is by far the most ambitious in its comprehensive coverage and the extensive range of specialist authors who are well known in their fields. Its detailed analyses carry a certain weight of authority: they are

[3]The structure of transfer payments was not part of the agenda, but was subject to a separate review process, following the recommendation of the Tax Working Group.

[4]For a discussion of tax reform in New Zealand, see Gemmell (2010).

[5]For further discussion of the review process and the recent tax changes, following the Tax Working Group's proposals, see Buckle (2010).

likely to be cited in academic articles and to stimulate many further detailed analyses. Yet it clearly remains to be seen how much policy influence it will have. This raises the difficult issue of the political aspects of tax policy and, as Chote (2010, p. ix) put it in his preface, the tension between 'what is economically desirable and what is politically practical'. The perfectly reasonable view was taken that there would be little point in trying to 'second guess' what is politically acceptable in the short term, so that the policy recommendations arise from a public finance rather than a political economy perspective.[6]

Nevertheless, readers may sometimes feel that more sensitivity to the latter issues might have modified some of the strong wording of criticisms of existing features which, while not adhering to familiar economic theory arguments, are readily explained by the types of wider consideration recently discussed by, for example, Auerbach (2009) and Brennan and Brooks (2010).[7] Indeed, these authors make the point that, while tax reviews of this kind are warranted in a 'longer cycle' (of something like 20 to 30 years), a case can be made for tax structure stability in order to reduce rent-seeking behaviour and enable taxpayers to have clear expectations about future taxes. These arguments have long been recognised and were stressed by the classical economists, in particular Smith and McCulloch.

[6]This reader was often reminded of Michael Caine's well-known comment (used in several of his books, and by many impressionists) that, 'not many people know that'. It carries the implied suggestion that if only policy advisers and politicians had read the right text books and journal articles, we would have a superior tax structure.

[7]An example concerns discussions of exemptions to VAT for redistributive reasons. It is well known that such exemptions provide a poor redistributive instrument, and generate inefficiencies as a result of the higher taxes on other goods (as approximate excess burdens increase in relation to the square of the tax rate). But there is the practical issue of the confidence of the electorate and others that 'compensation' through direct tax will occur and be sustained. It was clear that there was no such confidence in Australia during the introduction of GST. But in New Zealand, as a result of the considerable attention to such issues in planning, the very broad base was accepted. The subsequent increase to 12.5 per cent was not compensation, but in the recent further shift towards GST in New Zealand, the compensating changes in marginal tax rates were examined closely and discussed publicly.

Another feature of the three reviews may also be mentioned. As indicated above, the Henry review of *Australia's Future Tax System* and *Tax By Design* make a number of specific proposals for tax reform, with the implicit suggestion that these are the unanimous views of those contributing to the reports. In contrast, the Tax Working Group's *A Tax System for New Zealand's Future*, in explicitly recognising that complete agreement regarding tax policy design is virtually impossible to achieve, stresses the implications, using a range of criteria, of alternatives and is comfortable reporting that not all members of the Group agree. It may be said that the New Zealand report is an exercise in 'rational policy analysis'. By encouraging an understanding of why different people may not agree about the best way to proceed, it allows for rational discussion rather than heated argument. In *Tax By Design*, the authors do indeed regularly remind the reader that people have different views about income redistribution, and the volume is fortunately largely free of rhetoric.[8] Yet – and here I am happy to concede that this is something of a 'hobby horse' – I would like to have seen more discussion of the importance and nature of value judgements in tax design.

The reader is not surprisingly (given the role of Mirrlees in the review) informed that optimal tax theory is 'the foundation of the idea of "tax by design"' (p. 17). The authors state that, as a method of analysing the trade-offs involved in balancing redistribution objectives and the need to raise revenue against the associated efficiency losses, 'the conclusions of optimal tax theory inform the way we discuss policy' (p. 21). This suggests somewhat misleadingly that, rather than providing a broad 'welfare economics' approach to modelling taxation which tries to allow for tax disincentive effects, and which indicates the sensitivity of results to model specification

[8]Yet it seems rather unfortunate that the final sentence of *Tax By Design* insists that it is 'time for government to grow up and map out a rational course for tax policy'. And the claim in the previous paragraph that 'economic welfare could be improved by many billions of pounds annually if ... taxation ... were reformed in the ways we have suggested', is a further resort to rhetoric.

and objectives, there is indeed a clear set of policy conclusions provided by optimum tax theory.[9]

Furthermore, reference is often made to 'society's views' about redistribution, rather than those of a single disinterested judge whose value judgements are described by a 'social welfare function'. Given the well-known problems of preference aggregation, the use of a social welfare function as the method of evaluating the outcome of a tax structure is a cornerstone of optimal tax theory. It seems implicit that the authors have in mind a 'welfarist' social welfare function of the standard utilitarian kind which has utility as a welfare 'metric' and an aversion to inequality.[10] However, other welfare metrics and policy objectives (which may not necessarily be 'welfarist') may legitimately be investigated. And in discussing the 'conclusions of optimal tax theory' much weight is given to elasticity results regarding the responsiveness of individuals to changes in tax rates, with little indication that strong assumptions lie behind such unambiguous statements. Regarding the approach to redistribution, it is true that the authors state (p. 3) that, 'at the core of our analysis' is the desire to reduce distortions and their associated efficiency costs, without significantly altering the degree of redistribution of the present system. But with this implicit value judgement, there is perhaps an example of the 'tyranny of the status quo' which is elsewhere (as in p. 18) lamented as preventing much-needed tax reform.[11]

[9] The concluding chapter begins by suggesting that, 'the tax and benefit system should have a coherent structure based on clearly defined economic principles, such as those laid down in this volume'. This again suggests that the use of value-free economic principles – those adopted by the authors – is sufficient for the design of a tax structure.

[10] The term 'welfarist' is usually used to describe an evaluation in terms of measures, such as utility, which are clearly of concern to individuals involved. In contrast, 'non-welfarist' evaluations are in terms of measures, such as income-based or consumption-based poverty indices or the aggregate level of employment, which are specifically of concern to the judge.

[11] However, the authors do not seem to be aware that 'the tyranny of the status quo' is in fact the title of a book by Milton and Rose Friedman (1984).

16.2 The Contrast with the Meade Report

Tax By Design follows in the footsteps, some 30 years later, of the earlier IFS-sponsored review, *The Structure and Reform of Direct Taxation*, which was chaired by Meade (1978). It is therefore tempting to make some broad general comparisons, though of course the circumstances are very different and the scope of the earlier review was much more limited, being confined to direct taxation.[12] One approach is to consider the critical comments made at the time in the *Economic Journal* by Prest (1979), an eminent British public finance economist – though it would not be unfair to describe his review article as rather 'bad tempered', or at least of reflecting a degree of irritation with the report.

Prest (1979, p. 243) began his review by pointing out that the composition of the committee was 'star-studded', including 'five economists, four people with accounting connections, one solicitor and one ex-administrator', but he lamented the fact that it did not include businessmen or a 'fall guy' to represent 'the proverbial man in the street'. He also complained that its discussions of the literature reflected a degree of insularity and poor historical perspective. *Tax By Design* has undoubtedly also been produced by a 'star-studded', but more international, cast. Yet it is composed, with the exception of a QC, of professional economists. By comparison, the New Zealand Tax Working Group certainly benefited from the presence of tax experts drawn from a wider range of businesses and government departments.

One complaint made by Prest (1979, p. 260) was that the authors 'were not sufficiently able to repress a crusading spirit in the zeal for reform' and 'they might perhaps have done well to remember that Crusaders do not

[12]For example, the earlier review, coming at the end of the 1970s and its years of high inflation, paid much attention to the problems of designing taxes in the face of inflation. This receives little discussion in *Tax By Design*, though it will be interesting to see how this will become more prominent as governments inflate their way out of the current debt problems.

always make fast progress'. Fortunately, the same cannot be said of *Tax By Design* where a more balanced approach is evident. Prest (1979, p. 256) suggested that those 'who put heavy emphasis on distributional matters ... are more likely to find it to their taste than if they do not'. Notwithstanding the point made above about implicit values in supporting the status quo in terms of distributional objectives, the stated bias of *Tax By Design* is on efficiency rather than distributional aspects of taxes.

Prest (1979, p. 250) was particularly scathing about the discussion of social security, saying that he found it, 'less than satisfactory, both in coverage of the relevant considerations and in analysis of the issues'.[13] He suggested that they should not 'venture into the quicksands of social security without the benefit of help from the experts'. Here again the present report is not guilty of neglecting the intricacies of the social security system, and indeed several of the authors have substantial expertise in the area. In this context, Prest's review provides an example of the great difficulty of trying to judge what is or is not politically feasible. The Meade report favoured a type of 'New Beveridge' system having flat-rate benefits, but Prest's (1979, p. 251) response was that this was 'totally unrealistic. Short-term earnings related benefits are now a well-established fact of life in this country, as in others'. Yet, mere weeks after the publication of Prest's comments, a start was made in dismantling earnings-related social transfer payments.

16.3 The Style of Exposition

One aspect which received much praise from Prest concerned the clarity of the exposition. He suggested that 'what did Meade say about that?' would be an 'automatic response' when considering problems in direct taxation. The Meade report did indeed have the stamp of its chairman over every

[13]For example, Prest (1979, p. 251) reported finding only a one-line reference to the (at that time) new state pension scheme.

page: one instinctively felt, without knowing the situation precisely, that Meade's authority was behind each sentence and that he would have defended each point. In the case of *Tax By Design*, the wide range and extent of proposals relating to detailed elements of the tax and transfer structure make it harder to identify the review with a single dominant leader, who would need something like the breadth of a Richard Musgrave.

The writing style of *Tax By Design* is admirably transparent, and its structure has obviously been given very careful consideration, so that the reader is always well aware of how the discussion is moving forward. A self-imposed constraint was clearly followed, such that not a single equation or piece of mathematical notation should be used, and diagrams should be restricted to charts showing data rather than analytical figures. References to a wide range of literature have been confined to footnotes. All these features succeed, as the authors obviously hoped, in making the argument flow smoothly. And yet at times this reader is conscious of a certain lack of an unambiguous vision of the nature of the intended audience. Sometimes, simple points are rather laboured, while in other places the reader is rushed over the surface of a problem, such that where a complex concept or analysis is involved a decision seems to have been made simply to avoid mentioning it, and instead to jump to the final conclusions. Some of those conclusions therefore cannot avoid seeming as if they were 'pulled out of a hat'. Writing clearly for a wide audience of non-specialists involves working really hard to simplify and to find imaginative ways of communicating the essential features of an analysis, rather than simply avoiding mention of complex material. One wonders about the extent to which *Tax By Design* was 'road-tested' on a sample of the kind of audience the authors wanted to reach.

For example, it is unlikely that a non-specialist reader who had not previously come across the concept would be capable of giving a precise summary of the important concept of the excess burden of a tax, after reading the several 'explanations' in the review. It seems likely that those new to the idea would associate it with a Marshallian, rather than a Hicksian, elasticity. However, the difference between the two elasticities can be non-trivial.[14] Could someone new to the idea understand from the brief statements in *Tax By Design* the precise sense in which an optimal tax is supposed to be 'optimal'? And would such a reader have an appreciation of the strong assumptions needed to make use of a concept such as the elasticity of taxable income, assumed furthermore to take a common value for a wide range of individuals? Also, it seems most unlikely that the uninitiated reader is given a proper appreciation of the sensitivity of results to small variations in parameter estimates. When discussing the top marginal income tax rate (in section 4.3.2), the fact that this raises a disproportionate amount of revenue is stressed, but the difficulty of raising further revenue from small increases in the rate may well be opaque to many readers new to the idea.

To continue this example, the 'result' is given on p. 33 that an elasticity of taxable income of 0.46 implies a revenue-maximising effective top marginal tax rate of 56 per cent which, after allowing for National Insurance and indirect taxes, implies an income tax rate of 40 per cent. This means that the introduction of a top income tax rate of 50 per cent in the UK is expected to reduce rather than increase revenue. This may well appear to the general reader to be a piece of sleight of hand, if it is not actually pulled out of a hat.

And what is the experienced reader to make of this result, knowing that there are some unspecified assumptions involved in the calculation? If no income is diverted into a lower-taxed source, these figures imply that the ratio of the average income in the top tax bracket to the difference between that average and the income threshold is 1.708, which is around the value that one would anticipate for the UK (and hence average income in the top

[14]Much of the discussion appears – though it is not explicit – to be taking a consumer's surplus view of welfare changes (where income effects are ignored), rather than using Hicksian measures.

bracket is 2.41 times the threshold).

No mention was made in *Tax By Design* of the excess burden in this context, though the use of the elasticity of taxable income is usually accompanied by an assumption that income effects are zero (so that the elasticity is sufficient for providing a welfare change measure). In this case the marginal welfare cost of taxation in the top bracket can be calculated as 3.67: hence the marginal excess burden is very high, at 3.67 pounds per extra pound raised in revenue. If the elasticity of taxable income were instead assumed to be slightly higher, at 0.5, the marginal excess burden would increase to 5.85, showing how sensitive it is to the elasticity. On the other hand, if half of any reduction in taxable income is assumed to be diverted to another income source attracting, say, a 30 per cent tax rate, the reported elasticity of 0.46 implies that the revenue-maximising rate for the top bracket would instead be 62.6 per cent, and the marginal welfare cost would be just 0.38, or 38 pence for each pound of extra revenue.[15] These results, particularly the welfare costs in terms of excess burdens, demonstrate the sensitivity to some basic assumptions.

Furthermore, without any reference to excess burdens and associated inefficiencies, the review goes on to say (on p. 33) that non-marginal increases in tax rates would nevertheless impose significant losses on those in the top bracket and, 'Society's attitude to those losses is therefore as important as the precise revenue effect. The significance of the 50% income tax rate is less the paltry sum it might raise (or cost) than the substantial hit on high earners it represents'. Apart from the presence here of another reference to

[15] If η is the elasticity of taxable income, and the ratio of arithmetic mean income in the top bracket to the difference between that arithmetic mean and the income threshold is γ, the revenue-maximising rate (if no income is diverted to a source attracting a lower rate) is given by $(1+\gamma\eta)^{-1}$. If a proportion, s, of taxable income is diverted to a source attracting a lower rate of t, then the marginal welfare cost in the top bracket, where τ is the tax rate, is equal to $\eta\gamma(\tau - st) / \{1 - \tau - \eta\gamma(\tau - st)\}$. This expression requires the further assumption that utility functions are such that income effects of tax changes are zero, and taxable income can be expressed as a log-linear function of the net-of-tax rate $1-\tau$. On the assumptions behind these results, see chapter 12 above.

'society's views', it is not at all clear how the discussion contributes to practical policy analysis, other than emphasising the difficulty of obtaining precise estimates of important magnitudes and the need to specify value judgements more clearly for purposes of rational policy analysis.

16.4 Theory and Practice

One temptation when considering tax design is to compare an existing structure with an 'ideal' alternative. Prest made this point when he suggested (1979, p. 246) that the Meade report 'is somewhat prone to indulge in the old sport of comparing an impure income tax with a pure expenditure tax'. The need to compare practical alternatives was nicely made by Overstone (in O'Brien, 1971, vol. II, pp. 560–1) when he wrote that, 'all practical questions are questions of alternative. We must judge and decide, not by reference to an Abstract Standard but by the relative merit of one plan as compared with another'.[16] The same point, in a different context, was made in characteristic style by George Stigler when he referred to an audition in which the second singer is selected after only the first has sung.[17]

It has to be said that *Tax By Design* is occasionally guilty of favouring an ideal structure, according to stated principles, without sufficient elaboration of its practical difficulties. The emphasis on 'principles' rather than practical implementation problems is illustrated by the discussion of work-related expenses, where the authors recognise (in chapter 20) that 'it is not always easy to distinguish expenditure related to income generation from consumption'. They immediately add, 'But the principle at least is clear'. Similarly, in concluding that there is a strong case for a land value tax, the qualification is vaguely made regarding the 'difficulty of valuing land sepa-

[16] This comment by Overstone, made in a letter to Granville in 1853, is cited by O'Brien (2010, p. xxxv) when pointing out that George Warde Norman, in his writings on taxation, also fell into the trap of comparing an actual system with his ideal alternative.

[17] This comment was attributed to Stigler by Gwartney and Wagner (1988, p. 23), though no precise source was cited by them.

rately from the buildings on it'. Similarly, a member with practical business experience would have warned the authors that the 'principle' of allowing research and development expenditure to be fully deducted from profits gives rise to enormous practical difficulties and opportunities which would simply provide work for accountants.

The emphasis on 'principles' relative to practical considerations is perhaps also illustrated by the discussion, in the context of the taxation of income arising from savings and the taxation of corporate profits, of the deduction of a 'normal' rate of return. As with most discussions of this issue in the literature, the argument proceeds by setting up a range of numerical examples: one is reminded of Ricardo at this point. The analysis and policy recommendations are built on a single crucial assumption, that there exists a measurable 'normal rate of return' which would command wide agreement. Despite the importance of this concept, it receives very little explicit discussion indeed. The reader is told in chapter 13 that this is associated with 'the' risk-free rate of return and that, 'One would have to choose the appropriate risk free rate. Typically, this can be approximated by the interest rate on medium-maturity government bonds'. This rate is of course not constant over time, so 'There will always be a trade-off between varying the rate too frequently and maintaining strict neutrality'. In chapter 17, it is said casually that 'All that would be needed would be to specify ... which particular "risk-free" nominal interest rate is used'. The authors do not suggest who would be given the responsibility for making this choice.

Even ignoring things such as exchange-rate risk, the argument that certain government bonds provide a risk-free rate of return measure, which is not subject to medium-term fluctuations, requires much more justification. The recent sovereign debt crisis in the European Community has led to substantial costs of insuring Greek, Spanish, Italian, Portuguese and Irish government bonds against default risk.[18] This demonstrates that the concept of a 'normal' rate of return which can be measured by a medium-term government bond needs much more analysis before it can (as an assumption in small numerical examples) be used as the foundation of a major tax reform.

16.5 Conclusions

Different readers of *Tax By Design* will of course have different value judgements and different opinions about the relevant orders of magnitude of things which are notoriously difficult to measure or estimate, especially where responses to entirely new tax regulations are concerned. Furthermore, in a volume that is so wide-ranging, any single reader is likely to agree with, or be persuaded by, some arguments while being unable to agree with others. What is clear is that the authors have achieved their major aim, in their own words, of 'contributing to the debate'. Those interested in public finance cannot afford to ignore this volume.

[18] And of course insurance markets exist even for US and UK government bonds.

Bibliography

[1] Aaberge, R. and Colombino, U. (2008) Designing optimal taxes with a microeconometric model of household labour supply. *Centre for Household Income, Labour and Demographic Economics Working Paper* 06/2008.

[2] Ahmad, E. and Stern, N.H. (1984) The theory of tax reform and Indian indirect taxes. *Journal of Public Economics,* 25, pp. 259–298.

[3] Ahmad, E. and Stern, N.H. (1991) *The Theory and Practice of Tax Reform in Developing Countries.* Cambridge: Cambridge University Press.

[4] Amiel, Y. and Cowell, F.A. (1992) Inequality measurement: an experimental approach. *Journal of Public Economics*, 47, pp. 3–26.

[5] Amiel, Y. and Cowell, F.A. (1994) Income inequality and social welfare. In *Taxation, Poverty and Income Distribution* (ed. by J. Creedy), pp. 193–219. Aldershot: Edward Elgar.

[6] Amiel, Y., Creedy, J. and Hurn, S. (1999) Measuring attitudes towards inequality. *Scandinavian Journal of Economics*, 101, pp. 83–96.

[7] Atkinson, A.B. (1970) On the measurement of inequality. *Journal of Economic Theory*, 2, pp. 244–263.

[8] Atkinson, A.B. (1983) *Social Justice and Public Policy.* London: Harvester.

[9] Atkinson, A.B. (1995) *Public Economics in Action: The Basic Income/Flat Tax Proposal.* Oxford: Oxford University Press.

[10] Atkinson, A.B. and Stiglitz, J.E. (1980) *Lectures in Public Economics.* London: McGraw–Hill.

[11] Auerbach, A.J. (2009) Public finance in practice and theory. Unpublished paper, University of California, Berkeley.

[12] Australian Government Department of Family and Community Services (2004) *Annual Report 2003–04*, Canberra, available on http://www.facsia.gov.au/annualreport/2004/toc.htm.

[13] Australian Taxation Office (2006) *Taxation Statistics 2003–04 A Summary of Tax Returns for the 2003–04 Income Year and Collections for the 2004–05 Financial Year*, Canberra, available on http://www.ato.gov.au/content/downloads/70906_2004TAXSTATS.pdf.

[14] Auten, G. and Carroll, R. (1995) Behavior of the affluent and the 1986 Tax Reform Act. In *Proceedings of the 87th Annual Conference on Taxation of the National Tax Association*, pp. 70–76. Columbus, Ohio.

[15] Auten, G. and Carroll, R. (1999) The effect of income taxes on household behavior. *Review of Economics and Statistics*, 81, pp. 681–693.

[16] Auten, G., Carroll, R. and Gee, G. (2008) The 2001 and 2003 tax rate reductions: an overview and estimate of the taxable income response. *National Tax Journal*, 61, pp. 345–364.

[17] Banks, J., Blundell, R. and Lewbel, A. (1996) Tax reform and welfare measurement: do we need demand system estimation? *Economic Journal,* 106, pp. 1227–1241.

[18] Banks, J. and Johnson, P. (1994) Equivalence scale relativities revisited. *Economic Journal*, 104, pp. 883–890.

[19] Bastable, C.F. (1903) *Public Finance*. London: Macmillan.

[20] Bénabou, R. (1996) Inequality and Growth. In *NBER Macroeconomics Annual 1996* (ed. by B.S. Bernanke and J.J. Rotemberg), pp. 11–74. Cambridge, MA: National Bureau of Economic Research.

[21] Besley, T. and Coate, S. (1992) Workfare versus welfare: incentive arguments for work requirements in poverty-alleviation programs. *American Economic Review*, 82, pp. 249–261.

[22] Blackorby, C., Laisney, F. and Schmachtenberg, R. (1993) Reference-price-independent welfare prescriptions. *Journal of Public Economics*, 50, pp. 63–76.

[23] Blum, W.J. and Kalven, H. (1953) *The Uneasy Case for Progressive Taxation*. Chicago, IL: University of Chicago Press.

[24] Blundell, R. and Shephard, A. (2009) Employment, hours of work and the optimal taxation of low income families. *Institute for Fiscal Studies Working Paper*, WP08/01.

[25] Boadway, R., Marchand, M., Pestieau, P. and Racionero, M. (2002) Optimal redistribution with heterogeneous preferences for leisure. *Journal of Public Economic Theory*, 4, pp. 475–498.

[26] Borck, R. (2007) Voting, inequality and redistribution. *Journal of Economic Surveys*, 21, pp. 90–109.

[27] Bourguignon, F., Fournier, M. and Gurgand, M. (1998) Distribution, development and education: Taiwan, 1979–1994. (Unpublished paper) Delta (Joint research Unit, ENS–CNRS–EHESS), Crest (Laboratoire de Microéconométrie) and Centre d'études de l'emploi and Lamia (Université Paris I).

[28] Bourguignon, F. and Spadaro, A. (2006) Microsimulation as a tool for evaluating redistribution policies. *Journal of Economic Inequality*, 62, pp. 1179–1205.

[29] Bradbury, B. (1999) Optimal taxation theory and the targeting of social assistance. (Unpublished paper) University of New South Wales Social Policy Research Centre.

[30] Brennan, G. and Brooks, M.A. (2010) The Henry tax review: a view from constitutional political economy. In *Australia's Future Tax System: The Prospects After Henry* (edited by Evans, C., Krever, R. and Mellor, P.), pp. 417–438. Sydney: Thomson Reuters.

[31] Brent, R.J. (1984) On the use of distributional weights in cost-benefit analysis: a survey of schools. *Public Finance Quarterly*, 12, 213–230.

[32] Brewer, M. (2003) The new tax credits. *IFS Briefing Note*, no. 35.

[33] Broome, J. (1975) An important theorem on income tax. *Review of Economic Studies*, 42, pp. 649–652.

[34] Buckle, B. (2010) Tax policy reform New Zealand style. *New Zealand Economic Papers*, 44, pp. 129–136.

[35] Buddelmeyer, H., Kalb, G. and Creedy, J. (2007) *Tax Policy Design and Behavioural Microsimulation Modelling*. Cheltenham: Edward Elgar.

[36] Cai, L., Kalb, G., Tseng, Y.-P. and Vu, H.H. (2008) The effect of financial incentives on labour supply: evidence for sole parents from microsimulation and quasi-experimental evaluation. *Fiscal Studies*, 29, pp. 285–325.

[37] Caminada, K. and Goudswaard, K. (1996) Progression and revenue effects of income tax reform. *International Tax and Public Finance*, 3, pp. 57–66.

[38] Carter, R.M., de Freitas, C.R., Goklany, I.M., Holland, D. and Lindzen, R.S. (2006) The Stern review: a dual critique. *World Economics*, 7, pp. 165–232.

[39] Cassel, G. (1901) The theory of progressive taxation. *Economic Journal*, 11, pp. 481–491.

[40] Chang, C-H. (1994) On the optimum rate structure of an individual income tax. *Southern Economic Journal*, 60, pp. 927–935.

[41] Chote, R. (2010) Preface. *Tax By Design*. Oxford: Oxford University Press.

[42] Christiansen, V. and Jansen, E.S. (1978) Implicit social preferences in the Norwegian system of social preferences. *Journal of Public Economics*, 10, pp. 217–245.

[43] Claus, I., Creedy, J. and Teng, J. (2010) The elasticity of taxable income in New Zealand. *University of Melbourne Department of Economics Working Paper*, no. 1104.

[44] Cohen Stuart, A.J. (1889) On progressive taxation. In *Classics in the Theory of Public Finance* (Edited by R.A. Musgrave and A.T. Peacock, 1958), pp. 48–71. London: Macmillan.

[45] Colwyn, Lord (Chairman) (1920) *Report of the Royal Commission on the Income Tax*. Cmnd. 615. London: HMSO.

[46] Cowell, F.A. and Gardiner, K. (1999) Welfare weights. STICERD, London School of Economics.

[47] Creedy, J. (1979) Income averaging and progressive taxation. *Journal of Public Economics*, 12, pp. 387–97.

[48] Creedy, J. (1984) Public finance. In *Economic Analysis in Historical Perspective* (ed. by J. Creedy and D.P. O'Brien). London: Butterworths.

[49] Creedy, J. (1996) *Fiscal Policy and Social Welfare*. Cheltenham: Edward Elgar.

[50] Creedy, J. (1998a) *Measuring Welfare Changes and Tax Burdens*. Cheltenham: Edward Elgar.

[51] Creedy, J. (1998b) Means-tested versus universal transfers: alternative models and value judgements. *Manchester School,* 66, pp. 100–117.

[52] Creedy, J. (1998c) The optimal linear income tax model: utility or equivalent income? *Scottish Journal of Political Economy*, 45, pp. 99–110.

[53] Creedy, J. (1999) Marginal indirect tax reform in Australia. *Economic Analysis and Policy,* 29, pp. 1–14.

[54] Creedy, J. (2001a) Tax modelling. *Economic Record*, 77, pp. 189–202.

[55] Creedy, J. (2001b) Indirect tax reform and the role of exemptions. *Fiscal Studies,* 22, pp. 457–486.

[56] Creedy, J. (2001c) Labour supply, welfare and the earnings distribution. *Australian Journal of Labour Economics,* 4, pp. 134–151.

[57] Creedy, J. (2005) An in-work payment with an hours threshold: labour supply and social welfare. *Economic Record*, 81, pp. 367–377.

[58] Creedy, J. (2007) Policy evaluation, welfare weights and value judgements: a reminder. *Australian Journal of Labour Economics*, 10, pp. 1–15.

[59] Creedy, J. (2008) Choosing the tax rate in a linear income tax structure. *Australian Journal of Labour Economics*, 11, pp. 257–276.

[60] Creedy, J. (2009) Explicit solutions for the optimal linear income tax rate. *Australian Economic Papers*, 48, pp. 224–236.

[61] Creedy, J. (2010a) Tax and transfer tensions: designing direct tax structures. *Australian Economic Review*, 43, pp. 103–113.

[62] Creedy, J. (2010b) Reflections on 'A Tax System for New Zealand's Future'. *Agenda*, 17, pp. 63–73.

[63] Creedy, J. (2010c) The elasticity of taxable income: an introduction and some basic analytics. *Public Finance and Management*, 10, pp. 556–589.

[64] Creedy, J. (2010d) Personal income tax structure: theory and policy. In *Tax Reform in Open Economies: International and Country Perspectives* (ed. by I. Claus, N. Gemmell, M. Harding and D. White), pp. 137–165. Cheltenham: Edward Elgar.

[65] Creedy, J. (2011) Reflections on 'Tax by Design'. *Fiscal Studies* (forthcoming).

[66] Creedy, J., Duncan, A.S., Harris, M. and Scutella, R. (2002) *Microsimulation Modelling of Taxation and the Labour Market: The Melbourne Institute Tax and Transfer Simulator*. Cheltenham: Edward Elgar.

[67] Creedy, J., Enright, J., Gemmell, N. and McNabb, R. (2010) Income redistribution and direct taxes and transfers in New Zealand. *Australian Economic Review*, 43, pp. 39–51.

[68] Creedy, J. and Francois, P. (1993) Voting over income tax progression in a two-period model. *Journal of Public Economics*, 50, pp. 291–298.

[69] Creedy, J. and Gemmell, N. (2002) The built-in flexibility of income and consumption taxes: a survey. *Journal of Economic Surveys*, 14, pp. 509–532.

[70] Creedy, J. and Gemmell, N. (2003) The income elasticity of tax revenue for income and consumption taxes in the UK. *The Manchester School*, 71, pp. 641–658.

[71] Creedy, J. and Gemmell, N. (2004) The built–in flexibility of income and consumption taxes in New Zealand. *Australian Economic Papers*, 43, pp. 459–474.

[72] Creedy, J. and Gemmell, N. (2005) Wage growth and income tax revenue elasticities with endogenous labour supply. *Economic Modelling*, 22, pp. 21–38.

[73] Creedy, J. and Gemmell, N. (2006) *Modelling Tax Revenue Growth.* Cheltenham: Edward Elgar.

[74] Creedy, J. and Gemmell, N. (2007) Tax revenues and fiscal drag: an introduction. *Australian Economic Review*, 40, pp. 323–338.

[75] Creedy, J. and Guest, R. (2008) Population ageing and intertemporal consumption: representative agent versus social planner. *Economic Modelling*, 25, pp. 485–498.

[76] Creedy, J. and Hérault, N. (2011) Welfare–improving income tax reforms: a microsimulation analysis. *Oxford Economic Papers* (forthcoming).

[77] Creedy, J., Hérault, N. and Kalb, G. (2011) Welfare change measures in behavioural microsimulation modelling: accounting for the random utility component. *Journal of Applied Economics*, 14, pp. 5–34.

[78] Creedy, J. and Kalb, G. (2005) Discrete hours labour supply modelling: specification, estimation and simulation. *Journal of Economic Surveys*, 19, pp. 697–734.

[79] Creedy, J. and Kalb, G. (2005) Measuring welfare changes in labour supply models. *Manchester School,* 73, pp. 664–685.

[80] Creedy, J. and Kalb, G. (2006) *Labour Supply and Microsimulation: The Evaluation of Tax Policy Reforms.* Cheltenham: Edward Elgar.

[81] Creedy, J., Kalb, G. and Scutella, R. (2006) Income distribution in discrete hours behavioural microsimulation models: an illustration. *Journal of Economic Inequality*, 4, pp. 57–76.

[82] Creedy, J. and McDonald, I.M. (1992) Income tax changes and trade union wage demands. *Australian Economic Papers*, 31, pp. 47–57.

[83] Creedy, J. and Moslehi, S. (2011) A loglinear tax and transfer function: majority voting and optimal rates. *Australian Journal of Labour Economics* (forthcoming).

[84] Creedy, J. and Scutella, R. (2004) The role of the unit of analysis in policy reform evaluations of inequality and social welfare. *Australian Journal of Labour Economics*, 7, pp. 89–108.

[85] Creedy, J. and Sleeman, C. (2006) *The Distributional Effects of Indirect Taxes: Models and Applications from New Zealand.* Cheltenham: Edward Elgar.

[86] Dalton, H. (1954) *Public Finance* (4th Edition). London: Routledge and Kegan Paul.

[87] Dasgupta, P. (2006) Comments on the Stern review of climate change. (Unpublished paper) University of Cambridge.

[88] de Viti de Marco, A. (1936) *First Principles of Public Finance.* Translated by E.P. Marget. London: Jonathan Cape.

[89] Deaton, A. (1983) An explicit solution to an optimal tax problem. *Journal of Public Economics*, 20, pp. 333–346.

[90] Delorme, C.C. and Hayakawa, H. (1977) The specification of the demand for money and the built–in flexibility of taxation in a multiplier–accelerator model. *Public Finance*, 32, pp. 48–54.

[91] Diamond, P.A. (1998) Optimal income taxation: an example with a U–shaped pattern of optimal marginal tax rates. *American Economic Review*, 88, pp. 83–95.

[92] Donaldson, D. (1992) On the aggregation of money measures of well-being in applied welfare economics. *Journal of Agricultural and Resource Economics*, 17, pp. 88–102.

[93] Dorrington, J.C. (1974) A structural approach to estimating the built-in flexibility of United Kingdom taxes on personal income. *Economic Journal*, 84, pp. 576–594.

[94] Duncan, A.S. and Giles, C. (1996) Labour supply incentives and recent family credit reforms. *Economic Journal,* 106, pp. 142–155.

[95] Dye, R.F. and McGuire, T.J. (1991) Growth and variability of state individual income and general sales taxes. *National Tax Journal*, 44, pp. 55–66.

[96] Edgeworth, F.Y. (1881) *Mathematical Psychics.* London: Kegan Paul.

[97] Edgeworth, F.Y. (1897) The pure theory of taxation. *Economic Journal*, 7, pp. 46–70, 226–238, 550–571 (Reprinted in *Papers Relating to Political Economy, Vol. 2*, pp. 63–125. London: Macmillan).

[98] Edgeworth, F.Y. (1925) *Papers Relating to Political Economy.* London: Macmillan.

[99] Eissa, N. and Hoynes, H. (1999) The earned income tax credit and the labour supply of married couples. *NBER Working Paper*, no. 6856.

[100] Ericson, P. and Flood, L. (2009) A microsimulation approach to an optimal Swedish income tax. *IZA Discussion Paper*, no. 4379.

[101] Evans, C., Krever, R. and Mellor, P. (2010) *Australia's Future Tax System: The Prospects After Henry. Essays in Honour of John W. Freebairn.* Sydney: Thomson Reuters.

[102] Evans, D.J. (2005) The elasticity of marginal utility of consumption: estimates for 20 OECD countries. *Fiscal Studies*, 26, pp. 197–224.

[103] Feldstein, M. (1995) The effect of marginal tax rates on taxable income: a panel study of the 1986 Tax Reform Act. *Journal of Political Economy*, 103, pp. 551–572.

[104] Feldstein, M. (1999) Tax avoidance and the deadweight loss of the income tax. *Review of Economics and Statistics*, 81, pp. 674–682.

[105] Fleurbaey, M. and Maniquet, F. (1999) Optimal income taxation: an ordinal approach. *THEMA Discussion Paper*, 99–43.

[106] Freebairn, J. (2010) Overview of Australia's Future Tax System. In *Australia's Future Tax System: The Prospects After Henry* (edited by C. Evans, R. Krever and P. Mellor), pp. 11–62. Sydney: Thomson Reuters.

[107] Friedlaender, A.F., Swanson, G.J. and Due, J.F. (1973) Estimating sales tax revenue changes in response to changes in personal income and sales tax rates. *National Tax Journal*, 26, pp. 103–113.

[108] Friedman, M. and Friedman, R. (1984) *The Tyranny of the Status Quo*. New York: Houghton Mifflin Harcourt.

[109] Fries, A., Hutton, J.P. and Lambert, P.J. (1982) The elasticity of the US individual income tax: its calculation, determinants and behavior. *Review of Economics and Statistics*, 64, pp. 147–151.

[110] Frisch, R. (1959) A complete scheme for computing all direct and cross demand elasticities in a model with many sectors. *Econometrica*, 27, pp. 177–196.

[111] Gans, J.S. and Smart, M. (1996) Majority voting with single-crossing preferences. *Journal of Public Economics*, 59, pp. 219–237.

[112] Gemmell, N. (2010) Tax reform in New Zealand: current developments. In *Australia's Future Tax System: The Prospects After Henry* (edited by C. Evans, R. Krever and P. Mellor), pp. 63–92. Sydney: Thomson Reuters.

[113] Gevers, L., Glesjer, H. and Rouyer, J. (1979) Professed inequality aversion and its error component. *Scandinavian Journal of Economics*, 81, pp. 238–243.

[114] Giertz, S.H. (2007) The elasticity of taxable income over the 1980s and 1990s. *National Tax Journal*, LX, pp. 743–768.

[115] Giertz, S.H. (2009) The elasticity of taxable income: influences on economic efficiency and tax revenues, and implications for tax policy. In *Tax Policy Lessons from the 2000s* (ed. by A.D. Viard), pp. 101-136. Washington, DC: AEI Press.

[116] Giles, C. and Hall, J. (1998) Forecasting the PSBR outside government: the IFS perspective. *Fiscal Studies*, 19, pp. 83–100.

[117] Giorno, C., Richardson, P., Roseveare, D. and Van den Noord, P. (1995) Estimating potential output, output gaps and structural budget balances. *OECD Economics Department Working Papers*, no. 152.

[118] Glesjer, J., Gevers, L., Lambot, Ph. and Morales, J.A. (1977) Professed inequality aversion among students. *European Economic Review*, 10, pp. 173–188.

[119] Goode, R. (1964) *The Individual Income Tax*. Washington: The Brookings Institution.

[120] Groenewegen, P. (1990) Progressive personal income taxation – an historical perspective. In *Flattening the Tax Rate Schedule* (ed. by J.G. Head and R. Krever) Melbourne: Longman.

[121] Gwartney, J. and Wager, R.E. (1988) The public choice revolution. *Inter-Collegiate Review*, Spring, pp. 17–26.

[122] Hashimzade, N. and Myles, G.D. (2004) The structure of the optimal income tax in the quasi-linear model. *PEUK Working Paper*, no. 2.

[123] Heady, C. (1993) Optimal taxation as a guide to tax policy. *Fiscal Studies*, 14, pp. 15–41.

[124] Heinemann, F. (2001) After the death of inflation: will fiscal drag survive? *Fiscal Studies*, 22, pp. 527–546.

[125] Hersoug, T. (1984) Union wage response to tax changes. *Oxford Economic Papers*, 36, 37–51.

[126] Hicks, U.K. (1946) *Public Finance*. Cambridge: Cambridge University Press.

[127] Hindriks, J. and Myles, G.D. (2006) *Intermediate Public Economics.* Cambridge, MA: The MIT Press.

[128] Holder, R. (2008) Leisure and redistribution. *European Journal of Political Economy*, 24, pp. 354–363.

[129] Hutton, J.P. and Lambert, P.J. (1980) Evaluating income tax revenue elasticities. *Economic Journal*, 90, pp. 901–906.

[130] Hutton, J.P. and Lambert, P.J. (1982a) Modelling the effects of income growth and discretionary change on the sensitivity of U.K. income tax revenue. *Economic Journal*, 92, pp. 145–155.

[131] Hutton, J.P. and Lambert, P.J. (1982b) Simulating the revenue elasticity of an individual income tax. *Economic Letters*, 9, pp. 175–179.

[132] Hutton, J.P. and Lambert, P.J. (1983) Inequality and revenue elasticity in tax reform. *Scottish Journal of Political Economy*, 30, pp. 221–234.

[133] Jenkins, S.P. and Cowell, F.A. (1994) Parametric equivalence scales and scale relativities. *Economic Journal*, 104, pp. 891–900.

[134] Jevons, W.S. (1871) *Theory of Political Economy.* (5th edition, ed. by H.S. Jevons, 1957). New York: Kelley.

[135] Kalb, G. and Ghantous, S. (2006) Tables with elasticities broken down by individual and household characteristics. (Unpublished paper) University of Melbourne Institute of Applied Economic and Social Research.

[136] Kalb, G. and Lee, W.-S. (2007) Wage and Labour Force Participation in Australia: Accounting for Categorised Observations on Wages. Final Report for Treasury.

[137] Kalb, G. and Lee, W.-S. (2008) *Labour Supply in the Australian Population: Using Data from 1999 to 2004*. Final Report for Australian Treasury.

[138] Kanbur, R., Keen, M. and Tuomala, M. (1994) Optimal non-linear income taxation for the alleviation of income-poverty. *European Economic Review*, 38, pp. 1613–1632.

[139] Kanbur, R., Pirttilä, J. and Tuomala, M. (2004) Non-welfarist optimal taxation and behavioural public economics. (Unpublished paper) University of Tampere, Finland.

[140] King, M. (1983) Welfare analysis of tax reforms using household data. *Journal of Public Economics*, 21, pp. 183–214.

[141] Lambert, P.J. (1985) Endogenising the income distribution: the redistributive effect, and Laffer effects, of a progressive tax-benefit system. *European Journal of Political Economy*, 1, 3–20.

[142] Lambert, P.J. (1988) The equity–efficiency trade-off: Breit reconsidered. *Oxford Economic Papers*, 42, 91–104.

[143] Lambert, P.J. (1993) *The Distribution and Redistribution of Income: A Mathematical Treatment*. Manchester: Manchester University Press.

[144] Madden, D. (1996) Marginal tax reform and the specification of consumer demand systems. *Oxford Economic Papers,* 48, pp. 556–567.

[145] Marini, G. and Scaramozzino, P. (1999) Social time preference. *Journal of Population Economics*, 13, pp. 639–645.

[146] Marshall, A. (1890) *Principles of Economics*. London: Macmillan.

[147] McCulloch, J.R. (1845) *A Treatise on the Principles and Practical Influence of Taxation and the Funding System*. Reprinted with editorial material by D.P. O'Brien (1975). Edinburgh: Scottish Academic Press.

[148] Meade, J. (Chair) (1978) *The Structure and Reform of Direct Taxation.* London: George Allen and Unwin.

[149] Mera, K. (1969) Experimental determination of relative marginal utilities. *Quarterly Journal of Economics*, 83, pp. 464–477.

[150] Mill, J.S. (1848) *Principles of Political Economy.* Reprinted, with editorial material by W.J. Ashley (1920). London: Longmans, Green and Company.

[151] Mirrlees, J.A. (1971) An exploration in the theory of optimum income tax. *Review of Economic Studies*, 38, pp. 175–208.

[152] Moreh, J. (1981) Income inequality and the social welfare function. *Journal of Economic Studies*, 8, pp. 25–37.

[153] Mueller, D.C. (2003) *Public Choice.* New York: Cambridge University Press.

[154] Musgrave, R.A. and Thin, T. (1948) Income tax progression. *Journal of Political Economy*, 56, pp. 498–514.

[155] Myles, G.D. (1999) On the optimal marginal rate of income tax. (Unpublished paper) University of Exeter.

[156] Nolan, P. (2004a) When work does not pay: family structures and poverty traps in New Zealand's social security system. (Unpublished paper) Victoria University of Wellington.

[157] Nolan, P. (2004b) Welfare reform for low-wage workers in New Zealand: will working for families work? (Unpublished paper) Victoria University of Wellington.

[158] Nordhaus, W.D. (2006) The Stern review on the economics of climate change. *National Bureau of Economic Research Working Paper, no.* 12741.

[159] O'Brien, D.P. (ed.) (1971) *The Correspondence of Lord Overstone*, 3 vols. Cambridge: Cambridge University Press.

[160] O'Brien, D.P. (ed.) (1999) *History of Taxation.* 8 vols. London: Pickering and Chatto.

[161] O'Brien, D.P. (2009) Introduction. In *Taxation and the Promotion of Human Happiness: An Essay by George Warde Norman* (ed. by D.P. O'Brien with J. Creedy). Cheltenham: Edward Elgar.

[162] O'Brien, D.P. (2010) Introduction. In *Darwin's Clever Neighbour: George Warde Norman and His Circle* (ed. by D.P. O'Brien and J. Creedy). Cheltenham: Edward Elgar.

[163] Okun, A.M. (1975) *Equality and Efficiency: The Big Trade-off.* Washington: The Brookings Institution.

[164] Onrubia, J. and Sanz-Sanz, J.F. (2009) Reported taxable income and marginal tax rates: evidence for Spain based on fiscal drag. *Universidad Complutense de Madrid Working Paper.*

[165] Özmucur, S. (1979) More on built–in flexibility of taxation. *Public Finance*, 34, pp. 443–451.

[166] Pearce, D. and Ulph, D. (1998) A social discount rate for the United Kingdom. In *Economics and Environment: Essays on Ecological Economics and Sustainable Development* (ed. by D. Pearce). Cheltenham: Edward Elgar.

[167] Peel, D.A. (1979) On the built–in flexibility of taxation and the deterministic and the stochastic stability of macro–models under alternative expectations schemes. *Public Finance*, 34, pp. 258–266.

[168] Persson, T. and Tabellini, G. (2000) *Political Economics: Explaining Economic Policy.* New York: MIT Press.

[169] Peter, K.S., Buttrick, S. and Duncan, D. (2007) Global reform of personal income taxation 1981–2005: evidence from 189 countries. *Georgia State University, Andrew Young School of Policy Studies, International Studies Program Working Paper*, 07–21.

[170] Pike, T. and Savage, D. (1998) Forecasting the public finances in the Treasury. *Fiscal Studies*, 19, pp. 49–62.

[171] Pohjola, M. (1985) Built-in flexibility of progressive taxation and the dynamics of income: stability, cycles, or chaos? *Public Finance*, 40, pp. 263–273.

[172] Preinreich, A.D. (1948) Progressive taxation and sacrifice. *American Economic Review*, 38, pp. 103–117.

[173] Prest, A.R. (1979) The structure and reform of direct taxation. *Economic Journal*, 89, pp. 243–260.

[174] Radcliffe, Lord (Chairman) (1955) *Final Report of the United Kingdom Royal Commission on the Taxation of Profits and Income*. Cmnd. 9474. London: HMSO.

[175] Ram, R. (1991) Elasticity of individual income tax in the United States: further evidence from cross-section data. *National Tax Journal* , 44, pp. 93–99.

[176] Ramsey, F.P. (1927) A contribution to the theory of taxation. *Economic Journal*, 37, pp. 47–60.

[177] Richter, W.F (1982) From ability to pay to concepts of equal sacrifice. *Journal of Public Economics*, 20, pp. 211–229.

[178] Robbins, L. (1935) *An Essay on the Nature and Significance of Economic Science* (2nd Edition). London: Macmillan.

[179] Roberts, K.W.S. (1977) Voting over income tax schedules. *Journal of Public Economics*, 8, pp. 329–340.

[180] Sabine, B.E.V. (1980) *A Short History of Taxation.* London: Butterworths.

[181] Saez, E. (2001) Using elasticities to derive optimal tax rates. *Review of Economic Studies*, 68, pp. 205–229.

[182] Saez, E. (2004) Reported incomes and marginal tax rates, 1960-2000: evidence and policy implications. In *Tax Policy and the Economy* (ed. by J. Poterba), pp. 117-173. Cambridge, MA: MIT Press.

[183] Saez, E. (2009) Do tax filers bunch at kink points? Evidence, elasticity estimates and salience effects. *University of California at Berkeley Working Paper.*

[184] Saez, E., Slemrod, J.B. and Giertz, S.H. (2009) The elasticity of taxable income with respect to marginal tax rates: a critical review. *National Bureau of Economic Research Working Paper*, no. 15012.

[185] Samuelson, P.A. (1947) *Foundations of Economic Analysis.* Cambridge, MA: Harvard University Press.

[186] Saunders, P. (2006) *Taxploitation: The Case for Income Tax Reform.* Sydney: Centre for Independent Studies.

[187] Saunders, P. and Maley, B. (2006) Tax reform to make Work pay. In *Taxploitation: The Case for Income Tax Reform* (ed. by P. Saunders), pp. 104–122. Sydney: Centre for Independent Studies.

[188] Shehab, F. (1953) *Progressive Taxation: A Study in the Development of the Progressive Principle in the British Income Tax.* Oxford: Oxford University Press.

[189] Shorrocks, A.F. (2004) Inequality and welfare evaluation of heterogeneous income distributions. *Journal of Economic Inequality*, 2, pp. 193–218.

[190] Slemrod, J. (1990) Optimal taxation and optimal tax systems. *Journal of Economic Perspectives*, 4, pp. 157–178.

[191] Smith, A. (1776) *An Inquiry into the Nature and Causes of the Wealth of Nations.* (Cannan edition reproduced, 1776). Chicago, IL: Chicago University Press.

[192] Smyth, D.J. (1978) Built-in flexibility of taxation, the government budget constraint, the specification of the demand for money function, and the stability of an IS–LM system. *Public Finance*, 33, pp. 367–375.

[193] Sobel, R.S. and Holcombe, R.G. (1996) Measuring the growth and variability of tax bases over the business cycle. *National Tax Journal*, 49, pp. 534–552.

[194] Spahn, P.B. (1975) Simulating long-term changes of income distribution within an income tax model for West Germany. *Public Finance*, 30, pp. 231–250.

[195] Stern, N. (1977) Welfare weights and the elasticity of the marginal valuation of income. In *Studies in Modern Economic Analysis* (ed. by M. Artis and R. Nobay). Oxford: Basil Blackwell.

[196] Stern, N. (2006) The economics of climate change. Available at http://www.hm-treasury.gov.uk/independent_reviews/stern_review_economics_climate_change/sternreview_index.cfm.

[197] Stern, N.H. (1984) Optimal taxation and tax policy. *IMF Staff Papers*, 31, pp. 339–378.

[198] Stevens, R. (1990) Flattening the tax rate scale in New Zealand. In *Flattening the Tax Rate Schedule* (ed. by J.G. Head and R. Krever). Melbourne: Longman.

[199] Tuomala, M. (1985) Simplified formulae for optimal linear income tax. *Scandinavian Journal of Economics*, 87, pp. 668–672.

[200] Tuomala, M. (1995) *Optimal Taxation and Redistribution.* Oxford: Clarendon Press.

[201] Tuomala, M. (2006) On the shape of optimal non-linear income tax schedules. *Tampere Economic Working Papers*, no. 49.

[202] van de Ven, J. and Creedy, J. (2005) Taxation, reranking and equivalence scales. *Bulletin of Economic Research*, 57, pp. 13–36.

[203] van den Noord, P. (2000) The size and role of automatic fiscal stabilizers in the 1990s and beyond. *OECD Economics Department Working Paper*, no. 230.

[204] Veit-Wilson, J. (1999) The tax threshold: policy, principles, and poverty. *Twentieth Century British History*, 10, pp. 218–234.

[205] Wagstaff, A. and van Doorslaer, E. (2001) What makes the personal income tax progressive? A comparative analysis for fifteen OECD countries. *International Tax and Public Finance*, 3, pp. 299–316.

[206] Waterson, M. (1985) On progressive taxation and risk taking. *Oxford Economic Papers*, 37, pp. 510–519.

[207] Young, H.P. (1987) Progressive taxation and the equal sacrifice principle. *Journal of Public Economics*, 32, pp. 203–214.

Index